Smile!

and other practical life lessons
your dogs can teach you
while you are training them

Lynne Swanson, DVM

Smile! and other practical life lessons your dogs can teach you while you are training them

Copyright 2016 © Lynne Swanson

First Printing

Library of Congress Control Number: 2016908935

1. Animal behavior
2. Dog training
3. Personal improvement
4. Psychology
5. Self-help
6. Animals
7. Pets

ISBN: 978-0-9887460-8-4

Copies available at: www.givesmiles.us

*Are you seeking the big pictures in life
with a dog at your side?*

This book is written for you.

ACKNOWLEDGMENTS

Smile! is written with sincere thanks to Hans, for pointing out how applicable the approach taken with dogs at Safe Harbor Farm K9 Rescue and Rehabilitation Center is to life, and for suggesting it may be helpful to people in positions of management. Hans: I took your idea a step further.

Many thanks also go to the dedicated volunteers at that facility, and to Samantha, for all of her help at the Learning "DOG" Conferences. Much of the information presented in this book reflects what is taught to (and feedback from) rescuers, shelter personnel, veterinarians, veterinary staff and trainers at these conferences. This is the first time this material has been compiled with other dog lovers in mind.

Big smiles go to the people mentioned within, for sharing teachable moments. I have changed both names and locations (to protect the innocent and innocently guilty, alike), but whether you recognize yourself or not, I will always remember you.

Hugs and hand-wags go to my wonderful critique team: Patricia, John, Lali and Heather, and to Beki of Eastern Offset Printing. And extra butt-wiggles go to the swiftest of my Book Beagles: April K., April F., Jan, Melinda and Kelly. Your feedback has made this book a better one.

Above all, my gratitude goes to the dogs. They are the ultimate teachers, when we are ready to listen.

100% of the proceeds from this book
aid canine rescues and public libraries.

TABLE OF CONTENTS

JUST LET ME KNOW WHAT YOU WANT

GET MOVING, TO MOVE ON

HOW TO RESPOND TO GET THE BEHAVIOR YOU WANT

DE-STRESS!

TROUBLESHOOTING UNWANTED BEHAVIORS

STARTING OFF ON THE RIGHT FOOT

PRACTICAL LIFE LESSONS, FROM THE DOGS

INTRODUCTION

Canine culture values balance.
Our lives can only be better when we do the same.

CHAPTER 1
INTRODUCTION

Could your days use a few more smiles? How about some more laughter? A little light-hearted dancing, anyone? What about some good old-fashioned (but never out of style) tail-wags and butt-wiggles?

Uh, what was that last line?

You read it right.

If the thought of responding to a dog's happy butt-wiggles with a few of your own doesn't sound bizarre to you, you are going to love this book. If it does, then – dare I suggest it – you may really need this book.

Why is that? Because the average dog has so very much to offer the average person. Not simply in terms of joyful moments and shared adventures, but in terms of life lessons. Have a not-quite-average dog – a canine problem child – at home? Excellent! The more challenging the dog, the more profound the lessons he can offer us.

Hold on! Are we talking about the same species...the one that licks their genitals, takes full-body rolls in mud puddles and sticks their noses into garbage cans?

Absolutely. Because, no matter what life throws at a dog, he doesn't booze it up. He doesn't reach for mind-numbing drugs, and he doesn't live for the soaps. He also doesn't hold a grudge. Really. Dogs readily get moving, so they can move on to better things. As a rule, they prefer balance to drama.

Dogs naturally live in the moment, and in that moment they are usually willing to give things a chance. And when we come together, dogs only want to know that they are safe with us, something we can convey with the most basic of body language, starting with a simple smile.

Smile! discusses body language. It explores canine culture, with the goal of helping you shape the kind of dog you love to be around. Will it help you to train your dog? Definitely. Will it help you to be a better (and happier) person? Perhaps. After reading it, will you be able to view your dog the same way you do now? I doubt it.

A perusal of chapter headings will tell you that this is not your average dog book, nor is it your average self-help tome. It is about the energy we share with our dogs, the state of mind behind that energy and how a better understanding of the way dogs view life and communicate can provide tremendous insight into our own behavior.

Have you ever gazed at your reflection in a mirror, seeking a glimmer of understanding into life as you know it? Consider your dogs to be that mirror, and let this book be your interpreter. The journey will be a life changer.

Smile! came about after more than a decade spent living with twenty to forty dogs at a time, three hundred and sixty-five days a year. Big ones; little ones; young ones and old ones. Purebreds and mixes; boy-dogs and girl-dogs. Dogs from good backgrounds and some from hard-life hellholes. Dogs from sane households, dysfunctional households and shelters both large and small. Many came right off the streets, with no ascertainable history whatsoever. A large percentage of them were temporary residents at Safe Harbor Farm K9 Rescue and Rehabilitation Center in coastal North Carolina, where dogs get to enjoy safety, security and well-thought-out, canine-centric routines – some for the first time in their lives – on their way to finding well-matched new homes.

Add to those dogs several thousand more, encountered at veterinary hospitals where I was employed. A vet hospital is a lot like a pediatrician's office, except the "kids" have four legs as opposed to two. Nervous mommies and daddies – check. Youngsters reflecting the energy (for better or worse) of their parents – check. The need for a calm, collected and confident professional to guide everyone through life decisions, both simple and complex – double-check.

Together, the dogs and I shared learning curves and a few great big un-learning curves. I taught them things that made them better individuals, and it is safe to say that they taught me even more.

Life is a bunch of learning curves and un-learning curves. Given both, I propose that the un-learning curves can be the most life-changing and life-affirming. They occur when we enter a situation quite confident in our knowledge, only to find that we knew nothing at all. This sounds rough, but these curves can be quite wonderful, especially when the process encourages us to put aside past assumptions and quiet our minds, the better to listen and learn from others.

So, is this a book on dog improvement or is it one on life improvement? It is actually a book on both. It is about removing tension from your life and replacing it with joy while working on your relationship with your dogs. It is about being clear in your communication with others and honoring pivotal differences. It is about letting go of the stuff that isn't working.

Reflecting upon what works (and why it works) and what doesn't work (and why not) when observing groups of dogs promotes an awareness unlike anything else. Dogs are very good at teaching us new tricks, even when we strive to teach them what we want. All we need to be is ready to listen. But I'm getting ahead of myself…

Canine culture values balance. Our lives can only be better when we do the same.

CHAPTER 2
WHY SMILE?

Whether or not anyone is watching, please look up from this book and smile. Even if you don't feel like smiling, do it anyway. Allow yourself an honest, up-to-your-eyes, laugh-line-creating smile. I'll wait.

Did you notice how your body responded with a relaxed breath? Smiles trigger them. Do you have less tension in your shoulders and neck? Perhaps less stiffness in your posture? Smiles help there, too. Smiles are very, very powerful. If a stranger smiles at you from across the room, you tend to smile back, don't you? You may feel, in the moment, a little happier about yourself and even more trusting of others.

That is how dogs feel when people offer genuine smiles. Smiles convey a heck of a lot more than words do, and what our facial muscles do to all the other muscles of our body when we smile says volumes about us when we communicate with a nonverbal species. As a pretty darn verbal species, we tend to forget about that.

At Safe Harbor Farm we reward our dogs with sincere, relaxed smiles. What, no dog biscuits? No "good dogs?" No clicker clicks? That's right, smiles ninety-five percent of the time. Why is that? Because smiles don't lead to mouthiness the way treats can. Smiles don't elevate a dog's energy the way "good dogs!" often do. Smiles are always with you. They can't be dropped by arthritic hands, and they don't leave crumbs in your pockets. Smiles can be used selectively when working with multiple dogs, and we don't even have to be looking at a dog for them to send their message.

Plus, giving smiles to others helps us let go of a lot of our unwanted stress, through the release of endorphins (our very own happy-molecules). This further helps us to communicate with our dogs! Because dogs aren't happy where there is tension. Dogs just don't love the drama. Have you ever tried to smile and be dramatic at the same time? Fortunately, it is hard!

When do we say "good dog!" (or my favorites, "good job!" or "good decision!")? We use verbal praise when a dog makes the right decision after thinking things through. We want him to know that we are especially pleased with his <u>choice</u> of alternate behaviors, because we want to see similar choices made in the future. We also use it to pick up a dog's pace, when we want more pep in his step.

We save treats for times when we want to build happy new associations with things that have less-than-positive past associations. For example: when we reintroduce crates to dogs that have come to dislike them. We use food to engage a dog's nose if he psychologically shuts down. We also use biscuit pieces and lots of "good jobs!" to make treadmilling — a higher-energy activity — even more fun.

When a dog anticipates a treat, his focus naturally drifts to the treat. But when he is rewarded with your smile, his focus is on you. So smile at your dog when he is quiet, and you will get more quiet behavior. Smile at him when he relaxes, if you want him to be more relaxed. Smile at him when you are pleased with what he is doing, and you will be more apt to get the dog you want!

Many of you have attended traditional training classes where a certain emphasis was placed on tools. Different types of neck collars, head collars, harnesses and leashes. In many cases, the style of training utilized clickers and treats. In all cases, you were urged to set aside time in your week to practice new commands.

Some of you may have left your dog with a trainer, hoping to get back the dog you want after they did the heavy lifting. Either you thought it was the only way to fix your misbehaving pet, or the thought of following lesson plans made you long to avoid them. You may or may not have been happy with the results.

Some of you are newly looking for help. You have dogs that jump on you, pee on the couch or eat your stuff. Your dogs bite people, retreat under tables or fight with other dogs. Are these problems, in and of themselves, or symptoms of something else? When you see these behaviors, what is your reaction? Perhaps after reading this book, given some new skills and new ways of looking at canine (and human) psychology, it will be "I know what to do!"

Your dogs will support you bringing out your best, and if your experience learning about the way they view the world is similar to mine, you will find your life is more than a little changed. At Safe Harbor Farm, we are always learning from our dogs: how to live in the moment (and what that really means); how to get enjoyment from the simplest of things; how to be clear in our communication; how to be patient, and how to leave the drama behind.

When you choose to put specific concepts or techniques into practice, I ask that you do so with respect for other species, a sense of humor about your learning curve, a ton of patience for the process and an interest in earning the respect of others through calm, consistent leadership.

Why leadership? Because it is when we lead the way – and when we practice the skills, energy and characteristics that mark us as leaders and not just owners of our dogs—that we get the happy, sane and well-behaved dogs we want.

The smile-based training used at Safe Harbor Farm takes a natural approach, one that you can apply moment to moment. And moment to moment is how you practice it, not simply at a set time on a given day in a given environment. Taking a more dog-centric than human-centric approach, it honors the way dogs think and the way they communicate with each other. Easily utilized with single dogs yet applicable to groups of dogs, both large and small, it uses well-thought-out routines and focused movement. It emphasizes calmly confident, directed energy, and it will complement any approach that you have taken thus far.

Most importantly, it is good for you. After all, your life could use a few more smiles!

TRY THIS EXERCISE: Every day this week, when you first wake up (or should you wake during the night), allow yourself a relaxed smile. Then turn onto your back and gently stretch out your limbs. Enjoy the spontaneous cleansing breaths that your smile triggers. Regardless of what is going on around you or the thoughts that come up in the moment, enjoy a soft smile for a few seconds more. Then, if it is time to get going, get out of bed and see how you feel about what the day brings.

TAKE IT A STEP FURTHER: The first time you see your dogs each day, give them a quiet smile if they are calm and quiet. Nothing more; just a soft smile. (But don't respond if they are excited or boisterous. The reason why will become apparent in the next chapter.) The effect, at first, will be subtle, but over time it will be cumulative.

CHAPTER 3
IT HELPS TO KNOW THE RULES

When it comes to dogs and their behavior, knowing a few basic rules really helps. Following them allows us to communicate clearly (something that is only fair), and it encourages our dogs to do what we want them to do because they want to do it, too!

These rules share a universality. That is, they are applicable to relationships well beyond the ones we have with our dogs. To what extent? I will let you be the judge.

GOLDEN RULE #1 AND GOLDEN RULE #2

I travel a lot with my dogs, especially my Doberman, Hiker. We visit stores. We walk at the beach. We stay at hotels together. Groups of four to six dogs at a time (all from our shelter) have also attended conferences with me, where they lie down patiently, blending with the crowd without calling attention to themselves. Behaving otherwise is not the behavior they choose. In this way, they are good citizens of our community and good representatives of their species.

At home, everyone can run around the yard. They can play in gleeful abandon. They can offer up a few alert-barks to let me know someone is walking up the road. They know, however, that there is a time and a place to be vocal or energetic, and a time and a place to be quiet and polite.

How can you get your dogs to demonstrate the behavior you want when you want it, more often and for longer periods of time? How can you get them to choose better behaviors when multiple choices are available? And how can you get them to be good canine citizens, given the option to interact in public settings? The answer is pretty simple, and yet there are complexities. It makes perfect sense, but it can be pretty darn hard for a lot of people to do. It is so incredibly easy, and yet you will probably have to work at it. And it will teach you patience and frustrate you at the same time. Golden Rule #1 is:

Reward what you want.

To illustrate:

Tom leads three young dogs into a large fenced play-yard. The dogs know what lies ahead, and they are eager to race and roll. Tom encourages them to walk quietly through the yard's gate. At that point, they begin to bounce around.

"Uh uh," he responds, patiently utilizing a leash skill explained in Chapter 10. The dogs settle down, and they focus their attention on him.

Tom now has two choices:
  (a) He can unclip their leashes and step back to protect his legs as the dogs race off with raised tails.
  (b) He can gently unclip the leash of the calmest dog while rubbing behind her ears. Enjoying the ear-rub, she stays close to Tom rather than launch off his feet to barrel around the yard. Tom repeats this process with the other dogs, rewarding each one's relaxed energy with a gentle scratch. All three dogs then trot off, to begin their boisterous play a few feet away from Tom and not on top of him.

The second option rewards what Tom wants (a calm transition into play), so he isn't bowled over by rowdy, unruly dogs.

Alice, the owner of two dogs, opens her home to foster a third. After a period of extended play outside, all three dogs enter her house to curl up on comfy mats in the same room.

Alice now has three options:
(a) She can turn her attention to the next thing on her to-do list.
(b) She can walk over to the biscuit jar, which encourages the dogs to follow.
(c) She can pause to give each dog a big smile – a quiet way of letting everyone know that this relaxed, communal behavior is what she wants.

Choosing option (c) is more important than you might think, and not simply because Alice gave herself another reason to smile. With dogs, as well as with humans, offering calm positive responses for calm, quiet behavior is going to lead to what? More calm behavior!

Option (b) is also a positive response, but the problem with it is: it pops the dogs out of the very calm, quiet behavior Alice wants. The biscuits excite the dogs, and they foster competition instead of cohabitation. Plus, the dogs receive them not when they are lying quietly on their beds but when they are up and milling around.

When you work with your dogs be sure to ask yourself: what is your behavior, in the moment, telling them about their behavior?

After Golden Rule #1 comes the often-harder-to-follow Golden Rule #2:

Stop rewarding what you don't want.

To illustrate:

Flash, a Poodle-Bichon mix, circles in excitement when it is time to eat. Dancing on his hind legs, he is quite the engaging clown. He follows the same routine when visitors come to the house. That is when Tori, his owner, wishes that he wouldn't get so excited. Many of her houseguests dislike being jumped upon.

But how is Flash to know this? He is only exhibiting a behavior that has been rewarded. Too, Tori tends to express her frustration with him in an excited tone of voice, further upping his energy.

"Flash! Get down!" she commands before picking him up. "I don't know why you do this!"

Flash, on the other hand, knows exactly why he does what he does. He gets food for it, every day, twice a day. He gets picked up for it when houseguests arrive. And he has never been taught alternate behaviors, such as lying down respectfully a few feet away.

Cindy calls her Corgi, Puff, inside. Puff hears her, but he chooses to sniff a nearby bush instead. In exasperation, Cindy walks into her yard to pick him up, scolding him for ignoring her. Two points to Puff. He has trained her well. From his perspective, Cindy comes to him when he ignores her, and she gives him lots of excited attention, to boot. No points to Cindy earned here.

If these scenarios sound familiar, don't despair! Help is on the way. Right now just know that Golden Rules #1 and #2 reflect how our dogs view our behavior and the energy and state of mind behind that behavior. If we want to get better choices of behavior from them, the big picture is:

You will get more of what you reward.

The dogs at our shelter are excellent teachers when it comes to reminding us what works and why it works, and what doesn't work and why that is. When we calmly reward individuals choosing calm, quiet behavior, and when we don't feed into (or when appropriate, we correct) higher levels of energy, we get so much more of the polite behavior we all love. This, in turn, keeps our dogs happy, sane and healthy, and it makes them all the more adoptable.

Are the dogs at our shelter perfect little angels? Of course not…no more than any playground of six-year olds is always on its best behavior. It is just that whenever our dogs decide to indulge in a wild and crazy moment, they settle down in a reasonable amount of time. Their aroused activity doesn't escalate, and it less often spreads to the others.

The practice of following Golden Rule #1 and Golden Rule #2 fosters awareness, and it encourages mindfulness on our parts. It has many applications in life, with or without our dogs. Common media may make light of mindlessness, but it isn't a trait that is funny in real life, and it isn't a trait that our dogs can respect.

CANINE SOCIAL RULES

Gaining a dog's respect begins with gaining his trust, and it is easier to gain his trust when you understand certain social protocols common to all dogs. These are the rules of the road taught to them by their mama-dogs and enforced by their peers. They are integral to their species.

Every animal species has its unique set of social rules, not unlike the diverse customs of different countries. Body language that reflects comfort in one species may trigger unease in another. What indicates friendliness in one case can prompt distrust or alarm in the next.

The best of animal handlers are good at communicating with their charges using each species' own <u>nonverbal</u> body language. When it comes to working with dogs, they do it in the way another dog would; when working with cats, then the way a cat would, or with horses the way a horse would.

Consider how two members of our species and culture greet each other. We look into each other's eyes. We reach for each other, and we are vocal. (*Hi! How are you? I'm Lynne.*)

In the world of dogs, if two individuals that don't know each other look each other in the eye, and if they are vocal and if they reach out, in all likelihood they are headed for a fight. Polite dogs lead with their noses, and not with their eyes, their ears or their limbs. Their noses seek out each other's back half before exploring each other's front half.

This is instinctual. It is canine culture, and dogs are programmed to do this from birth. Unlike humans, when puppies are born, only their noses, and not their eyes or their ears, are functional for many days. It helps them to better develop this quiet, powerful sense.

Learning not to reach for new dogs before they have had the chance to politely sniff us involves a huge un-learning curve for most of us. After all, what are dogs other than the living, breathing embodiment of the stuffed animals we have loved since we were children? And isn't the purpose of dog-training to get them used to us, so they respond to our cues the way we want? No, and not really. You can go ahead and head-butt another culture all you want. You can try to reshape it into your own image. But neither approach reflects the best or the easiest way to get everyone on the same side.

Think of it this way: when we politely honor canine social protocol, it gives our dogs immediate license to be polite in return. They don't have to think about it. They don't have to get used to it. And they don't have to practice it. Rather, it will come natural to them. To demonstrate, let me use an example in which two women independently enter a room shared by three dogs that they don't know:

Susan enters first, at a relaxed pace with a smile on her face. She doesn't look directly at any of the dogs. She doesn't greet them vocally, and she doesn't stop at the entrance. Rather, she walks confidently toward the center of the room. There she pauses as the dogs approach to sniff her lower half and arms (which hang in a relaxed fashion). She breathes in a comfortable manner, and she smiles some more before crossing the room to sit in a comfortable chair.

The dogs follow her, still sniffing. Once they have completed their sniff, they walk a few feet away to show their comfort with her before turning around to come back with tails wagging. At that point, Susan greets everyone by name, rubbing their ears in greeting.

Janice enters with a big smile on her face, stopping at the entrance to the room.

"Hi guys!" she says enthusiastically with arms outstretched. "Come here and give me a big hug!"

Jackie, a fifteen-pound terrier mix, darts under the chair. Rox, a hundred-pound Rottweiler, warily watches from afar, his pupils newly dilated. Dalli, a twenty-pound Cocker-mix, wiggles toward her, piddling on the floor as he goes, to wind up on his back six feet away. At this point, Janice hesitates, holding her breath in the hope that the other dogs will approach. They choose not to.

She holds out the back of her hand, bending slightly (a posture that she had been taught as a youngster). None of the dogs come closer.

Both Susan and Janice are friendly, dog-loving women. But where one took a dog-centric approach to introductions – using postures and positions consistent with canine social protocol while projecting calm, relaxed energy – the other followed human social protocol and projected excited energy (which many dogs mistrust) followed by hesitant energy (which dogs will naturally avoid) coupled with a bent-over posture.

Both hoped to communicate "I love dogs. Come here and get some loving!" but with Janice that is not the message the dogs received. Very socialized dogs might forgive her verbal, hovering and hesitant approach, and they might bound up to her, ready to party, but not every member of the canine population falls into that category. A large percentage do not. Too, socializing a dog doesn't make him any less a dog, and it is in every dog to follow the social rules of his species more than ours. Those rules come from his DNA, his nature as opposed to his nurture.

The good news is: the body language of dogs isn't that hard to learn. It is much easier than learning French or Spanish or Russian! How to better communicate with our dogs using posture, position and movement, and how and when (and when not) to use our voices to get the behaviors we want, and how to troubleshoot problem behaviors will all be visited in the pages to come.

STATE OF MIND

"I get him to sit, but then he bowls me over when I open the door," is a common lament I hear from dog owners. "How do I convince him to walk through doorways politely?"

"She is walking well at my side, but then she jumps at the cat we are about to pass," is another one. And then there is: "They get along most of the time, but all of a sudden they are at each other's throat."

The common denominator in all of these situations isn't so simple as a dog's choice of behavior and its outcome, and it goes deeper than the energy level underlying his behavior (an important element in its own right). It is each dog's state of mind: the thought, instinct or trigger that underlies what is about to happen next.

By state of mind I mean: Is he hyperaware? Is he anxious? Is he fearful? Is he disengaged? Is he wary and on guard? Is he visually-cued? Is he anticipating the next step? Is he unsure? Is he following the dictates of his DNA (using his prey drive, for example) or the dictates of his hormones?* Or is he engaged, respectful, relaxed and ready to follow your lead?

Misreading a dog's state of mind only perpetuates behaviors we hope to change. For example, misinterpreting an anxious dog's pacing as happy excitement misses the boat completely. Misreading a visually-triggered dog's heightened focus as quiet curiosity equally misses the boat.

Throughout this book, I will revisit the very important concept of state of mind and why rewarding the right state of mind while redirecting (or correcting when needed) the wrong state of mind allows us to get what we want from our dogs, as

---

* *Since horror-mones hijack a dog's thought process and disrupt his behavior like nothing else, you can assume all dogs discussed in this book have been neutered.*

opposed to behaviors that may or may not "stick." I will also discuss the importance of commanding our own state of mind, because our dogs will know what it is, often better than we do ourselves.

WHEN EMPHASIS ISN'T NEEDED

You will notice that I use the word "calm" and the term "matter-of-fact" a lot. Taking a calm approach to shaping our dogs' behaviors makes all the difference in the world. Being equally matter-of-fact about things is pivotal when emotion would otherwise get in our way.

Our species loves to emote, for better or worse. We love to infuse moments with emphasis, many times for fear of being overlooked. Unfortunately, dogs don't understand this extra emotion, just as they don't feel comfortable around nervous energy. They respond with behaviors contrary to what we want: hyperactivity, nervousness, anxiety and avoidance.

When I help people troubleshoot troubled dogs, I frequently have to remind them to relax and dial back emotion that doesn't help. It is something that takes practice but, more often than not, those that practice it tell me they are much calmer and happier people for the process. This is something that echoes my own experience working with dogs.

TENSION WILL ALWAYS WORK AGAINST YOU

I would like to plant this seed in your mind. It is one that we will revisit a lot in this book, especially in Chapter 10 when leashes and other tools are discussed. Tension, especially when it works its way from your shoulders to your hands, will always work against you when you communicate with dogs. Their nature is to avoid it or pull against it.

Removing tension from any situation can only help you, and it isn't as difficult as it may seem. How to do this requires first, a recognition that it exists (the hard part), and second, mindfully letting it go (actually the easy part, as you will soon learn).

TIMING IS EVERYTHING

Good timing is vital whenever we pair A (what we do) with B (what comes next). Our dogs aren't going to sit and ponder, "I wonder how I feel about that. Let me get back to you."

Good timing is equally important when C (a dog's behavior) connects with D (our response). Our dogs aren't going to connect our pleasure or displeasure in the moment with something that they did five minutes, let alone thirty minutes, ago. Not at all. For them, the connection, or association, between cause and effect is immediate. The better our timing, the clearer our communication will be.

Let me use Katie, a Golden Retriever, as an example:

When I call Katie inside after an hour outdoors, I see that her lovely coat is caked with dirt, leaves and fine gravel. She's been exploring the underside of my deck. Sigh. I'd be lying if I said that I wasn't annoyed. I just finished cleaning my house! But I know better than to let my annoyance linger. If I project annoyance when I call her to get brushed out, it is less likely that she is going to trot my way. And if I project tension of any kind when she stands still to be brushed, the message that I will send is: I am upset with her standing still (as opposed to her going under the deck).

Since that is not the message I want to send, I really have to live in the moment and let my annoyance go. It won't change the fact that I have a dirt-encrusted dog. It is time to put a smile on my face, to reward Katie's excellent grooming manners. It will allow the job of cleaning her to be more pleasurable for both of us. It will also help me to let this bump in my day go, so I don't carry it into the next moment.

Good timing dictates that we live in the moment, the better to respond when a response is indicated. Of course, every moment doesn't necessarily require a response. Sometimes good timing means waiting before you take the next step. This is most true when approaching dogs that are in an unstable state of mind. Let me use a Chihuahua named Ziggy to illustrate:

On a summer day, we get an email about fourteen dogs needing rescue placement out of a county shelter across the state. The same email, with attached pictures, goes to six other organizations. Some of the dogs are pretty cute, and some look quite cuddly. A few appear frightened by the camera. And then there is Ziggy: four-and-a-half pounds of Mako Shark Chihuahua poised to attack the photographer. By the time the rescue transporter makes her way seven hours east on I-40, to where we are located on the coast, only one small dog is left. You can guess who.

When Ziggy arrives at our Center, he is glowering from the back of his carrier. His posture is guarded. His hackles are up. His pupils are wide, and he is growling, deep and serious. Oh yes, this little guy is not enjoying himself! What do we do?

We have to give credit to the woman doing the transporting. Despite his growling and baring of teeth, she actually offers to take him out of his carrier for us! Of course, she nearly bursts into tears when we assure her that it won't be necessary. Instead, we find a carrier similar to the one holding him, one that she is very happy to take back with her instead of her own.

Honoring good canine social protocol (no direct eye contact and no conversation or touching until Ziggy is ready), our plan is to give him three things:

❖ Time, so he feels relaxed enough to use his nose (the better to be polite), as opposed to just his eyes and mouth.

❖ Space, so he isn't put into the position of having to make decisions. He is way too reactive to make good decisions right now.

❖ Peace of mind, so he will see our facility as a place of security and comfort, first and foremost.

Without a word spoken, we leave him in his carrier under some pine trees in the middle of one of our dog-yards. For three hours we ignore him, and so do the eight other dogs playing in that yard: Dobermans, Pekingese, Shih Tzu and other Chihuahuas.

This gives Ziggy plenty of time to observe his surroundings. From the safety of his carrier, he can see the relaxed nature of the dogs around him. He can watch their interaction with people who come and go. And he can begin to relate to the smells of the place and unwind after his stressful trip.

When three hours have passed, I grab a good book, and I sit on a dog blanket with my back against his carrier for twenty minutes, the better to follow good canine butt-first social protocol (plus, I love any excuse to enjoy a good book). Rubbing my scent all over a slip-lead, I then open the carrier door a few inches and place all but a foot of it inside before returning to my book for five more minutes.

I want Ziggy to relate to the lead using his nose, so it raises no concern. (Hyper-reactive little guys like him often arrive loathing and fearing these leash-collar combinations due to prior yanking around.)

Time is on my side, because the longer he sits in his carrier, the more interested he is in leaving it to eliminate. It is a win-win situation when he gets what he wants (the chance to poop and pee) by giving me what I want (a dog who comes out of his carrier willingly and without any undue emotion).

With three-and-a-half hours behind us, we are both ready for the next step. With a picture of total success in my mind (something I will discuss later in more detail), I open Ziggy's carrier and wordlessly slip the lead over his head as if we have done this a hundred times before. He comes out of his carrier without incident (he is ready to do so now), and we visit a corner of the yard where he gets the chance to relieve himself. At this point, the little shark follows me as if he has always been my shadow. No fuss. No commotion. No gnashing of teeth or blood spatters.

Moral of the story: One of the first rules of communication is to know when to communicate and when to hold off on your communication. Simply put, you cannot rush the Ziggys of the world. Push them when they are in an unstable state of mind, and they will push back. Give them time and give them space, instead. Offer them your most calm, confident, non-reactive energy. That is all they need, and it is the only approach that will work with them.

EXERCISE FIRST

Hyperactive dogs are often referred to obedience classes. Come; sit; down; stay: all good lessons to learn. Unfortunately, many of these dogs get a lot less out of (or are even turned away from) these classes because they are not psychologically ready to learn, especially in a group situation. They are chronically excited and lacking in basic social skills, and their owners play second fiddle to their demands.

Getting a hyperactive dog (of any size, age or breed) in the frame of mind to focus and learn, and to apply what he has learned, requires exercise first and foremost, to burn off tension and bring his energy level down. Getting a hyperactive dog to exhibit quiet homebody behaviors also requires regular exercise, as dogs who have worked off their extra energy naturally seek to rest and not rabble-rouse. For this reason, the dogs at our facility enjoy group exercise every morning. Focused walking or treadmilling leaves them happy to relax together for the rest of the day, and this allows our facility to be a very pleasant place. Exercise is another theme that you will find interwoven throughout this book.

Treadmills are a wonderfully versatile all-weather tool that most dogs love. Like all tools, they must be used properly and with respect for the dogs to reap their benefits. How to do this is detailed in Chapter 17.

DOGS ARE NATURAL FOLLOWERS

Most dogs are followers by nature. In any situation, given a calm, confident individual who provides for their needs, they will gladly follow.

Dogs who have the DNA of natural leaders are much less common than people think. When I discuss testing for temperament and choosing the right dog for a given household or situation, I will discuss how to identify them and the importance of doing so.

GET THINGS RIGHT THE FIRST TIME!

Dogs are incredibly observant by nature. They look for patterns, and they recognize inconsistency. Like little kids, they are very capable of distinguishing life's loopholes, and they are not above exploiting them, if it is to their advantage.

For this reason, it is important to be clear about what we want the first time we ask for it. And for this to happen, we need to be clear with ourselves about what we really want. The chapters to come will discuss being clear in body, mind and action. They are all greatly important. For now, simply consider the following three scenarios:

Anna, a new shelter volunteer, wants to take Sydney, a hound mix, for a twenty-minute walk. Sydney sees her approaching his kennel, and he is raring to go. Anna has several options:
(a) She can open his kennel, prepared to catch fifty pounds of hopping hound on the fly.

(b) She can attempt to calm him down by talking to him, just enough to open his kennel door.

(c) She can wait outside his kennel wordlessly until he sits on his own, and then open the kennel before he gets up.

(d) She can wait outside his kennel wordlessly until he sits and eventually lies down. Giving him a relaxed smile at this point, she can wait a little longer, until his pupils come down in size and he gives her a big sigh (releasing some of his pent-up energy) before tucking his feet under his chest. At that point, she can open the kennel door.

With any approach other than (d), Sydney will not get the message that complete calmness equates to getting leashed for a walk, and the next time Anna approaches, she will face the same excited hound, no better behaved for their original experience. When option (d) is chosen, the message Sydney gets is: Anna is not someone persuaded by hopping and jumping. Fussing, whining and pawing at the kennel door won't work with her, either. The fastest way for him to get what he wants (a pleasurable walk) is to give Anna what she wants (calm relaxation), and that is the choice Sydney is more likely to make the next time that she approaches.

Tom would like his new cocker, Angie, not to harass the neighborhood cats. On the day he brings her home, he has three options:

(a) He can open the car door and let her out, prepared to dart after her should she chase a cat.

(b) He can tie her to a nearby tree as he unpacks boxes from his car, so she can see but not chase the cats.

(c) He can forego unloading his boxes to take her on a pleasant side-by-side walk around the block, bringing her back (still leashed) to sniff at the neighbor's cats once the walk has relaxed her and put her in a quietly curious state of mind.

Tom is more likely to keep the peace in his neighborhood and get the behavior he wants from Angie if he chooses option (c). Option (a) can result in unnecessary issues and corrections. Option (b) will promote barking and increased excitement when she sees, but cannot approach the cats for a good sniff.

Options (a) and (b) set Angie up for failure and Tom up for frustration.

Tonisha prefers that her dogs defecate at the back of her yard, far from her pool and deck. When it comes time to add Veggie, a goofy Cattle Dog mix, to her household, she has several options when she first lets him into the yard:
  (a) She can simply hope for the best, as she watches Veggie through her kitchen window.
  (b) She can stand outside to chase him away from areas she wishes to keep clean, until he eliminates in the right spot.
  (c) She can hook him to a long cable (roughly fifteen to twenty feet), attached to a tree at the back of the yard, and watch him from a distance so she can release him the moment he has sufficiently emptied both bladder and bowels.
  (d) She can leash him and stand outside with him in the preferred place, until he does his business.

Option (a) gives Veggie no guidance at all, setting him up for failure. Option (b) does nothing but bring an element of tension into a situation that should be matter-of-fact and stress-free. Option (d) is better than (a) or (b), but it sets a pattern that Tonisha may not wish to continue into the future.

Option (c) provides a more flexible way to set Veggie up for future success. It may need to be utilized a few times a day for several days, to establish the pottying boundaries that Tonisha desires, but beyond that, it shouldn't be needed.

Always take the time to get things right the _first_ time you do them with a dog, the better to clearly communicate what you want. To this end, patience will be your most valuable tool. Don't have a lot of patience to spare? Fear not; I will help you work on that. After all, patience is free (and yet it pays you back with big dividends). It weighs nothing (so you don't have to worry about buying it, carrying it, maintaining it or storing it). And it can be both empowering and incredibly effective (as the dogs, themselves, will show you).

THE BASIC RULES AND THE BIG PICTURE

Following a few basic tenets simply makes life easier and more pleasurable. For example:

 ❖ Deeply respect and don't fight Mother Nature. (She will always get the last laugh.)
 ❖ Simple solutions beat out complex ones. (Don't make things harder on yourself.)
 ❖ Treat others the way you wish to be treated. (It is only fair.)

Similarly, life with our dogs is made easier when we:

 ❖ Calmly reward behaviors that we want to see again.
 ❖ Stop rewarding behaviors that we don't wish to see repeated.
 ❖ Honor canine social rules, rather than force dogs to honor our own. (They are not into hugs, handshakes and how-do-you-do's the way we are.)
 ❖ Exercise our dogs before teaching them new skills.
 ❖ Patiently take the time, the <u>first</u> time, to get things right.
 ❖ Willingly lead the way, in a calm and matter-of-fact manner.
 ❖ Watch the timing of our actions and reactions.
 ❖ Identify the state of mind behind a dog's behavior, the better to address the problems involved and not just the symptoms.

Being mindful of these tenets makes it easier to get the dogs we want, the ones that we can take out in public and the ones who are a joy to be around. Following them won't always be easy, no matter how commonsense they are. The good thing is: recognizing when something could have been done better is the first step toward doing things better next time. In this way, as in so many others, our dogs are excellent teachers.

TRY THIS EXERCISE: As you interact with your dogs, identify times when you have been rewarding behaviors or states of mind that you actually don't want. For example: talking to them, picking them up, petting them or feeding them when they are rowdy, vocal or pushy. Then practice reversing your actions, one situation at a time.

TAKE IT A STEP FURTHER: Identify times when you have missed rewarding your dogs for tranquility or quiet attentiveness. Reward more of those times, moment by moment, with a relaxed smile. Watch your timing, and try to get it spot-on, to more clearly communicate what you want.

GO ANOTHER STEP FURTHER: Consider how Golden Rules #1 and #2 (and possibly some of the other rules discussed in this chapter) apply to our own species. Where in your life are you <u>not</u> rewarding what you want to see more of, and where may you be rewarding what you actually don't want? Where might your communication be clearer? And when could your timing be better?

END THINGS ON A CALM NOTE: Ensure that your dogs are in a calm and non-anticipatory state of mind before they enter your home after any time spent outside. When you return from a walk together, pause by your door for a long minute or two before opening it, to give them time to shake off extra excitement before coming inside. If they have been playing outdoors, wait in the doorway for as long as it takes for them to calm <u>completely</u>, before you let them pass. Use the extra time to relax with a few cleansing breaths, and be ready to offer a big smile when they, too, choose to relax. Never end things on a note of excitement (no, not even ten percent excitement) if you want dogs who know how to be calm!

BUILDING THE BEST BRIDGES

Canine mathematics is simple stuff. Dogs, by their nature, don't use multiplication or division, less than, more than or pi. It is all plus and minus and mostly equals with them.

CHAPTER 4
WHAT IS THE ASSOCIATION?

To understand why a dog responds the way he does (which may or may not be the way we would like), it pays to understand the associations he is making. By this, I mean the way he connects one thing to another in thought, either consciously or unconsciously.

Is his association with X positive or negative? What does X do to his energy level? Does X calm him, or does it get him excited? And does you doing X induce him to do Y?

Every new circumstance that you face with a dog is an opportunity to build or reinforce positive associations (as opposed to negative ones). What is commonly called socialization reflects this: the building and reinforcing of calm, confident, accepting associations with things, people and events. We take this a step further when we train our dogs, building conscious associations along the line of 'when you do this, he knows to do that' (also called conditioned responses).

Association is the simplest of concepts, and yet it is often overlooked when people expect certain behaviors from their dogs, moment to moment. I say 'moment to moment' because a dog's nature is to live in the moment, and prior associations can be changed if they are not too deeply seated. To make this concept practical, consider this scenario:

Leon approaches Sinda, a young Husky mix, with his leash in hand. In response, Sinda can:
(a) Jump all over him in excitement.
(b) Duck her head to pull away.
(c) Delight in a game of "catch me if you can."
(d) Extend her neck to quietly accept being leashed.

How Sinda responds to Leon's leash depends upon her association with him and her association with the leash. If Leon wants her to quietly accept the leash, he needs her to associate <u>him</u> with both trust and authority and the <u>leash</u> with something pleasurable. It is not enough that she associates the leash with something good but nothing more – that is choice (a) – and not enough that she trusts Leon, but doesn't honor his position in her pack – that is choice (c).

If Sinda chooses response (b), Leon knows that he has some work to do. He plays a simple game designed to help her see the leash (and his approach with it) in a better light. He moves her to another room (the change in location indicating a clean slate and a chance to do things differently), where he ties her to a secure object before leaving her, without a word spoken, to retrieve a second leash. He does this in a relaxed, matter-of-fact manner, as if these actions reflect his original plan. He times his return to match a moment when she is sitting quietly (not wanting to reward any fussing). Walking up to her without fanfare, he gives her a short, very pleasant massage with the second leash. That done, he leaves it on a nearby table and busies himself with a short, neutral task (he straightens up the room a little).

Picking up the leash again, he approaches her for a second massage with it. Over the next five minutes, he repeats these two steps five more times (the value of repetitions is explained in Chapter 13). His goal is for Sinda to see both the leash and his approach in a calm, positive light, and he has laid the groundwork for (d) to be the choice she makes in the future.

Our job, when we <u>train</u> our dogs, is to build positive associations with the behaviors we want, and doing so is often quite simple. For example, when Jackson, a German Shepherd, walks quietly across a threshold, I respond with a quiet smile and a whispered "good job." I am laying the foundation for him to cross other thresholds just as politely.

Our job, when we <u>rehabilitate</u> dogs, involves identifying associations that need to be modified, so we can change them into better ones. This doesn't mean overthinking them or analyzing their origins. Just recognizing their existence is enough, so we can build better associations that reflect calmness, confidence, safety and acceptance.

Calli, a retriever, backs off when you urge her to jump into the backseat of your car. It may be that she associates car rides with being taken to places she doesn't like. She may have been injured while jumping into a car at one time or another. She may expect to be picked up, based upon past experience. Or she could simply be responding to your mood. Are you projecting frustration, impatience or sadness?

To re-set your state of mind and the quality of energy that you are projecting (after all, you are only human, and the fact that Calli didn't jump right into your car is a source of minor annoyance), you direct her away from the car and tie her leash temporarily to a nearby pole. Ignoring her for the time being, you then busy yourself with a mundane task, such as loading a few items into the car or pulling a few weeds from the side of your driveway. That done, you then smile and open a door on the other side of the car (new location = a clean slate and a brand new request).

Untying Calli, you take her for a twenty-foot jog, to reengage her so she follows you. Smiling, and with some pep in your step, plus the picture in your mind that she is going to follow you into your vehicle without hesitation (the importance of which will become clear as you read on), you jog up to the car and enter it with a loose-but-not-too-long leash and an encouraging, "Let's go, Calli!" Balking only slightly, she then does what you ask, especially when you face forward (as opposed to look back at her), and you ignore her let-me-try-this and let-me-try-that tugs in other directions.

You can now reward her with a short massage and a whispered "good girl" before you close the car door. No excitement. Nothing over the top. Simply a new X (her calm follow-through) associated with Y (your matter-of-fact direction to hop into the car).

Now, if you are tight for time, you start up the car and head out. If you have a little time, you get into the driver's seat only to get out again. You then urge Calli out of the car for a very short jog and a repeat of what you just did, possibly a few times over, reinforcing the behavior you desire. This way it will become her choice of behaviors, given the next car she is asked to enter.

Why is it important to take each of these steps? The answer lies in the various associations that can come out of the situation:

(a) car = tension
(b) car = excitement
(c) car = a calm, matter-of-fact, pleasant situation
(d) balking = a chance to get picked up
(e) balking = increased tension (frustrated human)
(f) hopping into the car = a soft massage and a happy person
(g) your direction = something worth trusting and following

Results (c), (f) and (g) all build good associations, both for Calli and for you. Results (a), (d) and (e) will only reinforce her concern about cars. They will result in future behaviors that you don't want to see. Result (b) is also to be avoided. Chapter 7 will explain why.

Taking each step with an air of calm matter-of-factness is important. Consider how mama dogs guide and correct their young ones. Do they get emotional? They don't. Do they project more energy than is required? Not at all. Mama dogs are the epitome of matter-of-fact. Practicing this same calm matter-of-factness when helping our dogs form good associations keeps our message from getting lost in emotion.

This is especially true when rehabilitating dogs with associations deeply rooted in muscle memory (also called neuromuscular programming); for example, with puppy mill survivors and victims of abuse and terrifying injury. Stemming from episodes of fight-or-flight, their associations may be fear-derived and more instinct-driven than thoughtful. Consider Hera, an older Doberman who came to our shelter:

Hera was emaciated, heartworm-positive, Ehrlichia-positive, unspayed, incontinent and in heat. She also had a broken rib and multiple small mammary tumors. It was pretty clear that she had a history of neglect and abuse. Years later, with all of her medical problems addressed and in good health, this well-socialized, happy and outgoing dog still "goes someplace else" mentally if anyone raises their right hand above their waist quickly. Her pupils dilate. Her eyes glaze over. She vocalizes in panic, and she snaps. Her body responds automatically, without thought, and it is as if she really isn't with us in the moment.

A short time later, responding to calm, quiet energy around her and her name being called softly, she is back to being the dog we all know and love. There is no need for further intervention. There is no need for medication or correction. Just calmness, a little bit of time, and the understanding that what just happened has roots far in the past. The best thing that we can do to help Hera let go of her past is for us to let it go. No more; no less.

This depth of muscle memory can affect humans in a similar fashion. To illustrate:

Lisa lies face-up on a massage table, enjoying a shoulder massage as part of a day-at-the-spa gift from her daughter. As the massage therapist reaches over her, Lisa's head suddenly whips to the right. It is a completely unconscious action that she didn't knowingly start and she cannot stop. Her muscles clench, and her head jerks violently. It happens again, just a minute later, when the therapist reaches over her head another time. What is going on?

Sadly, Lisa had been a victim of spousal abuse for many years, and her right-handed husband always slapped her in the face from left to right. Her past may not be part of her conscious thought anymore, but deep down in her subconscious, the muscle memory is there.

A few years later, a second woman is enjoying an hour-long massage at the same spa, with a different massage therapist. When it comes time for her to get up from the table to head home, she finds that her arms are no longer resting comfortably on her abdomen. Rather, they are rigidly pinned in place, and they do not respond to any of her attempts at movement. For forty-five terrifying (and increasingly painful) minutes, she lies unable to move anything from her neck down as Lisa's more experienced (but still rather nervous) massage therapist relates Lisa's story to her, trying to convince her, and the small crowd of spa employees that have gathered, that this is a passing muscle memory phenomenon and not a permanent situation.

"Have you ever been abused?" the woman is asked. The answer is no.

"Have you ever been in a car wreck?" The answer, again, is no.

"Have you ever been pinned in this same position before?" To that question, the answer is yes. Twenty years earlier, the woman had been in a horseback riding accident, and she was pinned underneath her horse for an indeterminate amount of time before the horse rolled over her head, leaving her crushed and unconscious in the mud.

That woman was me, so I can tell you from first-hand experience that muscle memory is a very powerful phenomenon. It is stronger than the process of thought. At its most productive, it is what we utilize when we type without looking at a keyboard, and it helps both athletes and musicians bring out their best. At its most counter-productive, it plays a significant role in PTSD (post-traumatic stress disorder). When you come up against it in a dog, know that this is one of the few times your dog isn't living in the moment at all. Don't get stressed, and don't go back into the past with him. Rather, stay calm, centered and matter-of-fact for as long as it takes for him to be ready to be redirected back into the present. Then let the past go, so he can as well.

ASSOCIATIONS: PUTTING IT TOGETHER

I can't emphasize enough the importance of building good associations, especially when new dogs enter your life and dogs encounter situations for the first time.

For your dogs, it lays the foundation for good behavioral choices to come. For you, it helps you clearly communicate the kind of behavior and energy you want. (But know that if you aren't clear with yourself about what you want, your dog will know it, and he will draw his own conclusions!)

When problems arise, always ask yourself "What is this dog's association with what I am doing?" It is the key toward helping him form better associations in a calm and matter-of-fact manner.

Chapter 5 expands upon the topic of building good associations. Reinforcing them through repetitions is the topic of Chapter 13.

TRY THIS EXERCISE: In situations where you aren't seeing the behavior you want, ask yourself two questions: First, what is your dog's association with what you are doing? Second, what is his state of mind? (Is he fearful, excited, watchful, conflicted or anxious? Is he focused on the next step, or is he focused you?) Consider the associations and state of mind that you would rather he have. As you read on, you will find help creating them!

TAKE IT A STEP FURTHER: Try to replace any tension, anger, frustration or excitement that arises when your dog misbehaves with an air of calm, redirecting matter-of-factness. A technique that helps things seem less personal and easier to address is imagining that this is someone else's dog or someone else's kindergartner.

GO ANOTHER STEP FURTHER: Notice times when your emotions tend to overcome the message you want to send. Now practice addressing small issues that come up in a more matter-of-fact manner. You may find that your message better hits its mark.

CHAPTER 5
DOGS LOVE ROUTINE!

For better or worse and whether you know it or not, you train your dog every day. He watches what you do and when you do it. He notices the quality and quantity of the energy you project. He builds associations. He looks for patterns, and he recognizes routines. Routines are important to dogs, and in almost any environment, good routines can help them thrive. On the other hand, bad routines will reinforce behaviors and associations that you don't want.

Taking routines a step further, to include what I call rituals, relaxes the dogs that know them. It might be a feeding ritual, or a getting-leashed ritual or a now-we-go-out-to-poop ritual. If routine means what you do, ritual (in this context) means how you do it.

Dogs left to their own devices develop routines and rituals of their own. We have seen dogs consistently hop on two different moving treadmills before settling upon the one they use every day, dogs that circle twice before walking into their crates and dogs that drink out of the same three water bowls (out of many options), one after the other and always in the same order. These aren't behaviors that people taught and reinforced in them. They occur spontaneously, and they appear to serve no function other than to please the dogs that do them.

We have utilized a natural, smile-based, train-as-you-go approach to bring out the best in our Center's dogs for many years. This has allowed us to fine-tune the routines and rituals we use to:

❖ Introduce dogs to one another politely.
❖ Introduce dogs to their new households thoughtfully.
❖ Welcome dogs to our facility peacefully.
❖ Exercise numerous dogs every morning easily.

The routines and rituals we use all honor canine social rules, and they capitalize on a dog's nature. As a result, dogs take to them like proverbial ducks to water. Especially in the case of our morning exercise routine, they really enjoy demonstrating that they know what comes next.

Our routines and rituals also allow us to use time well. A little extra time spent up front (to communicate clearly) prevents a lot of wasted time later on (needed to address issues).

What they have in common are two things:

❖ They start with, or center on, focused walking.
❖ They aim to build trust, give our dogs the direction they need and form good associations from the start.

Each has elements that are applicable to the average dog-owning household, especially if two or more dogs share it.

INTRODUCING DOGS TO EACH OTHER

Our Center's four-step routine for introducing dogs of all sizes, shapes and temperaments to each other begins with walking. We don't stand in place, and we don't align dogs that don't know each other face-to-face. To illustrate:

Andy wants to introduce his Rottweiler, Frenchie, to Thor, Tom's Samoyed. In preparation – Step 1 – the dogs are allowed to urinate and defecate in different locations. They are then walked separately for as long as it takes to bring their energy levels down to a polite level. To understand the value of this, consider how you might feel about meeting a relaxed person as opposed to someone who is excitable. It is natural to find a relaxed person more approachable. Step 1 ends with both Thor and Frenchie walking calmly at their handlers' sides. (If you are having trouble visualizing your dog doing this, don't despair… help is on its way.)

Step 2 begins when Andy and Frenchie join Tom and Thor on their walk <u>without stopping</u> or slowing their pace. The men align themselves side-by-side, with their dogs on the outside.

dog – person – person – dog

This horizontal orientation is very important. It puts the dogs on equal footing, with their people leading the way. Without a word spoken, it fosters comradery, equality and unity, and it sends a message of common purpose. It also encourages the dogs to politely use their noses from a distance, and it should be continued until they comfortably ignore one another.

Once the dogs have been walking in a relaxed manner on loose leashes for five minutes, they are ready for Step 3. Now the men stop to chat. Keeping their leashes loose and paying no special attention to the dogs, they allow Frenchie and Thor to sniff each other thoroughly, in a relaxed manner. What results resembles a wiggly yin-yang symbol. The dogs get acquainted via a good nose-to-butt inspection, and this prepares them for Step 4 (walking side-by-side).

person – dog – dog – person

Andy and Tom resume their walk, now positioned far-right and far-left. Their continued horizontal alignment reinforces the idea that everyone is on the same team.

This four-step routine is both simple and safe for dogs of all sizes and energy levels. (It is also one that we have done with people in wheelchairs and golf carts, when mobility assistance was needed.) It puts the handlers at ease and in a positive frame of mind. It creates the associations we want, setting the dogs up to do well off-leash. It provides well-directed exercise, and it teaches polite manners.

WELCOMING DOGS TO THEIR NEW HOMES

Our routine for introducing dogs to their new households also strives to put them at ease. It helps them form useful associations, and it gives them a clear introduction to the rules that come with their new location. A dog's recipe for success begins the minute he enters his new owner's car for the trip home.

Picture a dog sitting on the lap of a family member in the front passenger seat of a car. Now picture the same dog seat-belted on the back seat of the same vehicle. In each case, what are we telling him as he embarks upon his new journey? Because we want our dogs to be terrific little followers of their new families (as opposed to decision-makers, when they may not make the best of decisions), we insist that they ride in the back seat. (How dogs communicate via posture and position is further discussed in Chapter 9.)

How about when everyone arrives home? Should they pile out of the car and race inside? Good grief, no! What kind of message would that send to the new dog? What kind of guidance would that give him? Instead, we walk him (together with any other dogs in the household) for at least a half-hour before approaching the front door. We want everyone to enter the house together in a quiet, relaxed state.

The associations that we want to make straightaway are:

> this home = a place of peace
> new dog = a member of the home-team
> you = head of the household, the decision-maker

By walking the dogs quietly at your side before entering your home in a peaceful, cooperative (and now rather tired) state, you are telling your new dog (as well as any others) that the behavior expected is one of tranquil coexistence and serene energy, not unbridled excitement coupled with an 'anything goes' attitude.

The order in which everyone calmly passes through the door, the first time, is also important. This is where you, as the head of the household, can dictate the pack order of your choosing. People without dogs enter first. People leading naturally less-assertive dogs enter next, and people leading naturally more-assertive dogs enter last, as a way to level the dogs' psychological playing field.

What next? To further reinforce that your new dog's job is the calm following of his people, and just as important, to give him a way to learn the rules of his new home in a quiet, wholly positive, hands-off manner, tie a loose belt or a second leash around your waist. Hook a small carabineer to it (they are available in the sporting and key-making sections of any large store). Then hook your dog's leash (shortened to three to four feet in length) to the carabineer in a way that allows it to pass behind your back to either side. This is called umbilical leashing.

Without a lot of conversation, take thirty minutes to walk around your house as you typically would, doing your regular routine with your dog at your side or just behind you. Do the dishes; retrieve your mail and sort through it; sit back and watch television; take a walk in the backyard; read a book… whatever you would normally do on a quiet evening at home.

This practice helps to build the following associations:

energy level desired = calm
state of mind desired = relaxed
behavior desired when questions arise = follow the
                                                  leader

When you pass a place that you would like your dog to frequent (e.g., his bed), quietly drop a small dog biscuit. Without words, he will get the message that this spot is a good place to be. If you would like to associate a word with the spot, simply drop another biscuit and say "*place*," and give him a big smile. Later, you can build upon this with repetition, and he will know where to go when you say the word *place*. *Place* is such a useful command, and it is so easy to teach!

If you would like your dog not to bark at doorbells, have a family member or friend ring the doorbell a few times. This helps to create an association between doorbell chimes and relaxing in place, a polite response that will be valuable later on!

Should there be a piece of furniture or another area that you don't want him to approach, pause by it for a moment using a loose leash. Say "no" or "uh uh" once, <u>without extra emotion</u>, before walking on with nothing else said. It doesn't sound like much, but it will be enough for your dog to understand.

Like little kids entering a classroom for the first time, dogs want, and need, to know:

- ❖ What is expected of them.
- ❖ Where they can go.
- ❖ Who they can trust.
- ❖ What they should do, to get their needs met.

Within minutes of their arrival, this thoughtful routine answers those questions. It is only fair. No one (dog or human) enjoys making mistakes because the guidelines weren't explained. No one likes the stress of uncertainty!

Umbilical leashing allows dogs to learn the lay of their new land quickly, and this helps them do well in the future. It is a routine that can be shared by multiple family-members, the better to involve everyone (even children) in the process. It is a routine that you can use to introduce dogs to new locations at any time, and to encourage calm watchful behavior in existing settings.

Dogs enter new locations incredibly observant. They look for routines and rituals, and they pick them up quickly. When a routine is done in a calm, confident, positive and authoritative manner, they lose their apprehension about what is coming next, where they might fit in and who will provide for their needs. They begin to feel safe, and their subsequent relaxation spreads to other dogs and to newcomers.

WELCOMING DOGS TO OUR FACILITY

Our Center, temporary home to many dogs, is a quiet and happy place to be, for them and for us. Did it get this way by chance? No. By luck? Most definitely, not! It is a quiet and happy place because each and every dog that comes to us is welcomed with a routine designed to build good associations from the get-go.

Similar to the other routines mentioned, introducing new dogs to our facility starts with a pleasant but focused walk. We don't bring new dogs inside right away, and we don't let a little inclement weather deter us. We head directly from their transporting vehicle to a quiet, out-of-the-way path far from our other dogs (for disease control). After stopping in one spot for urination and defecation, we walk side-by-side for twenty to thirty minutes. This is important bonding time. It gives us the opportunity to get to know one another. It gives our newcomers an all-important chance to unwind, too, since they have likely come from stressful situations.

On our first walk and with hardly a word spoken, new dogs learn that we are there to lead the way, and they learn that they can trust us to lead calmly and confidently. They learn that certain behaviors (such as jumping or pulling ahead) won't work with us, but when they make the right decisions (such as walking or sitting quietly at our side), they will be rewarded with a loose leash and appreciative smiles. The moment is much better than the ones just passed, and the associations now reflect calmness, direction and relaxation.

The leash skills necessary to do this will be discussed, in detail, in Chapter 10. The reason that most of our communication is nonverbal will be explained in Chapter 9.

After our walk, each newcomer is rewarded with a thorough, deep massaging bath. His flea control is applied, and he receives any vaccines that are needed. He is then left to rest in an isolated kennel. Since all of his needs have been met (his need to eliminate; his need to exercise and his need to feel clean, safe and secure), he is ready to rest quietly.

No matter where a dog originates, how old he is or what breed he is, our job is to be clear in our expectations from the start, so positive associations can be made with us and our facility. New dogs thrive with this routine.*

When the time comes for our new dog to join the others in our main building, we bring him in at the very end of the day, after another fifteen to twenty-minute walk. Matter-of-factly and without fanfare, he is put into a cage-condo next to but not across from the other dogs, and with a gentle scratch under his chin, his food is placed in front of him. This timing associates his arrival with dinnertime, a pleasurable event that fulfills everyone's needs. It also associates his arrival with peace and quiet, since the lights at our shelter go out for the night immediately after everyone is fed. The dogs then have the entire night to "meet" via some long-distance sniffing. No face-to-face interaction; just quiet cohabitation. As a result, come morning, the new dog will walk outside with the others (six to ten dogs at a time) as if he has always been with them!

This introductory routine is marvelous in its simplicity, and with hundreds of dogs of many breeds and different sizes added to our shelter in this way, we have <u>never</u> found it to fail. It also follows Mother Nature. In the wild, dogs exercise (chase down their prey), then they eat, and then they naturally seek to rest.

MAKING GOOD MORNINGS GREAT

If there is a time of day to have a good routine in place that provides exercise for your dogs, it is the morning. After all, dogs that get adequate morning exercise are happier to rest and relax the rest of the day.

Did you just say "I don't have enough time in my morning as it is!" It is a common sentiment. This is where resourceful

---

* *Contrast it with moving a new dog directly from the car that brought him into a kennel before walking away. Worse, make that a kennel next to and across from barking dogs that haven't had a focused walk in days. Not at our facility! Consider the kind of stress-driven associations that this kind of action creates… all negative ones that will take hours, if not days to undo.*

routines that allow for multitasking work well. Combine your routines with short rituals that reinforce good manners (such as the ones described below), and you can check 'train the dogs' off your daily to-do list.

Tina's routines and morning rituals are similar to the ones used at Safe Harbor Farm. Tina has three dogs of her own, and she fosters two others, at any time, for a local rescue organization. In addition to her volunteer work, she works as a nurse thirty hours each week. One busy lady, she needs a morning routine that addresses both her dogs' needs and her own.

6:30 am: Tina walks into her den, where three dogs rest in roomy crates. At her side are the two dogs who sleep on floor mats next to her bed each night. Quietly, she directs them onto dog beds placed to either side of the crates. All five dogs then watch her quietly, as she walks into her kitchen to retrieve their morning meal. Why are they so calm? They know that sitting or lying down quietly equates to being fed, and the calmest of dogs always gets fed first. Fidgeting, fussing or barking equates to missing a meal. One dog at a time, Tina places kibbles on their beds and blankets in two or more separate handfuls, each new handful a reward for a dog's continued relaxed focus on <u>her</u> and not the food. For a dog to get the signal to eat, he must remain calm. (Any excitement or anticipation is patiently waited out. Tina doesn't want to reward that energy or state of mind!) She rewards her dogs with a smile first, followed by a soft signal to eat. They see this as a fun game, but it is actually a little ritual that further teaches and rewards patience. It builds bonds and trust. It also helps to address resource guarding (discussed in detail in Chapter 19).

6:35 am: Once a dog has finished his food (this does not take long at Tina's house!), his leash is put on and (if he is crated) his crate door is closed with the leash's free end looped over the door. What results is five leashed dogs (three in crates; two out of crates) waiting quietly for the next step.

6:40 am: Tina gathers the leashes before walking the dogs outside to a large stone pen, so they can eliminate. At her side or just behind her, they walk as one unit (picture a flock of geese following their lead goose), pausing at each of two doorways between the house and the pen. Once in the pen, they stand quietly to be unleashed. Because leashes are never removed when a dog fusses or pulls, every dog quickly learns polite unleashing manners.

6:45 am: While the dogs get the chance to empty bladders and bowels (a group activity that builds bonds), Tina crosses a few things off her morning to-do list. Returning to the elimination pen, she then waits at its gate for the dogs to gather. They do so quietly, at a respectful distance of two feet or more from her toes (no crowding, please), before she waves them through, into the rest of her yard. Waiting together is another exercise that builds group spirit and rewards good manners. When her entire pack quiets at once, it is hard not to smile. And that, of course, is the right response!

6:55 am: Together, the dogs enjoy some fresh water that Tina replenishes in a mindful manner. What may appear to us to be the simple act of pouring water may as well be a Japanese Tea Ceremony to the dogs. Water is a gift that fulfills a very basic need. When Tina picks up her watering can, she does it with a smile and great love, and the moment she shares with her dogs is one of mutual respect and connection. It isn't what she does as much as how she does it, and what results sets an appreciative tone for the rest of the day.

7:00 am: The dogs gather at the rear door to the house, to go back indoors for a group walk on their treadmills. One by one, they are directed inside using a ritual that Tina calls 'competitive quiet.' In this case, the quietest and calmest dogs get waved in first, and it is fun to watch everyone try to out-quiet each other! Four of the dogs hop onto Tina's three treadmills (two of the smaller dogs sharing one). Bess, the old Labrador, moseys over to a big cushion placed next to one of the treadmills. Her routine is to keep the other dogs company while they walk. Each dog gets a short massage as he is hooked to his treadmill (reinforcing good associations). Tina then sets the controls for a relaxed walking pace (gentle exercise and bond-building are the goals, not cardiac conditioning). No dog jogs. No one even walks at a fast clip. As the dogs enjoy themselves, Tina sorts some laundry. She gets ready for work. She enjoys her breakfast. She makes calls, and she crosses a few more items off her to-do list, all while keeping half an eye on the dogs. To prevent "dread-milling," she varies their speed up or down every ten minutes.

8:00 am: The treadmills are turned off, and each dog is leashed and left in place for several minutes. This is another ritual that teaches patience. Everyone is then gathered to walk outside where, because they have had their exercise, everybody curls up for a long nap. Tina's home is a peaceful place, and she is free to address the balance of her day.

Are Tina's treadmills a substitute for a good walk? Not at all! They are, however, a wonderful all-weather tool that offers extra exercise to her dogs at times when she cannot offer a walk. She uses them five days a week, with weekends set aside for long walks in new locales.*

Routines like this create an environment of support for multi-dog peace and harmony, behavior that can be rewarded with frequent smiles and softly spoken "good jobs." It is conduct that comes naturally, since the dogs eat, drink water, eliminate and get exercised together. This kind of routine cements trust. It also:

❖ Teaches patience, acceptance of leashes, good crate behavior and general manners.
❖ Addresses hyperactivity and resource guarding issues.
❖ Rewards quiet natures, for everyone's peace of mind.
❖ Expands pack cohesiveness, for the mental health and safety of all. Yes, the dogs are individuals, but even more so, they are a team.

* You may be tempted at this point to run out and purchase a treadmill (or start using one that you already own), but please don't do that just yet. Chapter 17 discusses what you need to know first, since taking the right steps is vital.

Dogs that are well-versed in good routines and rituals help each other to do well. They see each other get rewarded for certain behaviors over and over, and this repetition accelerates their learning curve, with minimal effort on our part.

SOME OF THE BEST ROUTINES ARE SUPER-SIMPLE

A simple routine to teach your dog, and one with many benefits, is to tie him to a stable object (a table leg or chair next to a comfortable dog bed, for example) periodically throughout the day, for roughly fifteen minutes. Then go about your own routine, ignoring him for the time being. Especially when done shortly after eating, temporary tying encourages your dog to watch you and be restful. This teaches him patience.

Untie him when it is convenient, but only when he is lying down, <u>completely</u> relaxed (sleeping is good). Do not untie him or talk to him when he is excited or vocalizing in any way. (Remember: reward what you want, and don't reward what you don't want.)

Having a dog who defaults to peaceful watchfulness, whenever and wherever he is tied temporarily, is wonderful, and it is a sure way to get complements from passersby and visitors.

WHEN NOT TO FALL INTO A ROUTINE

There are two situations where having a routine can work against you:
- ❖ When leaving or returning home, with dogs suffering from separation anxiety.
- ❖ When a set routine encourages a dog to anticipate the next step at times when you would rather he follow your lead.

The first case (separation anxiety) will be examined in detail in Chapter 22. In the second case, know that a dog's anticipation can work against you. To illustrate:

Jeb is a smart little Beagle mix who likes to be a step ahead of everyone else. The trait is in his DNA, and we are not going to change it. We do want to temper his enthusiasm, however, so he doesn't perpetuate bad manners.

When he aims to be the first dog to enter his crate at night for his dinner, it isn't a bad thing (as long as he does so quietly), but when he starts to pull ahead of the pack when approaching a certain doorway, because he anticipates the next step in our routine, it is time to change the routine around and go through different doorways.

Routines don't have to be written in stone. Consider each one a tool in your dog-savvy toolbox, and allow for flexibility when situations call for it.

POSITIVE ROUTINES AND RITUALS: WRAPPING IT UP

Good routines naturally lead to good associations. For example:

leashes .... *I follow my person.*
vet visits .... *I trust my person.*
grooming .... *What's not to love?*
walks .... *I walk with my person.*
thresholds (doorways, steps, gates) .... *I wait for my person.*
treadmill .... *Let's go! This is fun!*
crates .... *I relax and watch the world quietly.*

Whether you choose to use some of the same routines and rituals that we use at our facility, use parts of them but not others, or develop ones that fit your circumstances better while honoring the way dogs think and communicate, your dogs will benefit from clear routines and supportive rituals.

We chose the ones we use because they are good for our dogs. They teach (and reinforce) valuable skills, address existing issues and stop new issues from occurring. They are good for us, too. They are simple and straightforward, and they create a peaceful and relatively quiet environment for all.

When disaster nearly struck, we found our routines also allowed us to be well-prepared for emergencies. With reports of a tornado headed our way, I began to leash up eight dogs sharing my cabin so we could all head to a safer building. I quickly realized that I didn't have the time needed to do this, so I just opened up the door and called for everyone to follow me. From Dobermans down to Teacup Chihuahuas (half my own dogs and half foster dogs), everyone followed me. Was this something for which we had all trained? Absolutely not. But since all of the dogs knew to follow their leader as a group, that was what everyone did. The fact that they were then added to twenty-six other dogs, many unknown, didn't matter. With a calm, confident person to show them what was expected, all thirty-four dogs filed into the building to ride out the storm.

TRY THIS EXERCISE: Consider, from <u>your dogs'</u> <u>perspective</u>, the routines and rituals that exist in your home, especially ones that involve their basic needs: feeding, walking, drinking water, going outside and coming indoors.

TAKE IT A STEP FURTHER: Identify where better routines and rituals might be helpful, ones that reward behaviors that you want to see, or stop rewarding behaviors you don't want to see. Look for ones that bring your dogs together, and ones that add more exercise to their day (or time it better).

As you read on, you will learn additional skills that will help you to bring out your dogs' best.

IT IS ALL ABOUT THE ENERGY!

*If you want to find the secrets of the universe,
think in terms of energy, frequency and vibration.*
Nikola Tesla

CHAPTER 6
THEIR ENERGY

An understanding of energy – basic levels of it, how to direct it to our advantage, what to do with too much of it and how to recognize different types – is absolutely vital if you wish to get the best from any dog. Knowing how to engage and how to direct him, how to match your response to his behavior or how to match him with the best of potential homes: it all requires an understanding of energy.

When we talk about energy, the size, breed and age of the dog doesn't really matter. We could be talking about a ninety-pound Malamute or a nine-pound Poodle mix, a seventy-pound Doberman or a six-pound Rat Terrier. We could be talking about a two-year-old hound mix or a twelve-year-old Havanese. A dog can be bred for hunting, guarding, sheep herding or simply companionship. No matter what potential comes from his DNA and upbringing, he won't be a pleasure to be around if he doesn't have an OFF button. And no, when he is sleeping doesn't count!

You may be the owner of a high-flying agility champion, the fastest dog in the ring, but you don't want him flying high over the back seat of your car on the way home from a competition. You don't want him vaulting over the exam table at your vet's office. You don't want him weaving through the legs of your elderly relatives. And you don't want him retrieving the next-door neighbor's toy truck, with the youngster still attached.

DEFAULT ENERGY

I define a dog's default energy as the level of arousal he returns to after any amount of exertion.

A dog is a pleasure to be around if he has a default energy of one. A dog at an energy level of one (out of ten) has a relaxed state of mind. He is not tense. He is not anxious. He is nonverbal. He introduces well to other dogs. He is mentally ready to learn new things. He is receptive to handling, and he is not disruptive.

A dog at an energy level of one doesn't pull on his collar. He doesn't jump up and knock you over. He doesn't run after the cat, knock food out of your hands or bite the veterinarian taking his blood. When you set off on a walk with your dog at an energy level of one, he is not going to pull ahead of you. Rather, he will walk at your side at a contented pace.

Give him the signal and he is ready to catch that ball, ready to take that long walk and ready to herd those sheep. But when it is time to stop, he goes back to his default energy at your direction, and it is time to chill, take a relaxing breath (and maybe have a little snack).

ENERGY LEVELS

What I call level-six energy, you may call level-seven. What I call level-five, you may call level-four. All of that is subjective and of minimal importance on a scale of one to ten. The most important two levels of energy are level-one and level-two. The difference is a dog's degree of alertness.

Alertness is a readiness for, and an anticipation of, action. Now there are times when a dog needs to be ready to take action… ears up, eyes dilated and ready to move at the twitch of a finger. That kind of readiness is a valued trait of sporting and terrier breeds and dogs in competition. It is not as valuable when you and he are visiting your relatives for Thanksgiving. In that case, you could have a dog prepped for action, when you would rather he rest at your feet.

What does a level-one dog look like, when compared to a dog at level-two? Picture two dogs sitting side-by-side. Yes, they are both sitting, and yes, they are both watching you. But one has relaxed shoulders. His tail is still, against the ground.

There is no tension in his body, and he is not leaning forward, nor is he showing any anticipation of your next move. The second dog's pupils are wider. He is leaning forward a bit. His tail is wagging. The first dog is at a level-one. The second dog is at level-two.

Golden Rule #1: Reward what you want.
Golden Rule #2: Stop rewarding what you don't want.

Now think back to our two Golden Rules. If we want a dog with hyperactivity or a history of poor manners to exhibit calm, level-one energy, should we ever reward him at level-two? Of course not! If we reward him at level-two one time out of twenty, the message he will get is: either level-one or level- two is fine.

Dogs at our shelter know that the fastest way to get fed is to sit calmly and quietly. We are not going to reward excess energy, especially when the other dogs are watching. By being rewarded for the behavior we want and not rewarded for what we don't want, our dogs learn quickly the kind of behavior that is expected.

This principle also applies to the walks we take. At our Center, it isn't uncommon to see a volunteer standing with several dogs to either side of her – just standing, and not walking, as a minute or more passes by. When it comes to taking her next step, she will not move unless the dogs at her side are on loose leashes at a solid level-one. For our volunteer, this is a short exercise in patience. For our dogs, it is a reminder of the calm focus we expect.

When people say that they have tried, but they can't seem to get their well-exercised dogs to walk quietly at their side, six times out of ten it is because they start walking before their dogs relax to level-one.* That bears repeating: six times out of ten, it is because they start walking before their dogs calm to a true level-one. Their dogs are focused on the next step, and not on them. Level-one dogs are relaxed; there is no anticipation in their posture.

People often worry that their dog will pop out of level-one if they wait too long before moving, but fear not! There is no need to rush. True level-one energy will tend to stay at level-one, especially when it is rewarded with a smile.

* The rest of the time this occurs due to tense leashes and poor handler posture. You will learn more about those issues in the chapters that come.

THE VALUE OF PATIENCE AND REPETITIONS

For some dogs, relaxation doesn't come easy. And for certain people, waiting for an excited dog to drop to a true level-one can be agonal. Nevertheless, it is easier to aim for good behavior and calm energy right off the bat than it is to correct misbehaviors and excess energy later on. A quiet start also encourages dogs to respond calmly to emerging situations and events, no matter what comes next. Patience, repetition and calm rewards for calm behavior are the keys.

When Cowboy (an Australian Shepherd) and I approach a door for the first time, I need to stand with him two long minutes until he understands that he can't pass in an excited frame of mind. I wait out his wiggles and a few whines. I ignore his panting and a nudge from his nose. I wait until he stops leaning forward, and I wait for him to look up at me quietly (since nothing else has worked for him). I offer him a big smile, and I wait another ten to fifteen seconds for his pupil size (a good measure of excitement) to reduce and for him to take a deep, energy-dropping breath. Only then do we quietly cross the threshold.

We turn to cross the threshold a second time, and this time I only need to wait thirty seconds for him to relax and look at me. The third repetition takes ten seconds, if that.

The whole process of politely walking back and forth through a doorway may seem as if it takes forever, the first time you try it, but really, three to four minutes spent calmly reinforcing this one particular practice can save a lot more time and frustration later on. (It will also help to keep you safe, since sixty pounds of eager dog can wreak havoc on a person.)

To use another example (one very important when it comes to preventing separation anxiety), consider your dog's level of excitement when you get ready to leave your home. If you leave when he is in an excited or unsettled frame of mind (especially if you project excitement, concern or frustration, yourself), he is going to look for ways to vent his extra energy in your absence (and you may not agree with the way he does this). On the other hand, if your morning routine has drained some of his energy reserves, and if you time your departure thoughtfully – to coincide with a moment when he is curled up on his bed – his energy level will tend to remain low (and your house remain safe). Higher energy has its place when jogging mountain paths or visiting deserted beaches, but its place is not in your home as you head out the door to run errands.

Once you get the hang of calmly waiting out a dog's higher energy, to get to level-one (and better behavior), it is really not that hard. Communicating this level of patience, even if only for five minutes at a time, is quite empowering, too.

I put an emphasis on doing things calmly because, if you convey any tension in your body language, your dog will match that tension. And tension will always work against you. In this way, our dogs reflect what we project, and they are entirely honest about the process.

In the last chapter, I alluded to how the dogs at our shelter are required to gather as a quiet, respectful group before they move from their potty pen to their play area. With multiple thresholds to cross several times a day – individually and in groups – our dogs get many chances to rehearse good threshold manners, three hundred and sixty-five days a year.

What everyone gets back from this practice goes beyond good behavior. Crossing thresholds as a well-behaved group generates a sense of unity and harmony. When an entire pack – twelve to twenty dogs, or more – settles down to a level-one energy at the same time, you can actually feel tension slipping away! Volunteers experiencing this for the first time turn to me in amazement. It is truly a wonderful sensation!

Our new adopters love how quietly non-competitive our dogs are, when it comes to passing through doorways. Some have never lived with dogs who let them pass first!

CERTAIN STARS JUST BURN HOTTER

Level-one energy keeps the peace, and it is an excellent goal to have. That said, there will always be dogs like Zoe.

Zoe is a happy-go-lucky, so-o-o-o-pleased-to-meet-you Brussels Griffon and Cairn Terrier mix. She is one of those little dogs who burns hot, and her furry furnace runs twenty-four/seven. Her tail is always carried high. She jumps up the second she sees a person. And she always has energy to spare, even when given good exercise.

You need to be patient, consistent and absolutely willing to stick to your guns with her, because her natural default energy is a two. It doesn't matter if she is standing, sitting or lying down. Achieving an energy level of one is simply not her style.

The problem with rewarding Zoe at a level-two is: it guarantees we will never reach her level-one. Worse, it sets a bad example for the dogs around her, opening the door to increased energy from them.

So when do I insist upon level-one from her, and when do I ignore or calmly redirect her natural level-two? How I respond at any given time reflects the answers to these questions:

❖ Are other dogs involved? (e.g., a group of dogs waiting to pass through a doorway.) In this case, I patiently wait out Zoe's wiggles and extra wags until she stands as still as the others. She can do it, and it is in the pack's best interest that she does. It is just a little harder for her to do it.

❖ What is Zoe's state of mind? Is she just being her happy-go-lucky, goofy self or is this a case where she isn't displaying the manners she has been taught. (I won't let playfulness trump good manners.)

❖ Is her energy likely to go to the next level (e.g., she's playing rough with another dog), or is this just Zoe having a gleeful moment by herself (she's playing rough with a toy)? In the first instance, I redirect her energy to something better. In the second instance, I simply enjoy watching her.

❖ Is this a no-harm/no-foul situation where I would needlessly be micromanaging against her nature? (e.g., Zoe's tail wags furiously as she waits to hop out of my car. She isn't fussing or whining. She isn't big enough to knock me over. She is simply exhibiting more excitement than I would accept in one of my Dobermans, given the same situation, since their energy could escalate to the next level where Zoe's energy won't. In this case, I do nothing more than give her the hand signal to hop out of the car.)

Know your dogs. Be consistent, and stick to your guns when it is important. But don't micromanage needlessly. In this way, leading the way for your dogs is an art, as much as a science.

"QUIET DOG"

An excited dog isn't necessarily a happy one. An excited dog is simply an excited dog. Despite the fact that excitement amongst dogs can be a recipe for disaster, excitement is often a behavior taught to dogs by their owners. "Look! He is excited to see me!" does not necessarily translate to "He likes me. He really likes me!" but good luck telling anyone that.

To give an excited dog the means by which to settle down quickly, I teach and reward the command *quiet dog*. It is a command used most often around dinnertime, when my dogs are brought inside. They are naturally excited. They know their dinner awaits, and they are anxious to dive in. But large excited dogs will bowl you over, and small excited dogs will bounce off your chest to get into an upper-level crate. I don't know about you, but I don't enjoy being bowled over or treated like a launching pad. So I teach *quiet dog*, a completely made-up, easy-to-teach command designed to promote polite behavior. Whenever a dog chooses to relax despite an air of excitement in the room, I say his name softly and whisper, "Good *quiet dog*." He soon associates his choice to remain quiet with the term (and my pleasure), and later, when he hears it, he will give me the behavior I want.

Naming behaviors that you want to see in this way, the better to turn them into commands that your dogs will follow, given repetition and positive reinforcement, is something that is discussed further in Chapter 11.

COUNTING

Counting, a practice used by elementary school teachers and parents to get and focus the attention of children, is another technique that works well to quiet mildly excited dogs. It switches their higher-energy, more visually-mediated focus to a lower-energy, more auditory-mediated focus.

Picture several large dogs having a grand time playing. I would like them to come inside, but whenever one leaves the playgroup to approach me, the most boisterous of the bunch tags him to continue the play. I call the instigator's name once, to get his attention, and I start to count slowly: one…two…three…four. By the time I get to seven, the dogs have stopped their play, and led by the dog I called, they have all trotted my way. By the time I get to eleven, they are sitting or standing quietly, watching me. At this point, I give everyone a big smile and a little wag of my hand (see Chapter 9), before directing them inside.

Picture your dog sitting on the other side of a doorway, waiting to pass at your direction. He is sitting, but his focus is on another dog behind you. His pupils are moderately dilated, his posture tilts forward and his ears are pricked. Technically he is waiting for your direction, but he is equally ready to jump up, knock you to the side and engage the other dog in play. Uh-uh-uh. You want him to stop thinking about the next step, to focus on you.

You start counting, slowly and softly: one…two… three… By the time you get to six, your dog is thinking with his ears and not his eyes. His pupils are smaller, his ears are down, and now he is really watching you. Give him a big smile. It is a calm, quiet reward for his calm, quiet behavior, and it doesn't increase his energy level the way a "good boy" can. He is now ready to pass through the doorway, and he does so at your nod or hand signal, in a relaxed state. The other dog is still on the other side, ready to play, but you haven't become a casualty in the midst of the action.

DOG PARKS

Several elements govern a dog's success at public dog parks, including his style of play (be it a gentle give and take, rowdy-but-never-over-the-top roughhousing or let's-take-it-to-the-limit/no-holds-barred) and the awareness (or lack thereof) of his handler. The way he is introduced to a park is pivotal, because this sets the tone for what comes next. Fortunately, most parks have excellent staging areas at their entrance to facilitate the process.

No matter what a dog's size or his play-style, good manners dictate that he enter a park in a relaxed state of mind, exhibiting respectful, level-one energy. To illustrate this, consider Sandi and Sally and their dogs:

Sandi takes her dog, Stella, on a well-paced walk <u>before</u> they approach their local dog park. Along the way she stops to play a few *'go out* and *come back'* games (Chapter 8), to engage Stella's focus. She then walks her slightly tired dog up to the park's entrance and quietly into its staging area. There, she drops her end of Stella's leash, so Stella can freely sniff the ground and the dogs on the other side of the gate.

Sometimes Sandi waits in the staging area for a minute, and sometimes more. She patiently waits for as long as it takes for all of the dogs involved to enjoy a good sniff and get into a completely calm, ho-hum (and not just relatively quiet) state of mind. She waits as long as it takes for all of the dogs to <u>ignore</u> one another (signaling their acceptance of each other) before entering the park with Stella following. At this point, she steps aside so her energy doesn't affect further introductions, and she takes Stella's leash off once everyone is comfortable with one another. Because she has laid the groundwork, it doesn't take long.

Sally brings her dog, Nutz, to the park without walking him first. He bolts out of her car in excitement, and he runs up to the park entrance with his tail up and pupils dilated. "Slow down!" Sally orders, pushing him away from the gate. "Sorry! He loves this park!" she then says to a bystander, as Nutz barrels through the staging area into the park.

Contrasting the two dogs and their park introduction, is there any wonder why Nutz gets into dog fights? When Sally doesn't set him up for success, other dogs can step in to correct him or match his heightened energy with some of their own.

Please don't be a Sorry Sally and don't let your dog be Nutz. Don't confuse excitement with happiness. Not in your dog. Not in other people. Excitement is excitement; pure and simple. It is extra energy, for better or for worse. Channel it; focus it, so you can have a fulfilled (and enjoyable) dog.

TRACKING THOSE CALORIES

Speaking of extra energy, it pays to know that overfeeding a dog does more than make him fat. It gives him additional energy to burn, and it creates more stool. Unless you have a malnourished dog who needs the extra calories, or you work with true working dogs or dogs in competition, it is in your own best interest and your dog's best interest that he ingest just a reasonable amount of food.

Voluminous amounts of food and treats are often fed by well-meaning people looking to brighten up a dog's day, but it doesn't help the dogs at all when they eat more than what they need out of boredom or a lack of appetite-inhibition (Labradors and Pugs come to mind). Creating more energy without an abundance of outlets for it – plus more poop to scoop – does not make for a better quality of life. Save on your pet food bill, and keep your dogs happier and their hearts, joints, liver and respiratory tracts healthier at the same time. Don't overfeed.

"But I don't overfeed my dog. My spouse does!" is a common lament heard at veterinary offices. If this situation sounds familiar, know that the "green-bean" diet can help. Simply swap an equal volume of green-beans or peas (any variety, as long as they are unsalted) for one-third to one-half of a dog's food. Same volume; more fiber; fewer calories.

Instead of extra treats, offer your dogs extra-large bovine hip bones to chew on. The rounded edges of these reasonably priced four to six-inch diameter roasted bones promote good dental health with minimal calories attached. Too, they provide dogs with a healthy natural outlet for their energy.

At our shelter, we take a one-size-fits-all approach to these bones. We never use smaller bones for smaller dogs (they would be dangerous for the bigger dogs), and we stay away from long bones like femurs, tibias and humeri (which are easy to crack). To prevent squabbles, we always have two more bones available than the number of dogs.

TRY THIS EXERCISE: Review the difference between level-one and level-two energy, so you can begin to recognize both levels. Then identify when your dogs are at level-one, and reward it with a smile.

TAKE IT A STEP FURTHER: Require your dogs to be calm before entering your home. Practice waiting out their higher energy, to get their level-one best in response. Be consistent; stay relaxed, yourself, and never settle for level-two in this case.

GO ANOTHER STEP FURTHER: View your dogs' waists from above. Can you see defined waists in every case? If not, cut the amount of food fed by one-third or try the "green-bean" diet.

CHAPTER 7
OUR PERSONAL ENERGY

For better or worse, dogs mirror the energy around them, be it from their handlers, other dogs or people passing by. Excitement feeds more excitement. Anxiety and frustration perpetuate more anxiety. Tension begets tension, while relaxation and composure reinforce equanimity. Since the energy we project in any given moment so greatly influences the behavior we get back from our dogs – and because the quantity and quality of our personal energy is well within our power to change – here are some practical generalities worth noting.

FEARFUL ENERGY

People who are afraid of being bitten by dogs get bitten more often. People who are afraid of being kicked by horses get kicked more often. Regardless of species, animals don't trust fearful energy, and they don't want to be associated with it. Predator or prey animal, they want that kind of energy gone from their midst.

There probably aren't too many readers of this book who are fearful of all dogs, but it is in all of us to be less self-assured with certain breeds. If you find yourself in that frame of mind, it is best to push all fear aside with a performance worthy of an

Oscar. Straighten your spine. Look up. Relax your shoulders, and project calmness and confidence in a non-threatening manner. Remember not to reach for, start talking to or elicit eye contact with dogs that concern you. Smile softly, the better to breathe normally. Pretend that an Akita–Mastiff–Rottweiler–Doberman mix is really an old Shih Tzu, if that works for you. Wait for him to lift his nose for a sniff, and then patiently wait some more. This allows him to show comfort with you by walking away, allowing you to move in a different direction.

We have a saying at our facility: noses don't bark, and noses don't bite. A curious dog engages his nose. A dog showing heightened awareness engages his eyes and his ears. We always smile when a dog we don't know lifts his nose to us. He is being inquisitive, rather than on guard, and this opens the door for everyone to get along just fine.

NEEDY ENERGY

Dogs that are used to getting their way love people to push around. Little dogs are especially good at this, using their own brand of psychological warfare, but any size dog of this character will actively seek out people who exhibit a sense of need, the better to be top dog. More balanced dogs may tolerate neediness in people and in other dogs, but they won't nurture it, and they may actively avoid it, given the option.

Few of us set out to be needy. It suits our nature more to be strong and capable. Unfortunately, neediness can creep into the energy we project when we want something to happen quickly. We want our friends' dogs to like us immediately. We want stray dogs to approach with their tails wagging. We really get disappointed when these things don't happen. And the message the dogs receive is: we are less than cool, calm, collected and self-assured.

When you meet new dogs, be willing to let them do what comes naturally, in their own time. In this way, you will project a sense of calm comfort (rather than neediness), which is what any dog seeks.

Speaking of neediness, dogs who have received positive feedback for projecting it may exhibit what veterinarians call "limping poodle syndrome." Most often these are small dogs who injured themselves at one point, got lots of attention for it, and now limp on occasion to get more attention from their humans (just one way dogs are good at outsmarting their people.) This isn't neediness as a state of mind. It is more a learned behavior repeated because it has been rewarded. Nurture your dogs when they need it, of course, but be careful not to support a culture of neediness in them. It doesn't support your dog's best, and what you reward is what you will get back.

HESITANT ENERGY

When you look for the best person to perform a task, do you choose someone who is hesitant? Probably not. Would you choose to see a hesitant doctor? Probably not. Would you trust directions given to you by a hesitant neighbor? Probably not. Dogs don't follow hesitant energy either.

Consider how often you see people hesitate, especially at thresholds, waiting to see what their dog does next. We see it happen all the time when we visit pet stores and veterinary offices. The sad thing is: these people then wonder what is wrong with their dog when he hesitates, too. Of course, there is nothing wrong with him! Dogs naturally follow leaders, not other followers.

Non-threatening does not mean hesitant. Have you ever approached a dog slowly, trying to appear non-threatening, only to see him freeze up or even back away from you? He wasn't responding in the way that you hoped because he read your actions as being hesitant, and therefore suspect.

A better practice is to stand upright and relaxed <u>with your side to him</u>, looking away long enough for him to approach for a good sniff. With smaller dogs, facing away in a crouch can help. You will then appear non-threatening in a confident manner that invites them closer.

Those of us who rescue dogs often encounter unsure individuals. These dogs, more than any other, look for people who exude confidence. Remember to breathe normally, move naturally, smile and use good canine social protocol around them, and they will be more relaxed in your presence.

Why is smiling important? Because smiles promote our personal relaxation. They relieve tension. Consider smiles to be the antidote to holding your breath, something that many of us do a lot throughout the day (in some cases, even in our sleep!). Recognizing this tendency toward hesitation in ourselves (and how holding our breath robs our bodies of relaxing, revitalizing oxygen) is the first step toward fixing the problem, the better to be kind to our bodies and send the right message to our dogs.

FRUSTRATED ENERGY

Frustration inserts itself into everyone's life. It is a reasonable and even justifiable response to many situations. Unfortunately, it gets us nowhere with our dogs. Rather, it will work against us one hundred percent of the time, resulting in a dog's avoidance or reactions that are nervous, fearful or defying.

Why is this? It is because, when bad stuff happens to us, the dogs don't get the details. The dogs don't get the history and the who-said-what-to-whom. They don't know (and they don't really care) who started it. They just know that there isn't peace in their pack, and what they do about it depends upon the dog. One might soil the carpet. Another might fight with his dog buddy. Yet another might withdraw completely, and the fourth…well, he is the one who finds and chews up your underwear.

Frustration weakens us in the eyes of our dogs. It affects our posture. It changes the positions we take (the importance of which will be explained soon). It is also not a trait that dogs look for, or understand to be a part of their leaders.

Acknowledge your frustration when it comes up (especially when it is justified), and then take a deep breath before putting it aside, if only for that moment with the dogs. Their behaviors will be so much better. Knowing how to do this is very empowering, and it has many applications in life. Chapter 20 offers several good techniques to help.

COOL, CALM, COLLECTED, MATTER-OF-FACT ENERGY

It is easy to say "Don't get frustrated. Your frustrated energy will work against you one hundred percent of the time." But it can be difficult to compartmentalize your frustration when you are working with a stubborn, seemingly irrational or misbehaving dog. This is where what I call 'the robot' works well. Imagine a robot saying:

"Oh, darn; you got into the garbage again. Let me take this tissue out of your mouth.

Oh, fooey. You are retreating into your crate when I want you to go outside. Here is your leash, so we can get on with our day.

Oh pickle-juice, you just knocked the Yorkie into the water bowl. Gee, that's a big puddle…"

Robots don't have feelings that sway all over the place. They don't get frustrated. Rather, they have the incredibly valuable attribute of being totally in the moment, and in a very matter-of-fact way. It may sound strange, but channeling your inner robot can keep you at your best when your dogs are giving you their worst.

You may utilize your inner robot several times a day, at first (especially when training puppies or working with adolescents). As time passes, you may find yourself using it less and less, as you learn to tackle bumps in the road in a more matter-of-fact way. It works very well for occasions where emotion is going to work against you, and it will help you to move on to a new moment without dragging the last one with you.

Remember that mama dogs don't get overly emotional. They don't project more energy than a situation requires. When guiding and correcting their young ones, mama dogs are the epitome of matter-of-fact. We do well when we do the same.

LEADERSHIP ENERGY

If your life depended upon it, what kind of person would you follow? If you were a student entering a classroom, what kind of professor would you prefer? If you were seeking an opinion, what kind of person would you ask? If you asked me, I would look for someone who is confident (not unsure), calm (not excitable), quiet (not loud), consistent (not unpredictable), assertive (not passive) and aware (not unobservant). Those are the traits of leaders.

Dogs follow the energy of good leaders, because the vast majority of dogs, like children, are natural followers.

Connecting with dogs is very similar to connecting with little kids, and in saying that, I am not anthropomorphizing dogs. I say it, instead, because the more I work with dogs in large numbers, the more I find that if I channel my inner kindergarten teacher – the quiet, watchful, calm, confident, patient, assertive, supportive, loving, responsive but not overly reactive sides of myself – the more receptive my dogs are... no different than if I was working with a group of five-year olds.

Dogs, like children, really enjoy their friends, but their lives revolve around their leaders. Leaders lead the way at forks in the road. They develop and direct mindful routines. How can you better lead your dogs? Recognize these forks, and be willing to direct what happens next in a calm, clear way.

Know that leaders aren't people without failures. Everyone experiences the occasional failure. What sets good leaders apart from their peers is: they don't let failure become a state of mind. Rather, they aim to learn from their experiences before moving on gracefully, and this, in turn, lightens the load that they carry.

DISAPPROVING VS. DOMINEERING

We are all on our learning curves, and people seeking to lead the way occasionally confuse important concepts. They mean well, but they haven't seen the big picture yet, something that only comes with experience. Some confuse <u>disapproving</u> energy and a calmly assertive disapproving posture (picture an unhappy school principal) with <u>domineering</u> energy and a domineering posture (imagine the Incredible Hulk). Please, please, please…they are not the same thing!

The first (disapproving) will be used fairly commonly, as you express your expectations so your dogs can do their best. It is crystal clear what you mean, but not challenging or over-the-top. The second (domineering) will be discussed in more detail in Chapter 23, when I discuss aggression and what happens when people don't understand the true nature of being the top dog.

For now, just know that, if domineering energy is projected when disapproval is all that is required, your dog won't feel a correction. He will feel a challenge, and that can only escalate into resentment or even worse…the need to challenge you back. Let me say that again: if domineering energy is used when disapproval is all that is required, your dog will feel not a correction but a challenge, and that can only escalate into resentment or even worse.

ASSERTION VS. AGGRESSION

Believe it or not, many people mix these two concepts up, much to the concern of their dogs! Let us pull out our Merriam-Webster Dictionaries, to be sure that we get these terms, and the energy behind them, correct.

<u>Assertion</u>: a positive statement
<u>Aggression</u>: an unprovoked attack; the practice of making attacks; hostile, injurious or destructive behavior or outlook, especially when caused by frustration.

It is not hard to see that aggression will lead to further instability, while assertion can be used to achieve balance. Balance, more than anything else, is what we seek.

VOCAL ENERGY

Vocal energy attracts a dog's attention, and it can raise his energy level fast. Valuable in spirited competition, it is a heck of a lot less valuable when a dog is excited and you don't wish to rev him up further. This is where nonverbal communication works best. Chapters 9, 11 and 24 will cover nonverbal and verbal communication in detail, both from us to our dogs and from the dogs to us.

Vocal energy also exists in the form of music and sounds from your electronics. Soft music is often promoted to soothe dogs, and if it equally soothes you, so much the better. Spare your dogs the loud and raucous; it just promotes stress.

GETTING EVERYONE TOGETHER

When multiple people are in the room, a dog is going to read both the collective energy of the group and the personal energy of each individual. Good canine handlers are aware of this, and they do what they can to keep excited energy and unsettled states of mind at bay.

My own policy (and that of our shelter) requires dogs and visitors, alike, to be calm and relaxed prior to introductions. I often spend ten to fifteen minutes with my guests, dispelling their excitement and nervous energy before they come within a hundred feet of my dogs. To do things any other way would necessitate corrections, and nothing is gained when issues arise that could have been avoided, given a little time and awareness.

For your dogs' sake (as well as your own sanity), when bringing visitors into your home, do what you can to bring out their composed and unruffled side before they meet your dogs. Do what you can to ensure that your dogs are <u>one hundred percent</u> quiet and calm, before they meet your visitors. Your home will be a quieter one. Your home will be a safer one. And everyone will reap the benefits.

TRY THIS EXERCISE: Identify times when your energy is "off." For instance: when you are fearful, frustrated or hesitant. Identify times when your words or emotions are working against you. Try being more calmly confident, quietly watchful and patiently assertive where you can (and notice how much time you save and how much more you accomplish with your dogs as a result).

TAKE IT A STEP FURTHER: Channel your inner matter-of-fact robot in response to some of your dogs' less-than-stellar moments, if only to keep the frustration of one moment from turning into tension in the next. Reward yourself with a big smile for doing this!

CHAPTER 8
TIME TO GET YOUR SNEAKERS ON!

Dogs naturally move a lot. They move to get from Point A to Point B. They move to adjust their posture and position, the better to communicate with their peers. And they readily move so they can move on psychologically. Our species would do well to do the same.

Sedentary lifestyles in dogs can lead to a vicious cycle of depression, circulatory issues and obesity, just as they do in people, but unlike with people, dogs with restricted activity just as often suffer from anxiety, hyperactivity and destructive behaviors. This is because dogs aren't couch-potatoes by design. Dogs are, by their nature, wanderers. They are predators, and not prey animals. A dog in the wild who doesn't walk doesn't eat. He doesn't find water. He doesn't find shelter, and his pack will leave him behind or even attack him for being the weak link.

WALKING HELPS TO ESTABLISH PACK ORGANIZATION

Pack structure is important to dogs, just as family and friendships are to people. It is not simply a matter of who might be 'alpha' and who might be 'beta.' In reality, most dogs are born to fit into and thrive in the middle of their pack, like birds in a flock or players on a football team. There is the spirit of unity, of security, of togetherness, and of 'us' and 'them' identities.

Walking, jogging and bicycling with our dogs at our sides (or just behind us, if need be) fosters this spirit of unity and group identity. Too, it keeps our dogs safer in situations where they may not always make the best decisions. In showing them the way, we become the teacher to the student, the captain of the team, the leader of our pack.

I mentioned, in Chapter 5, that taking a walk is the first thing I do with every dog I take in. The time of day, the weather outside and pretty much anything else doesn't matter. Walking next to one another – so we can connect as a team, and I can earn his trust and respect and begin to teach him the rules of the road ahead, right off the bat – sets the stage for our future together.

Although it definitely helps, please know that one doesn't have to stand upright to lead. People in wheelchairs and assistance vehicles can still be strong leaders to their dogs, because what matters most isn't their height. It is their movement and their direction of their dogs' movement. Due to strength issues in my own legs, I have directed dogs from wheelchairs, from a scooter, from an ATV and from a motorized bicycle. In all cases, we moved forward side-by-side. We enjoyed changes in scenery and time spent together. And we responded to what we saw as a team, which promoted and strengthened our bonds.

Who a family dog includes in his pack can vary greatly. In most cases, it will include his people (both old and young), some of their familiar friends, other pets in the household, plus a buddy or two from the neighborhood. Pack-inclusion dictates much of a dog's behavior. To illustrate:

I once faced a situation whereby some of my larger dogs (including my Doberman, Hiker) were harassing goats kept on the other side of some chain-link fence, a potentially dangerous behavior that was going to escalate if I didn't do something and do it quickly. When formulating a plan, I asked myself what I would do if I had two groups of dogs facing off. Fortunately, I knew the answer to that one! I would take all involved on a good, long, side-by-side walk together, an excellent way for everyone to experience being on the same team.

So that is what I did with the dogs and two of my leash-trained goats. We went on walks together several times over the following week, and all the harassment over the fence line stopped. Did it stop simply because the dogs got the chance to sniff the goats up close? No. They could have done that through the fence; and I didn't even permit sniffing until after we had walked together for ten minutes. It stopped because I gave both the dogs and the goats a common task (to walk politely on a leash) and a common direction (forward, at my side) and a common leader (me).

We still take group walks at least twice a year to reinforce that everyone is part of the same pack, and peaceful coexistence is required. Since each of the dogs involved knew to walk calmly at my side, and because the prey drive that each was exhibiting was at a fairly low level* (more curiosity than obsession), walking everyone side-by-side has been enough to mitigate further issues. Now whenever a new dog barks at a goat, Hiker purposefully looks away from them and toward me, to demonstrate how quiet and respectful he can be. Of course, he gets told (calmly) what an awesome dog he is for making that smart decision!

WELL-PACED WALKS ARE EXCELLENT EXERCISE

I define a working walk to be one where my dogs are walking at a moderate (not wandering) pace on either side or just behind me. We are moving as one unit, with me (and not my dogs) deciding direction, speed and pauses along the way. It doesn't matter if I am walking Great Danes or Norwich Terriers. A healthy dog of any size will shed tension when he walks in this manner, and he will enjoy the comradery.

Compare this to a dog dragging his human around on the other end of a leash. That dog isn't getting mindful exercise. He isn't sharing comradery. He is taking charge, leading the action and relegating his human to boat-anchor status.

In the same way, a dog running loose around a backyard is probably recharging his batteries as much as draining them.

* *Please know that I would __not__ have done this if the prey drive of any of these dogs was high, nor if any of them weren't willing to follow my lead in __all__ circumstances!*

Random movement around a yard doesn't make a dog focus and <u>think</u> the way a working walk does, and without a certain level of concentration on his part, his workout isn't nearly the same. Unfocused wandering does not equate to exercise.

Dogs that follow their person's cues are much more aware of their surroundings, and keeping that level of awareness burns calories. It is excellent mental and physical exercise. Waiting at their person's side when the person stops is also exercise. For some dogs, the biggest exertion comes when they are asked to stand still! Chapter 13 describes some of the benefits that come from short start-stop exercises.

Am I saying that dogs should *heel* at all times? Not at all! There may be times when I ask my dogs to *heel* (walk very close to my side), usually for safety reasons, but most of the time I ask them to *walk nice* next to or behind me. This allows for more relaxed and natural movement. When working with dogs, it doesn't pay to be rigid. Quite the opposite; to be flexible with the times is one of the great lessons we can learn from them.

Of course, if you really want a dog to *heel* beautifully, the command is very easy to teach if he already knows how to *walk nice*.

WALKING HELPS TO ADDRESS BEHAVIORAL ISSUES

Focused walking is of huge importance when it comes to addressing hyperactivity, and it is equally vital when it comes to mitigating aggression, anxiety and insecurity.

Chapter 23 discusses how walking can address many types of aggression. Chapter 21 discusses how brisk walks in quiet locales provide exercise and needed changes in scenery for dogs that suffer from anxiety. Having a job to do (which is what a good working walk is) focuses them. Wearing light backpacks on walks can help further, since backpacks help dogs to concentrate on each step.

Insecure and unsure dogs benefit from working walks for two reasons. First, it is hard for them to overthink things when they are moving. Second, walking next to good canine mentors helps them to gain confidence. I will discuss this more in chapters to come.

THE NEXT STEPS

We have established how important walking is to dogs, and how it can be an effective means of shaping good behavior. But how do you get the walking partner of your dreams if that isn't the case already? The answer lies in good communication* and in meeting two of your dog's basic needs, so he is ready and willing to step up to the plate:

❖ Let him eliminate first.
❖ Get him ready to focus.

Walks should be about bonding and enjoying time together. Walks should never be about eliminating for many reasons, not the least of which is: dogs that don't have to urinate or defecate will find the process of walking so much more enjoyable. All of our shelter's dogs are trained to associate a quick trip to certain locations with emptying both their 'yellow tank' and their 'black tank' thoroughly, and their new owners love them for this! By associating a place with a purpose, we have made these dogs more adoptable.

THE MALE DOG MYTH

In this vein, it is worth mentioning the male dog myth. That is the one that says male dogs must mark as much territory as possible with their urine. When you allow a dog to mark his territory all along your walk, you reinforce a strong association between walking and peeing, not walking and teamwork!

Urine marking is pretty obnoxious, and many people won't adopt male dogs (or they will adopt and then abandon them) for reasons having to do with this behavior. When we assure our potential adopters that our boys are trained to empty their bladders all at once, many are surprised that this is even possible. That is how prevalent the male dog myth is!

It is easy to train a male dog to empty his bladder completely. First, make sure that he is neutered (since it is possible to correct bad habits but impossible to correct hormones). Second, before you set out on your walk, take him to a place of your choosing and be prepared to wait as he pees, then circles, then pees again, then strains to the end of the leash, then pees again, then sniffs around, and then pees again. Just stand your ground and be patient until you believe he has emptied his bladder. Only then should you start your walk with your buddy at your side. Be sure not to let him sniff or mark his

---

* The following chapters will help you communicate what you want to your dog, both verbally and nonverbally. They will also help you choose and use the right tools for the job (most commonly, the right leash and the right collar, worn in an optimal way).

territory while you walk! After a few repetitions of this routine, your dog will know that he needs to empty his bladder quickly and entirely if he wants to go anywhere else.

This is a prime example of how a little time spent up front saves a lot of time and aggravation later on. The first time you do this, you may spend a long ten minutes waiting out your male dog. (To keep my cool, I often carry a paperback!) The second time, it may take five minutes, and the third time only two minutes…a seventeen-minute investment overall to end a lifetime of obnoxious behavior. I don't know about you, but I say it's worth it!

This same approach, consistently applied, works well when training puppies.

IS YOUR DOG READY TO FOCUS?

If you have reached this point in the book with a sense of dread because you cannot imagine your dog walking well at your side, your dog may be too full of pent-up energy to focus in any capacity, and nothing short of a few all-out sprints will allow him to settle down and connect with you. Bicycles, adult tricycles (trikes), in-line skates, golf carts and ATVs are all wonderful tools to use when you have a dog in need of a good run. If you don't have any of them, one of your friends might, and they may be willing to help.

Tell your dog to *go out* (explained below), and allow him to dictate the speed until he naturally falls in step with you. At that point, direct him to walk at your side for ten minutes or more, with occasional breaks for a few sips of water. After all, walking as a team is the point of your workout.

Have a bike (or a trike) and a friend or family member willing to assist, but not the strength and endurance to match your dog? Try this more controlled approach: Attach two leashes to your dog. Hold one leash as you mount your bike. The other is held by your assistant on your dog's other side. Now set off at a mutually comfortable pace in a horizontal line:

bicyclist – dog – assistant

At some point switch positions with your assistant, to walk next to your dog. This exercise does multiple things:
- ❖ It provides additional safety until you and your dog bike well as a team.
- ❖ It directs your dog to walk at your side, as opposed to walk in front of you (or your bike).

❖ It keeps your dog moving at a respectful, mindful, reasonable pace, allowing him to burn off extra energy.
❖ It helps you develop confidence walking your higher-energy dog, and it helps to put a positive picture in your mind of things to come (the importance of which will be discussed in the next chapter).

Springer Dog Exercisers and similar bicycle attachments (look for them online) are designed to keep dogs a safe distance from any bike, and they can be paired to allow you to bike with multiple dogs.

GO OUT!

When you want your dog to move ahead and explore, either on-leash or off (for his enjoyment and your own, since you get to watch him), be sure to stop and wait for him to <u>calmly</u> focus on you, first. Reward this with a smile before giving him the command to *go out*, with a point of your finger. This clearly releases him from your side.

Spontaneous *'go out* and *come back'* games are excellent ones to play with long-leashed dogs just learning to focus on you. *Go out* is a reward in itself. Small treats, interspersed with smiles, ear rubs and soft praise are used to encourage and reward a dog's return to your side. These five-minute games are another example of the out-of-the-classroom, train-as-you-go approach that I love to take.

TIME TO GET YOUR SNEAKERS ON!

People often add dogs to their lives in an effort to move more. Dogs are a reason to get up earlier in the day (they need to go outside). They are a reason to walk around the block (they need their exercise). And they are a reason to move around the house (they need an element of supervision).

If you aren't already a walker, taking the first step is the most important. Get some comfortable shoes or sneakers on! From there, it is simply a matter of getting outside so a short walk can awaken your senses. Bring along some dog biscuits, but don't feel the need to get conversational, since talking tends to deaden our senses. Simply give this time to yourself and your dog, and don't forget to smile whenever he chooses to focus on you!

NEED SOME EXTRA INCENTIVE?

Interested in meeting nice people? There are few better conversation-starters than a dog! People like to complement dogs. They stop and admire handsome ones, cute ones and unique ones. They are quick to ask questions about new ones. They would never cross a walking path or park to ask your name, unless prompted, but they would do it readily to ask your dog's name, opening up an opportunity to get to know one another better.

Interested in getting away from people for a while? A walk in the woods with no one but your dog is an excellent way to reconnect with nature, sans technology.

Want an event to brighten and lighten up your day? Interested in improving your circulation, toning some muscles or dropping some weight? Grab a leash and invite your dog for a mindful, well-engaged walk! You won't be sorry, especially if the activity allows you to discover new places.

TRY THIS EXERCISE: For each dog in your household, consider where you are on your walking learning curve. Prepare to take the next step, be it reading the next two chapters before doing anything else, choosing an elimination go-to spot (so your dogs don't eliminate on your walks together), or enjoying a few all-out sprints to release pent-up energy before settling into a good working walk.

TAKE IT A STEP FURTHER: Umbilical–leash your dogs around your house for fifteen minutes at a time. Use this time to perform quiet, mundane tasks that don't involve food preparation. Wash your dishes, make phone calls, sort the mail or do some gardening...and smile to yourself and your dogs when they follow you calmly and quietly. This exercise helps to generate good follow-ship, something that can be built upon when walking outside.

COMMUNICATING WITH CANINES

A thousand fibers connect us with our fellow man; and among those fibers, as sympathetic threads, our actions run as causes; and they come back to us as effects.
Herman Melville

CHAPTER 9
WHAT YOU SAY
AND HOW YOU SAY IT

Body language is really the name of the game when you work with dogs. They express themselves clearly through their posture, the positions they take and the energy they project. They read our posture and the positions we take, plus the energy we project, and they interpret them in the unique context of their species. With dogs, it is not so much what you say but how you say it.

HAND-WAGS AND BUTT WIGGLES

Take one of your hands and wag it back and forth at your hip. Just your hand; not your forearm. Now try this near your dogs when you approve of what they are doing, and watch their little faces light up! Dogs interpret our hand-wags the way they would the tail wags of a friendly dog. They understand butt wiggles, too. Hand-wags and butt wiggles (do I really need to describe how to do those?), that is Dog Communication 101. Like smiles, they work incredibly well when you want to tell dogs, both near and far, that you approve, nonverbally.

HAPPY FEET

Need to communicate with some cats? Try this: Let your hands come to rest a few inches below your waist. Now stretch out the fingers of one hand slo-o-owly before bringing them back into a relaxed fist. Do the same with your other hand. Alternate this motion unhurriedly, one hand at a time, as if you are a contented kitty kneading her paws. These low-and-slow "happy feet" work amazingly with cats, especially if you want to draw them in, from a distance.

Let me demonstrate the power of this nonverbal approach by sharing two past experiences:

I was at a large recreational vehicle social event, one with over one hundred motorhomers from around the country. The motorhomes were parked in long rows under shade trees, with their windshields facing out. Since a significant number of motorhomers travel with their pets, there were many cats and dogs curled up next to those windshields, basking in the sun. Being a veterinarian, I always looked out for them.

One cat stood out from the rest. She was a Siamese who turned up her nose and vanished whenever anyone stopped to admire her. She was such a little snob that I decided to play a trick on her. Standing twenty feet from her motorhome, I waited for her to see me and begin her nose-up ritual, but before she could disappear, I gave her some of my "happy feet," low and slow. The response was hysterical. Her body went one way and her head went the other, and she toppled off her perch. She reappeared immediately, and the astonished expression on her face said it all. Half indignant and half mesmerized, it was as if she was saying "Who taught you that?"

Two days later, I ran into her owner. Actually, her owner sought me out (word about a visiting vet travels fast at RV events). She wanted to know why her normally asocial cat kept walking by the windshield, as if searching for something. I showed her how to make happy feet, low and slow.

Several years later, I visited a municipal animal shelter that had a depressing room set aside for the temporary holding of "unadoptable" cats. I was standing in the middle of the room, talking to a staff member, when I started kneading my hands, low and slow. Within thirty seconds, nearly one-half of the cats in the room were kneading their paws with me, and one silly girl was on her back, kneading all four feet frantically in the air.

"These aren't feral cats!" I stated. "Please get them to the adoption floor." It was the first time any cats made it out of that room alive. Little Miss Four-Feet-In-The-Air was one of them. She came home with me.

Remember happy feet, tail wags and butt wiggles when you want to communicate with cats or dogs nonverbally. You will be amazed at how they respond!

WHAT THE TAILS WILL TELL YOU

You would have to be hard-hearted not to love wagging tails and butt-wiggles. That said, it is important to know that a wagging tail signals elevated energy, more than it does happiness (and by now you know that extra energy isn't always a good thing).

Tails communicate a great deal – both to us and to other dogs – even when they are motionless. They give us a peek into a dog's state of mind.

Fearful dogs hold their tails between their legs, tight against their abdomens. When dogs are relaxed, their tails hang down with no tension at all. A tail positioned up, without tension, belongs to an alert but not overly concerned dog. Often it conveys "I'm ready. What shall we do next?" The higher the tail is carried, the more alert and energized the dog.

A tail raised with tension and at full height, like a shark's fin, is saying "Who are you and what are you doing here?" or "I'm about to take charge." The more tension in the tail, the more you need to be aware, regardless of whether it is still or wagging. The more tension in the tail, the higher the intensity of a dog's focus, even if he isn't moving anything else. Some of the most lethal hunters stand perfectly still before pouncing.

Most of you have never seen, let alone worked with, feral dogs, but their body language is interesting. Feral dogs avoid humans as a rule. Everything about their body language says, "Stay away." I have been involved in a number of hoarding cases and similar situations where a mix of dogs were present: some obvious pets; some shy, withdrawn or frightened individuals and some dogs too feral to socialize. In every case, I watched the tails to identify which was which.

A shy, withdrawn or frightened dog holds his tail against his belly. A feral dog, on the other hand, carries his tail neutrally. He will exhibit avoidance and wariness, but not a fear of you. He simply wants no part of what you have to offer, and the chance that you will change his mind is small.

"But what about dog breeds with upturned tails?" you ask. In our experience, if one of them exhibits increased energy, his energy, combined with the position of his tail, can lead to conflict, even when he doesn't project a fighting stance. This is as true with hounds as it is with Huskies. Be sure to quietly reward these dogs with a broad smile when you see them carrying their tail in a neutral position, because a relaxed posture can keep other dogs from challenging them. They may carry their tails up high routinely, but they are capable of carrying them lower.

Whoever coined the phrase "the tail that wags the dog" probably didn't know how close to the truth he or she was. Just as tail position is dictated by a dog's state of mind, his state of mind can be influenced by his tail position! Tail position can be altered in many situations, and it is remarkable how a simple adjustment can change a dog's attitude!

Maggie, a Pomeranian mix, was incredibly timid when she came to us. She frequently kept her tail clamped between her legs. As part of her rehabilitation, we gently passed a hand below her tail when we saw it clamped, to support it in a neutral position. As a result and almost immediately, her entire body would relax. Our repositioning of her tail away from her belly let her know that there was no reason to be fearful. It was okay to be relaxed!

Maggie got the message clearly, and no words were needed. Very quickly and with renewed confidence, she stopped holding her tail between her legs.

Remember Zoe, the wild child from Chapter 6? We called her our little instigator, as her tail (her "excite-o-meter") was up and active from sun-up to sun-down. Sometimes we needed to reposition it lower (using a flat hand to calmly limit its height).

With her tail neutralized in this manner, her energized behavior and the tension in her body immediately dropped a few notches. She relaxed, as did the dogs around her.

Observe your dogs' tails when you seek to determine which dog started a ruckus. Watch their tails – and not simply their ears, eyes and hackles – when you have two dogs angling for a fight. I have never known an instigating dog to maintain a gladiator posture, if I quickly and confidently move to his side, to neutralize his tail position before another dog takes his bait. Instead, he stops what he is doing, and he looks back at his butt, completely thrown off guard. At that point, I use my position as the resident top dog to calmly redirect him to better things, and this puts an end to the fight.

Am I recommending that you dive into a fight between two unknown Dobermans in this way? Of course not! Redirected aggression, and any hesitation on your part, could get you seriously hurt. But if they are your two Dobermans, and if they accept you as the top dog in your household, chances are good that this technique, well-timed, is all you will need to keep David from chewing up Daniel in that moment.

USING ENERGY TO COMMUNICATE

People familiar with Tai Chi know the concept of moving energy between one's hands. Tai Chi is not a dance. It is a powerful martial art that harnesses, directs and projects energy. Dogs understand harnessing, directing and projecting energy. They respond to the energy around them, and they communicate using the same.

For those unfamiliar with this, consider how a pitcher throws a ball slow or fast. Consider how an actor projects his voice on the stage, be it loud or soft. It is not the physical nature of throwing the ball or projecting one's voice that makes it effective. It is the energy behind the ball or the voice that elicits the response desired.

Let me use two examples to illustrate the use of energy with dogs. The first involves Maggie, the very timid Pomeranian mix I just mentioned. When frightened or unsure dogs like her come to our shelter, we use calming energy, and not words, to earn their trust.

When Geoff approaches Maggie, she ducks her tail and runs into a corner, so he slows his momentum deliberately. Using good canine social protocol, he stops roughly three feet away, so she can lift her nose to him. (He wants her to "meet" him using her nose, and not her eyes.) Without bending over, he crouches to lower his center of gravity. At the same time, he calmly and wordlessly uses his hands (palms out and open, <u>from a few feet away</u>) to corral and cradle her with what can best be described as two pillows of warm air. He keeps his hands soft and still, as if touching a cloud, while he waits for her body to relax. This stops Maggie's cowering. Feeling cradled, as opposed to crowded, she now sees that Geoff means no harm. Rather, he embodies a safe ally! She relaxes some more, and Geoff smiles. Now he can move to her side and pick her up without difficulty.

Contrast Geoff's actions with what might have happened if he had pursued Maggie without pausing, or if he didn't stop to lower his center of gravity. Picture what might have happened if he didn't set comforting boundaries for her movement (using his palm-open hands), or if he didn't project calming energy. Imagine the results if he used only human social cues (such as talking and direct eye contact). In all of those cases, Maggie's concern would have increased.

A similar slow, step-by-step approach using calming energy to communicate helped us one day, when a volunteer came running, shouting that a large unknown dog was loose on the property. To put things into perspective, you need to know that our shelter is not a public facility. It is located more than a quarter mile down an unmarked dirt road, and it is protected on all sides by six-foot chain-link fence and equally tall gates. Any dog larger than a Rat Terrier finding their way onto the property has to have been tossed over the fence. Needless to say, the dog is usually scared.

Our biggest concern, when this happens, is our other animals. With dozens of free-roaming felines and ducks, plus a handful of goats, the last thing we need is a cat-aggressive or high-prey-driven dog appearing out of the blue. When we hear of a strange dog on the grounds, we all come running.

When we do, we see that this dog has no collar. And we learn quickly that he has no intention of approaching any of our volunteers, no matter how much they coax and offer biscuits. He bolts when they appear. He sees them as a threat, so I send them all away. Now it is just the two of us, one hundred feet apart.

Sensing which way the wind is blowing, I purposely stand so my scent can travel in his direction. I want him to use his nose to get to know me. His nose will keep him around when his eyes tell his brain to move on. I don't say anything. I don't reach out. I don't look directly at him. I stand quietly, with my side toward him, and I let thirty seconds or so go by.

When I get the sense that he is okay with this, I move ten feet closer, at an angle, and pause. After another thirty seconds, I move another ten feet closer, again at an angle and not straight on. I glance at the pond behind him, wondering if he is a swimmer (while hoping he is not), because our one-acre kidney-shaped pond surrounds him on two sides. I check out the goat pen to the left, knowing that a few goats may appear without warning. I move only ten feet at a time, and it takes me four to five minutes to get within fifteen feet of him.

It is time well spent, because my calm, indirect approach has prompted him to become curious. I crouch down, side-on, in a relaxed manner. A slip-leash is around my neck, and it is already loosened with a big loop at its end.

When I sense that he is at ease with this, I rise, and with smooth, confident movements and the picture in my mind that he is going to accept my leash willingly, I walk to his side and pass it around his neck without a sound. I then turn, pat my leg and start walking, and he is ready to follow. Twenty minutes later he is on our exam table, wagging his tail while we examine him and start a medical record.

Why did he respond to me when he ran away from everyone else? Because I took my time and utilized calm energy and proper canine body language. I didn't insist that he respond to human cues.

WHAT WE SAY WITH OUR HANDS

To be a dog's go-to person, his mountain and his port in every storm doesn't require a lot of touching or conversation. Simply trustworthy energy. Any dog in any situation looks for it. It is his nature.

When you pet a dog, especially for the first time, watch that your touch is calming, and not stimulating. A light touch or a gentle ear rub will convey trustworthiness more than any of the rougher stuff. What I call one-stroke devotion is a very powerful phenomenon. It is a perfect example of 'less can equal more' and 'leave them wanting more.' And more than just being gentle, you want your touch to be giving, as opposed to needing. Remember this the next time you pet a dog who may be a little shy, or one that you want to reward for being calm. Relax and reach for him less, so he feels comfortable reaching for you more. The alternative is to push a dog beyond his comfort level.

When a dog feels pushed or handled roughly, he has limited means by which to convey his discomfort. He can attempt to move away. He can growl, curl his lip or snap at the air. Or he can bite. He can't exactly say, "How about treading lightly, Bud?" People are often bitten when they don't have a sense of how forceful they appear. (More about this and a dog's need for personal space in Chapter 23.)

PICTURING SUCCESS AND GETTING IT

When it comes to communicating nonverbally, your posture and the positions you take form the framework for everything else. Having your energy right and picturing success in your mind solidifies that framework. This makes success all the more attainable when you work with dogs.

For a moment, let us consider the opposite. What happens to your posture when you question your abilities or take your next step, expecting to fail? Your body tends to curl into itself, in order to protect itself. Your mind-set becomes defensive, and that surely isn't the best state of mind with which to achieve success.

When you picture success in your head, it changes your posture for the better. Whether you channel your inner canine guru, your favorite powerful person or yourself at your best, this is the mind-set to have when you enter a dog's frame of reference. You are embodying leadership, and that is what the dogs seek. That is what they will willingly follow.

"What if you have no picture in your mind?" someone once asked me. "Isn't that better than a negative one?" The problem with no picture at all is: you wind up thinking things through as you do them. This creates a scenario that, at horse shows, is called "being behind the stride." People who ride horses in jumping competitions walk each course before the event begins. This helps them form a mental picture: which combination of jumps requires two strides and which requires three or more. In this way, their subconscious is better prepared for the course, and their bodies (and the energy that they pass to their horses) can follow suit.

Visualizing success does more than turn hesitant, thinking-it-through energy and posture into more relaxed and confident energy and posture. It also creates an efficiency of movement. For this reason, lugers visualize each turn on a luger course before they set off. Gymnasts visualize their routines before taking their first step. You may be walking up to an unknown dog or about to feed ten dogs at a shelter. If you visualize smooth confident movement on your part, it will show in your posture and the positions you take, and it will become the message the dogs receive.

As you read this book, you may find it hard to believe your dogs could be as well-behaved as some of those described. The first step toward getting the behaviors you really want is to banish all pictures of failure from your mind! In many cases, success is right around the corner. It might even be instantaneous, given some new understanding and skills! Never stop believing in your capacity to learn and your dog's capacity to step up to the plate when your communication is clear, even when your success occurs in layers over time.

LOOKING UP AND OUT

If you look down as you walk, what happens to the muscles of your chest, shoulders and arms? Where does your energy project? If you look up, what happens to those same muscles? Where is your energy projecting now? With which posture are you leading your dogs? With which posture do they lead the action, while you follow?

People just learning to walk with groups of dogs at their side often look down to see what the dogs are doing. Their shoulders tense up, their arms pull back and their leashes tighten at a sharp angle. Unfortunately, this urges the dogs to pull forward, away from their handler's tension.

Whether you walk one dog or six dogs, rather than look down, look up and use your peripheral vision (or the shadows ahead of you, should the sun be behind you) to maintain a relaxed awareness of them. In your mind, imagine them walking beautifully at your side (regardless of what they are really doing). Picture them tranquil, but aware of your movement, adjusting their stride with your stride. It will help you to better lead the way, so you can embody the picture in your mind.

Should you need to stop and adjust a dog's position, take the time to adjust his energy level, too, down to a true level-one. Then <u>smile</u> and shake out your arms, shoulders and hips, to encourage your own relaxation. Look up, and look out. Look for something worth laughing about, if it helps you to relax some more. Center your weight in your hips, and not above them. When you feel more like the letter H than the letter C, you will be ready to walk again, keeping your torso and your arms tension-free.

WHERE IS YOUR WEIGHT?

To better understand the importance of centering your weight in your hips and not in your shoulders (the better to stand like an H, as opposed to a C), take a walk without your dogs, paying attention to how you carry your weight. Do you tend to hike your shoulders? (It is a very common habit.) Do you feel top-heavy? Are you aware of your hips when you walk? Do you bounce when you move, or do you keep a low center of gravity? If any tension exists in your body, is it above or below your hips? (Here, tension equates to weight.) Are you smiling much?

People who study the martial arts, particularly Tai Chi, are familiar with centering their weight in their dan tien, a point located between and slightly above the hips. When we move with our weight centered there, we are more physically balanced than if we carry our weight higher. Dogs are quick to pick up on this, since they naturally recognize and honor balance.

To get the best from your dogs when you walk with them, always remember to:

❖ Look up and out.
❖ Center your weight in your hips.
❖ Smile, to support relaxed breathing.
❖ Straighten your spine while keeping your arms and shoulders loose.
❖ Put a positive picture in your mind.

Easy to say, and hard to do for many people, and it may take practice. Hum a happy tune in your head if it helps.

WHEN NOT TO LOOK BACK

Handlers often stop and look back when leading a reluctant dog. The problem with doing this is: while your leash and your voice may be urging him forward, your body language is telling him to stop. There is no forward movement in it! You are stationary, and you are urging him to move up to a stationary object.

Instead, if you face the direction that you want him to go, you then take the lead so he can follow, something that is more natural to any dog than the alternative. If your dog still shuts down, check the picture you have in your mind. Are you picturing success or anticipating failure? Check for any tension in your body, because dogs won't follow that!

When I discuss leashes in the next chapter, I will share a leash technique that helps to "reboot" the most reluctant of dogs so they are more apt to follow you, when you turn to lead the way.

REACHING OUT

Many of us have been taught to offer the back of our hands to strange dogs, but this approach is much more human-centric than canine-centric. (Think: shaking hands, as opposed to sniffing butts.) It isn't the safest approach to take with dogs that you don't know! Remember:

- ❖ Polite dogs don't introduce themselves eye-to-eye, and they lead with their noses, not with their limbs.
- ❖ Dogs will avoid energy that appears hesitant or needy. Hesitation out results in hesitation back.
- ❖ Dogs don't sniff each other's feet in greeting. They explore each other's torsos first.
- ❖ Reaching over a dog can appear predatory.

To review what was written in Chapter 7: if you want a dog to approach you in a calmly curious manner, allow him to come to your side without reaching out. With smaller dogs, present your side while crouching down. Smile softly, but don't be in such a rush to talk or make eye contact. If you want to do more, offer a little wag of your hand at your hip. These actions will never be seen as aggressive. Rather, they reflect the etiquette of a friendly dog.

When it comes to picking dogs up, even dogs that know you may be less than comfortable, if you reach out for them. This is where adjusting the angle of your back and arms can make a huge difference. Reaching <u>straight down</u> works better than reaching out, especially with very small dogs. (In Chapter 16, I describe how I encourage dogs to approach, so this can be done.)

What we did with Molo, a timid black-masked Chihuahua mix, illustrates another trick that we use, so as not to reach out for a less-socialized dog:

> At only seven weeks of age, Molo was taken away from his mother, and he was given to a couple who had mixed emotions about being dog owners. They left him outdoors and had little interaction with him day-in and day-out for nine months. With no other dogs to relate to, and no real bonds with humans, he got very little guidance and socialization. He was a very jumpy and mistrustful youngster when he came to us.
>
> Molo didn't like to be approached or picked up, and he cringed whenever he was touched. To earn his trust over time, we attached a soft cloth leash to his collar, and we left it attached twenty-four/seven. This allowed our volunteers to reach for the end of his leash (as opposed to him) when necessary. After a week of this indirect approach (and our shelter's routines and supportive rituals), he was running up to people with the rest of the pack, happy to be picked up and massaged.

When we use this technique with teething puppies, we use lightweight metal leashes that hold up to (and discourage) leash chewing.

WHAT YOUR POSITION COMMUNICATES

Just as our posture communicates volumes to our dogs, so do the positions we take. This is especially true when dogs encounter us for the first time.

For example, when a visitor comes to our facility, we encourage him to straighten his spine, relax his shoulders and smile (even laugh a little) as he walks in front of us into our dogs' main play-yard. Why in front of us? Because this tells our dogs that we accept him as a fellow leader, and not a follower.

How might our dogs view him, if he follows us? First, he could be someone who means us harm. Second, he could be a new follower (and it is up to the dogs to determine where in the pack he fits). Both situations promote excitement, and both encourage barking and unwanted behaviors.

Of the many things that the dogs at our Center have taught me, this was one of the most profound (and yet so simple). But time after time, we consistently found it to be true.

New person in front → dogs become curious
New person following → dogs become concerned

We remind our visitors to honor canine social rules (no reaching, no direct eye contact, and no talking, at first) while our dogs sniff them over. Once the dogs have taken a few steps away (signaling their acceptance of the situation), our guests are then encouraged to initiate eye contact, and to softly talk to and handle our dogs.

REINTRODUCING DOGS TO GROUPS

Position also plays an important role when dogs get returned to their play-groups, and the approach we take depends upon whether a dog is hand-held or leashed, at our side.

<u>Hand-held dogs</u>. Our canine Miss Manners dictates that hand-held dogs never be placed face-first into their groups. That would be confrontational, and it wouldn't be the fault of the dogs if conflict ensues. As I lean to put a small dog back with his buddies, I turn him around and place him into his group <u>butt-first.</u> In addition to following canine social protocol, this orientation does two things:

❖ It leaves all of the dogs facing the same direction.
❖ It gently reminds the dogs that they are on the same team.

<u>Dogs at our side</u>. When I return a leashed dog to his group, I walk a half-step <u>ahead of him</u> into the group. This encourages all the dogs to part politely. They focus on me (as opposed to the incoming dog), and my leading position reminds them that he is a follower and I am still the decision-maker.

THE LIGHT BEHIND US

Does your dog bark when people stand at your door? While there may be multiple factors contributing to this problem (prior associations, visitor off-energies, your own off-energies or excitement, or the need for alternate behaviors, to name a few), a halo of bright light around your visitor may be to blame. Sunlight behind us (especially in doorways) makes our features hard to discern.

To rule this out as a factor, evaluate the light on the other side of your door at different times of the day, and view people standing in the doorway from your dog's perspective. To put your dog more at ease, encourage your visitors to pass into your home quickly, without lingering by the door.

The same principle applies outdoors, when you approach dogs with the sun behind you. What they may see, instead of your polite and friendly expression, is a dark outline that can appear suspect or even predatory. Try never to position yourself between an animal and the sun. Reposition yourself ninety degrees, so he can see you more clearly.

CLAIMING SPACE

Dogs communicate a great deal to each other and to us via the claiming of space. Whose paw is on top; who goes through a doorway first, and who leans over whom when a dog wants to claim an item. It is how they determine which of them, in any given moment, are equals (as opposed to who should lead the action). It is also how dogs play with one another. Occasionally an individual may vocalize, to more strongly communicate what he wants, but for the most part, dogs use nonverbal positioning and simple calm assertiveness to get their point across. Dogs conceding a point simply back off and walk away.

In any group of dogs, this give-and-take communication occurs frequently, with peaceful outcomes. One dog postures "I want this space/object. May I have it?" and another dog responds, via his posture, yes or no. The answer established, they then move on to the next moment.

Can (and should) we communicate what we want from our dogs in a similar nonverbal way? Most definitely. When our dogs attempt to claim an area or an item they shouldn't have, we can view their actions as we would the simple question, "Is this okay?"

"Can I do this? Can I claim that? Can I move here? Can I lead the action now?" Sometimes our answer will be yes. Yes, it is fine to *go out* toward the car. Yes, that is your bone; enjoy it! Yes, you can lie on that dog bed. Sometimes our answer should be no. No, you cannot crowd me at the door and push me aside to greet newcomers. No, you cannot knock over that little kid; you must offer her extra space. No, you cannot stand on my toes; I want you to stand quietly at my side.

In all of the latter cases, the dog is claiming space that rightfully belongs to someone else. Why is he doing that? Most likely (and simply) because he hasn't been shown more polite behaviors. Also, his bid for that space hasn't been calmly, consistently and clearly denied. Calmly, because dogs communicate with each other through calm (not excited) assertiveness. Consistently, because dogs love exploiting loopholes. Clearly, because if we do not know what we want, or if we doubt that we can get what we want, our dogs will ignore our message.

Know that it isn't impolite to convey your need for personal space, be it from other humans or your dogs! There is a peaceful way to go about it, however, and it involves standing your ground in a matter-of-fact way, something that even children can learn to do. To reclaim your personal space back from a dog (or the space around an area or an item you want him to avoid):

❖ Keep your posture erect.
❖ Project quiet, sticking-to-your-guns, assertive energy in a way that backs him away.
❖ Calmly point to where you would rather he go.
❖ Claim back, not only your space, but also an additional two to three feet.
❖ Step forward a step or two, if needed, in a matter-of-fact way (that is, without projecting heightened energy or emotion).
❖ Don't turn away, or walk away, until he adjusts his energy level down and backs away.

The process may take a long minute, but your patient follow-through (defined below) is as pivotal as your body language. Together, they convey that this space (or item) and the space around it belongs to you. Period. No discussion. There is a line in the sand and having drawn it, well, you own that, too.

This is a simple and straightforward practice, but it can be hard for some people to do. They don't have a lot of inner confidence (which sets them up to lose their dogs' respect). Alternately, they get frustrated or verbal, and they push back at their dogs. Pushing creates problems because:

❖ It uses force, which projects tension (as opposed to calm, directive energy).
❖ It pulls your posture off-center.
❖ It encourages dogs to push back or hover several inches away. Several inches just isn't a respectful or practical distance (several feet is). Many dogs will see this as a game that they know well. They push you, and you push back, so they push back...

Watch peacefully coexisting dogs communicate what they want to each other, both in play and around your home. If you are like me, you will find many lessons worth learning. For example:

Maxx the Doberman wants the bone that Treble the terrier has. To convey this, he hangs his head over her, like a cloud blocking the sun. Treble grumbles a little – in the hope that it will send him on his way – but the rest of her communication is nonverbal.

She repositions herself, to move her bone farther from Maxx. It doesn't work. He shifts position to negate her efforts. She moves again, angling her body between him and the bone, but he calmly overshadows her, waiting her out. His persistence pays off. Tired of the game, Treble gives him one last grumble before walking way, leaving her bone behind. No fighting; no gnashing of teeth. Maxx's calmly assertive posture and position, together with his calm follow-through is all that is needed.

Alternately, Treble could have held her ground by continuing to chew on her bone, no matter what Maxx did. In that case, her own calm assertiveness and patience would have won out over his. In either case, the dogs go on to coexist peacefully. What happens in one moment doesn't pass to the next.

Visitors to my home are often surprised to see dogs (in groups of six to eight at a time) sharing resources without issue. The reasons are two. Resources, such as extra-large bones to chew, are plentiful in number. If I have eight dogs, there are always ten bones available. Also, my dogs know that every one of these bones, first and foremost, belongs to me (and not them). I will expand upon this when I discuss resource guarding in Chapter 19.

Living in a small log cabin with so many dogs, I require them to stay well back from my fireplace, my kitchen counters, my computer and breakable items that could easily get knocked over. Should someone get too close, a simple *chicht!* or the command *back up* directs them to reverse their gears and give me or my property not just inches, but a respectful amount of space.

When I travel with Hiker, his job (when I am not directing him otherwise) is to lie quietly on his blanket, be it three feet, thirteen feet or twenty-three feet away. By directing him to his blanket with a point of my finger when I don't want him to do something different, I am claiming the rest of the space as my own. I am telling him that other behaviors (such as wandering the room, leaving the area, or flirting with the ladies...yes, Hiker is a big flirt) are off the table as choices. I am setting parameters for his space and claiming the rest for myself.

To do this, I don't push him. I don't touch him. Rather, I use my erect posture, my choice of position, my calm and assertive energy, plus my earned authority to point him to where I want him to go, and I calmly follow through. When he walks over to his blanket, to curl up in a relaxed, non-anticipatory manner, I reward him with a great big smile, a gentle wag of my hand or a soft "good job." He loves this quiet acknowledgement, and he is happy to repeat this behavior the next time I ask for it.

THREE-FOOT RULE FOR INFANTS AND TODDLERS

Just as I require my dogs to give certain areas and items extra space, I require that they do the same with infants and toddlers. In this case, my three-foot rule dictates that a dog should *wait* (pause) and *watch me* (look to me for direction) before moving within three feet of an infant or toddler. This creates a bubble of personal space for the child.

This rule also dictates that no toddler moves within three feet of a dog without checking for adult permission, allowing each dog to have his own bubble of personal space.

Simple to teach to dogs, using a broad smile as a reward for good behavior and the command *back up* (or *give me space*) plus calm redirection when they get too close, this three-foot rule is important to teach to parents, too. We teach it in a way that gives both the dog and the child positive reinforcement for hanging back. This is definitely not a situation where negative energy (*"Watch out, Johnny, that dog might bite you"*...or..."*Bad, Bosco, back off!"*) is productive. We want our kids to enjoy dogs. We just want them to do it with an awareness of, and care and respect for, a dog's personal space. We want our dogs to enjoy children, too, but with the same care and respect that we expect from the kids themselves.

FOLLOWING THROUGH

Let me define what I mean by following through, since it is a very important concept. When I follow through, I simply stand in place calmly, refusing to move until I get the behavior I want. Following through is an important part of canine communication. Dogs that follow through get the resources they desire. Dogs that follow through direct the energy of others. And dogs that follow through gain the respect of others.

Doing something without following through, that is without ensuring that you get one hundred percent of the results you want, leads to confusion about what you want. Being clear means following through. (More about this in Chapter 12.)

WHAT WE SAY WHEN WE LEAVE

Just as we communicate our intentions when we patiently stand our ground, we also communicate important things to our dogs when we turn to walk away. This is something that people often get one hundred and eighty degrees wrong!

Consider the many times that you have walked away from another person to signal your disapproval. When one dog walks away from another, it means the opposite! A dog turning and walking away signals one of the following:

❖ Acceptance of a situation.
❖ Comfort with a situation.
❖ Approval of a situation.

When I approve of what a dog is doing, I smile. I may offer a little hand-wag. And I feel free to walk away. When a dog does something I disapprove of, I need to stay and deal with it, be it through calm-assertive patience (the message being: "I'm going to wait you out until you change your behavior and the energy and the state of mind behind it."), correction (discussed in Chapter 18) or redirection to a better choice of behavior. Then, and only then, will I move on.

At this point, you may envision the need to spend a lot more time modifying your dog's actions. The good news is: if you are clear in your communication, and if your energy is calm and patiently assertive, and if your actions are consistent, with time those modifications will be much fewer and farther between.

Getting the dogs you really want, those who are such a pleasure to be around, requires first and foremost good nonverbal communication.

CATS ARE CATS, AND DOGS ARE DOGS, RIGHT?

Allow me to end this chapter with a tale of two languages…

Cats enjoy rubbing their faces all over their friends and the furniture and the walls – you name it, they'll rub on it – but you don't see many dogs doing that. Cats are into face-first, head-on, head-butting communication. They leave it to the dogs to sniff the butts. That said, occasionally there comes along a cat like Sid.

At our Center, Sid tolerates the other cats, but they beat on him all the time. If they aren't hissing at him, they are swatting him or chasing him away. Poor Sid!

Silly us; we thought it might be because Sid is a single white cat amid multicolored ones. We were wrong. Sid loves to be around dogs, and he often visits their play-yards. One day he appeared, asking to join us, and what did we see? When the dogs approached him from the other side of the fence, he lifted not his head to them, but his rear end! It wasn't just what he did from the other side of the fence, either. When we let him into the play-yard, he proceeded to let every new dog in the place sniff his butt. No swats. No hissing. No complaints.

Over the next few weeks, we watched his body language closer, and while he was happy to wind through our legs in true cat style, we never once saw him offer a good head-butt.

We don't know Sid's history before he came to us, but I would be willing to bet that he was a kitten raised by dogs. He knows their body language, and he speaks it well, even to the point of preferring it to the language of his own species.

Moral of the story: If you want to tick off a tabby, communicate like a dog.

HUMAN NONVERBAL COMMUNICATION

We humans have a body language all our own, and just like other things that we take for granted, we may not recognize its importance until it is gone.

When we sit down, or look down, to use technology – be it a cell phone, tablet, laptop or desktop computer – we cease much of our communication with other people in the room. We may continue to speak as we type, text and swipe, but our primary focus shifts from one another to our technology. Why might this be concerning? Because nonverbal communication is as vital to our species as is the spoken or written word! Nonverbal communication promotes connection. It promotes empathy, and it tends to tell the truth at times when lips lie.

Nothing kills communication between two people faster than when one stops to view a text message!

If you are having trouble communicating or connecting with others, try putting your technology aside. Focus on the people around you, if you want their focus in return.

TRY THIS EXERCISE: Visit a dog park to observe how dogs use body language to communicate. Watch how they use postures, positioning and calm assertive energy more than their voices. Let the dogs be your teachers for a little while, and enjoy being their student.

TAKE IT A STEP FURTHER: Try the approaches discussed in this chapter with dogs that you know and some new to you. Make changes, as needed, to your posture, the positions you take and the energy you project (for the latter, a review of Chapter 7 may be helpful).

CHAPTER 10
USING TOOLS

When people want to communicate with their dogs, they often reach for tools such as collars, harnesses and leashes. Some get used correctly. Sadly, many do not. While it is important to choose the right tool for the job, of even more importance is the manner in which it is handled and how it is positioned.

HOW A TOOL IS PUT ON

When I work with dogs, I often reflect upon how what I put out in energy and in effort comes back to me, and it has made me a better person.

If you have read all of this book's chapters so far, you know that I enjoy finding ways to bond with my dogs. I look for reasons to give them a big smile! When putting on a collar, leash, harness or slip-lead, I do so only when they are relaxed, so I can do it gently, while sending a message of love and connection. This elevates an average moment to one that connects us, and it sets us up for good teamwork in the future.

When over-the-head items need to be put on or taken off, I use wide loops, so as not to tug on a dog's ears or bump him in the nose. It may not sound like a big deal to us, but our dogs really appreciate it, and it influences what they do next.

UNIDIRECTIONAL VS. BI-DIRECTIONAL TOOLS

Some tools (harnesses, martingale collars, buckle collars, head collars and prong collars, for example) are bi-directional. They function the same, regardless of whether you stand on a dog's right side or his left. This makes them easy to use.

Other tools (slip-leads and so-called 'choke' collars, in particular) are unidirectional, and therefore not ideal for many situations. They tighten and release correctly if you stand on one side of your dog, but not when you shift to the other side. To better understand this, put a slip-lead (or a leash and 'choke' collar combination) on your dog, and stand on his right side. Follow its path from your hand down to his neck where it passes through a ring, and see where it goes from there (over or under his neck). Now move to his left side, rotating (but not removing) the collar so the ring is on your side. Follow the path once more. (If it passed through the ring and over your dog's neck, it now passes under it. If it passed through the ring and under your dog's neck, it now passes over it.) Your slip-lead or collar will tighten and loosen correctly only when it passes <u>over</u> his neck after passing through the ring. It will maintain inappropriate tension, sending the wrong message to your dog, if it passes any other way.

COLLARS

Where a collar sits on a dog's neck is important, because positioning it optimally allows you to use a <u>gentler</u> touch, when direction is needed. Collars naturally rest at the base of the neck, against the shoulders. Unfortunately, this is where all of a dog's pulling power originates. Professional handlers know to move collars to the top of the neck, just behind the ears, as doing this completely changes a dog's behavior.

collar low on neck → encourages pulling, given any tension
collar high on neck → encourages focus and a proud gait

Since keeping a collar in this optimal position can be difficult, several alternatives have been developed to help. The four that we most often recommend, when people need extra help, are:

(1) A modified Pack Leader collar. This kind of collar, which you can find online, works well with short-necked dogs, and I hope that one day there will be a good version available for longer-necked dogs. The idea behind its construction is simple: keep a collar away from a dog's shoulders and closer to his ears, so a lighter touch can be used when direction is required. One loop sits against the dog's shoulders and three stiff bridges keep a second loop (which is attached to a cloth slip-collar) closer to his ears. As I much prefer bi-directional collars to unidirectional collars, I usually replace this slip-collar with a martingale collar.*

(2) A head-collar. I use Halti and Gentle Leader head-collars on occasion, both of which require careful fitting and people-training. Head-collars shouldn't bump into a dog's eyes, and they are definitely <u>not</u> designed for heavy-handed people.

(3) A chest-ring harness. This type of harness allows a leash to be hooked to a ring on a dog's chest (as opposed to his back), making it less comfortable for him to power forward.

(4) A no-pull harness. The kind of no-pull harness we prefer has soft sleeves that go under the arms. Gentle tension in an upward direction tightens its chest straps, making it harder for a dog to pull forward. It is perfect for little dogs who like to call the shots, matched with handlers happy to have them do it. (They just don't want to be pulled around that much.)

These tools serve to remind a dog to use good manners, but in no case will they create good manners in the absence of good leash skills, calm handler energy and confident, directive body language.

LEASHES

It is hard to write about leash skills, because as vital as they are, they aren't easy to learn from a book. Rather, they are best learned under the watch of a perceptive coach. Even so, some leash generalities are worthy of note.

* Depending upon the size of a dog's head, this may take some careful fitting. Don't cut the slip-collar off until you know that your martingale collar, when attached, will fit over your dog's head!

From the moment you pick up your dog's leash, whether it is attached to him already or simply sitting on a tabletop, you are communicating with him. Your posture and position, plus the picture in your head of things to come, all say many things. On a scale of one to ten, what is your energy like, and what is your state of mind? Are you calm and relaxed? Are you excited and ready to move? Or are you holding your breath, anticipating a frustrating walk with a rude and rowdy animal? Asking yourself these questions is worthwhile, because your dog already knows the answers, simply by watching what you do! Before you reach for a leash, take a minute to smile and get your energy truly calm and centered. Do a few slow stretches, if it helps. What follows will be a much better experience for everyone.

People are often hindered by their choice of leash. They choose leashes that are too long or too heavy, when they would be better served with a short, lightweight one. Alternately, they reach for flexi-leads. While these extendable leashes can be useful when watching your dog romp at a leashed-pet beach, or for letting your dog eliminate, when you don't have a fenced-in area for that use, their clunky handle and length thwart any communication with your dog. These leads are all about distancing your dog from you, and if you want the benefits of walking as a team, they are not the tool to use. They also can be terrifying to a dog should their handle be dropped, driving him into the street.

At our Center, we prefer lightweight cloth leashes that are three-eighths-inch wide and only three to four feet long. When walking with one dog or many, we don't want to deal with lengths of extra leash. Ignoring the loops at the end, we let our leashes drape over our fingers in a relaxed manner, similar to the way we would hold a horse's reins or the handles of a gym bag, secure but with no added tension. This allows us to make simple adjustments with our fingers, without using our arms or our shoulders. If you have never used a similar simple lead, give one a try. You may never wish to pick up a longer, heavier version again.

Using leashes to communicate with dogs takes some finesse. When they are used correctly, they hang loose ninety percent of the time. (Our dogs remain next to us by choice, and not through the use of a leash.) When they are utilized to redirect a dog, the direction in which this occurs is important.

WHEN PULLING BACK MEANS "GO FORWARD"

Here is an irony for you: pulling back on a leash can urge a dog forward, against the tension your leash has created. Whatever the dog was focusing on, now commands more of his focus because you are tugging him away from it. You tug back; he tugs forward. You tug back; he tugs forward. Sound familiar? If he is at a high level of excitement or agitation (a dog lunging to get at another dog, for example) pulling back on his leash without changing direction can send him over the edge, into some very dangerous behavior. Also, the more any dog's neck gets tugged unnecessarily, the more he learns to ignore it and his handler by extension.

So what should you do when your dog pulls ahead or begins to out-pace your stride? If a simple corrective sound (I use *chicht!*) isn't sufficient to slow him down, one of several other approaches can be taken. You can:

- ❖ Stop long enough for him (and you) to return to a calm, level-one energy. This may take fifteen seconds. It may take a minute or two before you <u>both</u> relax one hundred percent and stop anticipating the next step. Use this time to unwind with a smile and a few deep breaths, and then get your dog's attention so he can share in your smile. Look up and outward. Wiggle your torso and shake the tension from your arms. Reposition his collar to the top of his neck, then ensure that your leash is loose and held only two to three feet away. Is your dog exhibiting level-one energy? Is his focus back on you? If so, you are both ready to move on. If not, take a little more time to get things right.
- ❖ Hook his leash to your belt or to a second leash around your waist, for some umbilical leashing. (There are few better ways to guarantee that lingering tension isn't projecting from your arms and down your leash.)
- ❖ Use the command *watch me*, if your dog knows it, to get his attention while changing your pace or direction slightly. This turns his negative behavior into something that you can reward. (*Watch me* is taught by rewarding your dog with a big smile and a soft but cheerful "<u>good</u> *watch me*" whenever he looks at you.)
- ❖ Change direction momentarily. Pat the side of your leg (to show your dog where he should be), and smile when he responds well.

❖ Use gentle pressure <u>straight up</u>* to reboot his focus. (This is explained more in two pages).

❖ Reengage his focus with a treat, rewarding only <u>quiet</u> attentiveness. (This said, some dogs just aren't food-motivated. Others completely lose their focus when a treat is in the picture. My buddy, Hiker, is one of them.)

❖ If you are walking several dogs at once and you don't wish to stop your forward momentum: use your heel or a walking stick to give a soft tap to the chest of a fast-paced individual, to remind him to slow down. A soft tap is a lot more effective and humane than tugs on his collar.

In none of these cases do you want to lose your calm. (It would only create tension.) You don't want to reach down to your dog, either. (It would put you off-balance, drop your focus and weaken the energy you project.) Lastly, don't get vocal, beyond your disapproving *chicht!* (That would increase the energy of the moment when you want to decrease it.)

"But it will take me forever to get from Point A to Point B!" you may say. This is where remembering your long-term goal – a well-behaved dog who is a pleasure to walk – helps. It is also where clear, sticking-to-your-guns consistency pays off the most.

In the toughest of cases – the Persistent Pull-o-potomus – remember the big picture. Responding to a person's direction and walking calmly at a person's side are skills, and for any dog to be ready to listen and learn new skills requires that he be in a receptive state of mind. Whenever I am faced with dogs that are eager to pull, I get out my ATV or my three-wheeled bike, or I call upon a volunteer with inline skates. After an hour of rip-roaring exercise, these dogs are happy to walk quietly at my side. Having had their need for speed fulfilled, they are ready to listen and learn.

Different dogs respond to different approaches. The ultimate goal is to have yours do what you want them to do because they want to do it, and not because they are forced. And

---

* *The timing for this is important, and your collar must be positioned correctly. If you wait too long and your dog gets a step ahead of you, or if his collar slips down near his shoulders, your leash will be at the wrong angle to create upward pressure. It will create backward pressure, and your dog's response will be to tug against it.*

when any dog is doing what you want, his reward should always be a loose leash (and your smile).

WHEN PULLING FORWARD MEANS "GO BACK"

Ever have a dog balk at moving through a doorway? Whenever I foster dogs that do this, invariably they are Boxers or American Bulldogs who hate to get up in the morning. They have come to associate moving through a doorway with something negative, and many of them will have bladders ready to burst by the time they allow themselves to be coaxed outdoors. Pulling them forward only makes them dig their heels in deeper, for the same reason that pulling them backward urges them forward. Dogs move away from tension! Too, the more you pull these dogs forward, the more you reinforce the association they have between certain thresholds and irritated, aggravated people. And their bladders get bigger and bigger...

You need to form new and more pleasant associations with doorways. This may involve:

❖ Leashing them (in a relaxed and wholly unemotional manner) before walking them outside and back inside a half-dozen to a dozen times. (More about repetitions in Chapter 13.)

❖ Engaging their noses with high-value treats, to turn crossing certain thresholds into an enjoyable game.

❖ Using another route outside initially.

❖ Tying their leashes to the collar of a bigger dog who passes through doorways confidently at your direction.

Whatever your approach, be prepared to do it with a big smile and without conversation each time – the first time to make going outside into a positive, matter-of-fact experience, and the other times to reinforce it as the best action to take, given the next doorway through which they are asked to pass.

Don't get discouraged if a dog doesn't instantaneously get the message. If you get discouraged or frustrated or vocal, your negative body language and energy will only reinforce his original, negative association with the door. Take a few deep breaths and remain matter-of-fact, and with time and repetition (in really stubborn cases it can take a few days), you will help him form a new association, one in which you point to any doorway and he happily travels through it on his own.

REBOOT!

We have established that walks are pretty important to dogs, but every pup doesn't get with the program without a little help. (Young puppies, puppy-mill survivors with limited leash experience and dogs concerned about walking on non-carpeted floors all come to mind.) Given the option to move forward (even with good mentor dogs at their side), these uncertain dogs sometimes freeze up. And like computers going into sleep-mode, they need the right button pushed to reboot.

If I have treats available, I might offer one with a backward* hand, to engage a dog's nose (replacing his concern with curiosity). If this doesn't work, or if treats aren't handy, I will move his collar up behind his ears and draw his leash straight up, so his nose tilts down and his forelegs reach for (but do not leave) the ground. I then look forward, and ease all tension on his collar as I simultaneously step forward.

Most dogs will then follow, because gentle poll-bending like this reboots their state of mind. It mimics their mama-dogs picking them up as pups, and it triggers a sense of relaxation. With shutdown dogs:

I'm not sure, so I'm freezing up. →
I'm relaxed and willing to take the next step.

Two pages back, I mentioned using this same technique to slow fast-paced dogs. In that case, my collar-repositioning and slow draw up, followed by slow release, has this effect:

I'm forging ahead. → Okay, I'll slow down.

Should you need to draw upwards and release more than once, keep your motions slow and steady, and your energy calm. Put a picture of success in your mind, look up and don't look back at your dog as you move forward.

CANINE CLYDESDALES

Have you put off adopting a second (or third) dog due to a concern about walking multiple dogs? Then get ready to adopt your next dog! A simple practice that makes walking two or three similarly-sized dogs easy, with the added benefit of freeing up one of your hands, involves tying their leashes together! Tie one knot close to the dogs, four to eight inches

---

* So I can face the direction I wish to go, as opposed to face the dog.

from their collars, (enough to bring them side-by-side, but not enough to permit tangling). Tie another knot close to where you want to hold their leashes. This braces the dogs together like a little team of Clydesdales, and what results is more mindful walking. A knot can also be easier to hold than multiple flat leashes.

We frequently use this trick to walk two or three dogs on our right side and two or three dogs on our left.

WHO SHOULD HOLD THE LEASH?

There will be plenty of times when the answer to this question is: not the person holding it; that's for sure! And there will be times when the answer is: another dog.

One day, I invited one of our volunteers and her two dogs to join me and several of our shelter's dogs on a trip to the beach. She enthusiastically agreed. A moment later, she began to backtrack about taking one of them. Sidney, her Golden Retriever, would love it, she told me, but her hound mix, Agnes, hated the water and the waves.

"The waves will be too much for Agnes to take."

That was all I needed to hear. Of course, both dogs would come with us!

At the beach parking lot, all of the dogs hopped out of our van with tails wagging and tongues lolling. They all walked beautifully up to and halfway down the raised deck toward the dunes. That was where Agnes began to balk, and that was where my volunteer friend announced that this experience was going to be too much for her. I looked at my friend, at her tense shoulders, tense arms and concerned expression. I then took the end of Agnes' leash away from her, and I tied it to Sidney's collar.

"Now let's walk to the beach," I said, leading the way with six dogs from our shelter, leaving my friend with only Sidney's leash to hold.

With only the slightest hesitation, Agnes followed the very-confident Sidney down to the sand, and we all thoroughly enjoyed an hour at the beach.

Morals of this story:

❖ Make sure that the individual holding the leash is in a <u>relaxed</u> and <u>positive</u> frame of mind.
❖ Sometimes the best individual for the job will be another dog.

PATIENCE: ONE OF YOUR MOST IMPORTANT TOOLS

Back in Chapter 3, I mentioned that patience will always be one of your most valuable tools. It is certainly one of your most powerful ones.

Remember how dogs move away from tension. Remember how they avoid (or seek to correct) drama. Patience allows you to summon the inner calm needed to conquer both tension and drama when neither will suit your purposes.

To illustrate, consider a five-month-old puppy, whining in her crate. What should you do? If you let her whine herself out without direction, the process will take quite a while. Her fingers-on-a-chalkboard symphony will increase the stress level in the room for everyone. And she will learn next to nothing from the experience (or things that you don't want, such as a negative association with crates).

Telling her "no" will only match her vocal energy with your own, and that will lead to increased tension and increased noise on both sides of the equation. (The use of the word "no" is discussed in Chapter 24.)

What works well is responding with a short disapproving sound (*chicht!*) and a disapproving posture (like that unhappy school principal in Chapter 7), prepared to wait out her whines and wiggles and barked protests <u>from a few feet away</u>. Calmly and patiently stand your ground, knowing that she is expending a lot more energy than you.

As you wait her out, she will throw every trick she knows at you. She will dig at the door. She will lick at its bars. She will make plenty of noise, but all you need to do is maintain your calm but disapproving posture. One approach at a time, she will learn that her puppy tricks aren't going to work. You are not going to talk to her. You are not going to bend down her way. You are not going to give her something to do, nor will you open her crate. And she cannot win points by getting you frustrated.

Easy to say, you say, but not so easy to do (after all, standing in place is no fun for anyone). This is another good time to reach for a riveting book! Turning this waiting-for-my-puppy-to-decide-to-behave time into some I-can-now-read-another-chapter-in-my-novel time goes a long way toward turning a negative into a positive.

With no more tools in her vast puppy toolbox after three or four long minutes, the puppy gives up her tirade, replacing it with a great big yawn. At that point, she tries sitting quietly. Now is when you give her a great big smile. It calms her, and it encourages her to lie down. You then wait for her head to drop and the rest of her body to relax one hundred percent. You reward this with a happy wag of your hand before walking away. Your well-timed, quiet walking away tells her that her calm relaxation is what you wanted.

Because you took the time needed for her to quiet completely, she will now remain quiet as you tackle other tasks and walk outside the room and back in again. When you are ready to take her out of her crate, she will exit just as quietly, having learned that quiet behavior is worthy of reward.

This is patient nonverbal communication at its best, and it sets dogs up for better future behavior. The next time your puppy throws a hissy-fit, she will only play her sad-sack routine for thirty seconds, and not four minutes, before settling down. Episode by episode, things will get better. When you consistently utilize patience to wait out unwanted behaviors to get to the ones you want, I cannot emphasize how quickly dogs learn.

I mentioned the puppy's yawn. A yawn in this context is really good. It means that she is letting tension go. When a dog like this yawns, I always nod and smile. Let it go, baby. Let it go!

Fortunately, it is near impossible for a dog to perpetuate tension when everyone around her refuses to feed into it. In other words, she can throw energy at you for only so long before she runs out of it! This is what makes patience so empowering. It helps to keep us sane, while it helps to put situations right.

Practice with any tool makes perfect, and patience takes practice. The more you summon it on a case-by-case basis, and the more you use it, the better your results will be.

THE RIGHT TOOL FOR THE JOB

Here are a few questions worth asking before choosing a new tool:

- ❖ What are the symptoms you hope to correct, and what is the underlying problem? (For example, is the underlying problem a severe lack of focused exercise? Without adequate exercise, you are going to see more nuisance barking, more hyperactivity, more household destruction and all of that leash-pulling. No tool in the world is going to address these symptoms without exercise.)
- ❖ Are other options better suited to address the problem?
- ❖ Does this tool require proper fitting or training?
- ❖ Does this tool require supervision?
- ❖ Is this tool going to be utilized by the right person in the right frame of mind, using the right energy? Subtle corrections in the way a collar is positioned or a leash is held can make all the difference in the world, but this requires a calm, perceptive hand.
- ❖ Is the tool unidirectional (and might a bi-directional tool be better)?

The right tool should not maximize corrections. Put together with the fundamentals discussed in this book, it should help to minimize the need for them.

TRY THIS EXERCISE: Give your dogs some focused exercise (such as playing fetch or trotting alongside your bicycle), to put them in the frame of mind to follow you. Then find a quiet path and umbilical-leash walk with them for ten minutes or so. After that, walk side-by-side with their leashes in hand. If your dogs are more relaxed when you umbilical-leash them, than they are when you hold their leashes, look for ways to shed residual tension from your shoulders and arms. If they walk well next to you in both cases, congratulations! Enjoy your walks together!

TAKE IT A STEP FURTHER: If a dog is reluctant to follow you in a given situation, hook his leash to the collar of a more confident dog. Then walk on, holding only the leash of the more confident dog. Be sure to smile and relax, and put a picture of total success in your mind before you take your first step.

CHAPTER 11
USING OUR VOICES

Although it is always more effective to communicate with another species in the way that members of that species communicate with each other, human beings are human beings. We are a conversational bunch. For this reason, it pays to understand what happens when we get vocal around our dogs.

When we talk to our dogs, it increases the energy of their responses. It peaks their interest. It focuses their attention. It gets them thinking with their ears and their eyes, instead of their noses. Did you know that when we open our mouths to speak our blood pressure rises? It doesn't matter whether we are saying something nice or nasty. Oops! There goes our blood pressure! No wonder dogs respond to our voices with a higher energy of their own.

There are times when you want to increase a dog's energy, and there are situations where verbal communication has its place. But since, as we get more verbal with our dogs, it increases the chance that they will get more verbal with us, a good rule of thumb is: if you can communicate in a nonverbal way, do it. That is dog-centric (as opposed to human-centric) communication.

USING SOUNDS

Certain sounds work so much better than words do when we want to cool a dog's jets. Their vocal energy tends to back dogs up (the better for them to focus on us), whereas any amount of conversation would only excite them. I communicate a lot to my dogs using four simple sounds.

- ❖ "*Chicht!*" means stop what you are doing and focus on me.
- ❖ "*Tsst*" is a short reprimand, a sort of disapproving "*chicht!*"
- ❖ "*Tsssssssssssss,*" which sounds similar to a punctured tire, is used to claim my space, to back a dog up, and it works much better than any kind of touch (especially near thresholds). With boisterous adolescent dogs that like to dart past my legs, it communicates what I want without affecting my posture. With dogs following the movement of my hands when I don't want them to (for example, when I move an object from one location to another), it interrupts their focus so they concentrate on something else.
- ❖ "*Eh-h-h-h-h-h,*" which sounds similar to a buzzer, will be explained further in Chapter 24.

TEACHING OUR LANGUAGE TO THE DOGS

When it comes to words, dogs have a great capacity to learn and follow spoken directives. That said, some ways of linking words to behaviors work better than others. To demonstrate this when I taught obedience classes, I divided each group in two for a demonstration called Teaching Orange. One half of the class represented the "dogs" while the other half represented the "handlers." I sent the "dog" group to a corner while I spoke to the "handlers" across the room.

I told the "handlers" that we were going to teach a new command. Their job was to call out the command and see what their "dogs" did. We then paired the groups and, on the count of three, the "handlers" gave the command *orange!* Needless to say, everyone was confused. The "dogs" had never heard the term before. Some "handlers" repeated the command. Others just shrugged their shoulders, signaling that their "four-legged" partners were on their own when it came to figuring things out. It usually took a little while, but everyone involved got the point of the exercise.

As a species, we are so language-dependent that it can be hard for us to imagine our dogs don't understand the meaning of *sit, down, stay* or *come* the first time or the second time or the third time we say it, no matter how differently we say it.

NAMING BEHAVIORS

So what is the best way to teach new commands to a dog? Whenever possible, name the behaviors as they do them naturally! Consider three different scenarios:

Scenario 1: Give Jack a command that he hasn't learned yet. He doesn't understand it. Say it again. Jack still doesn't understand it. Say it again, with more emotion in your voice. Jack's tension (and your own) increases, and he still doesn't have enough information to know what you want. Jack may figure things out, but he now associates the command with <u>tension</u>.

Scenario 2: Say a command and use a treat to guide Echo into the position desired. Say the command again. Echo focuses on the treat and his behavior follows suit. He associates the command with getting rewarded (and with repetitions he can learn to associate it with the behavior you desire).

Scenario 3:   See Lilla sit calmly. Give her a big smile and softly tell her "Good *sit*, Lilla." Repeat this whenever you see Lilla sitting quietly. Lilla learns to associate sitting with the command *sit*, and she links both to your pleasure.

See Lilla lie down calmly. Give her a big smile and softly tell her "Good *down*, Lilla" (with *down* pronounced in a drawn-out fashion). Repeat whenever you see Lilla quietly lying down. Lilla learns to associate lying down with the command *down*, and she links both to your pleasure.

Notice Lilla focusing on you quietly. Give her a big smile and softly tell her "Good *watch me*, Lilla." Repeat whenever you notice Lilla quietly focusing on you. Lilla learns that *watch me* means 'focus on me.'

While Scenario 2 is a tried and true way of teaching behaviors, it doesn't fit into many practical circumstances. For instance:

❖ When you are working with more than one dog at a time.

❖ When you have dogs that get too excited when they see treats.

❖ When you want to reward dogs for good behavior from a distance.

For this reason, I prefer to teach commands to dogs <u>as they do them naturally</u>. Smiling and naming a behavior, as a dog does it, rewards not only his choice of behavior, but also the calm matter-of-factness associated with it.

Dogs quickly learn commands this way. How quickly? Let me use the command *hurry up* as an example. At our shelter, *hurry up* means 'poop or pee, please,' and it is taught simply by saying a dog's name and "<u>good</u> *hurry up*" in a soft voice whenever we see a dog emptying his bladder or bowels. New adopters love that their dogs know this command, especially on cold, rainy days!

That said, I need to mention Willy and Alberta, two little dogs who think *hurry up* means 'run over to a clump of grass and start grazing.' Willy and Alberta must have been chewing on some grass at a time when I was praising another dog for hurrying up (the way the command was intended) because now, whenever I urge the rest of the pack to *hurry up* before dinner, they sprint to eat as much grass as they can before joining the rest of the dogs on their trek inside. It just goes to show how easy teaching commands can be, using this approach!

Like what your dog is doing? Give him a big smile to calmly let him know that it pleases you, and then name the behavior. ("Good *sit*, Bosco." "Good *down*, Bella." "Good *come*, Fido." "Good *go slow*, Jenni.") You don't have to carry treats, and you don't have to worry about your dog not following through.

Feel free to create commands that suit your individual circumstances! *Quiet dog* (Chapter 6), *give me space, walk nice* (Chapter 8) and *let's go pack* are some of the commands that we have made up. (The dogs really perk up when they hear that last one.) This turns dog obedience from a course that is held once or twice a week into a way of life in which you and your dogs communicate to get on the same page, a few minutes here and a few minutes there, seven days a week, with excellent results.

This is a wonderful way to be verbal with your dogs, and when you have other people watching what you do, it helps to train them, too!

TONE OF VOICE

When you decide to be verbal, watch the tone of your voice. Your dogs will respond with increased energy when your voice rises in pitch, and unless you are revving a dog up to tackle an obstacle course, it is probably not for the better.

This is one area where my dogs often correct me. As long as my voice is of a normal conversational tone, they remain relaxed. If my voice rises in volume or inflection, they start moving around, and they may whine or bark. They are only following their leader. I don't correct them verbally, beyond a simple *chicht!* After all, my verbal energy is what prompted theirs. I correct myself, and my dogs quiet in response.

Good trainers know to be aware of the tone of their voices. They may use a higher-pitched, higher-energy voice (what I call my poodle-voice) with a dog that won't take it over the top, and a lower-pitched, soft voice with another that would fall apart with a higher one. One problem with newbie trainers schooling in only one method of training is: one method of training and one tone of voice doesn't work with every dog.

I was visiting a small training facility in Canada with Hiker when one of their trainers offered to teach him how to crawl through an agility tunnel. To be polite I said, "Sure," but it was against my better judgment. The moment she started utilizing a higher-pitched, higher-energy voice, he pulled back, confused by her energy (not the tunnel). Contrast this with how he learned to ride up and down airport escalators. In that case, I simply walked with him onto the moving steps as if we had done it a hundred times before, and not a single word was spoken. Yes, he jumped a little at first, as his front end and hind end moved in opposite directions, but when he saw that the entire event was no big deal to me, he settled in for the ride. At that point, I rewarded his calm acceptance of the situation with a soft scratch on his shoulder, and that was it. No "good boys" were needed.

Now don't get me wrong...I enjoy saying "good boy" as much as anyone else. I just know that calm, nonverbal energy gets me a lot farther with most dogs.

The excellent thing about Hiker riding escalators nowadays is: he gets lots of positive feedback from people traveling in the opposite direction. They point at him and give him huge smiles, and smiles are the way to this dog's heart!

Tone of voice is also important when you say commands. To demonstrate this, say the following words in a monotone:

Come*	Watch	That's enough	Get it*
Sit*	Heel	Watch me	Leave it
Stay*	Off*	Stand*	Walk nice
Down*	Seek*	Go out*	Place*

If this is how you sound when you communicate verbally with your dogs, you shouldn't be surprised when they get confused. Now say each of these commands again, changing the inflection of your voice while accentuating different syllables to make each term distinct from the others. For me, *sit* is a calm word pronounced as if it has two syllables, whereas *stay* is said as a short single syllable. *Watch* sounds more like "w-a-a-tch," while *leave it* is crisper; simply two short words. At our facility, the commands starred above are used together with hand signals, the better to be completely nonverbal in other circumstances.

AGREE UPON THE MEANING OF EACH WORD

If you teach your dog that *down* means 'lay your belly against the ground and don't move until released,' he will be confused if someone uses the command to direct him off a couch or to keep him from hopping against their legs. What you mean will be clearer if everyone around him uses *down* to mean 'lay down until you are released' and *off* (pronounced o-off, as if it has a second sing-songy syllable) to mean 'get off' something.

Two more commands that confuse dogs when people don't utilize one and only one meaning for them are *stay* and *wait* (the latter pronounced as if it has two syllables). *Stay*, in the traditional sense, means 'plant your bottom or belly down and don't move until I release you.' *Wait*, on the other hand, is utilized in cases where you want a dog to remain a step back. *Wait* doesn't require your release. Most commonly, it is used when you want to pass through a door without your dog joining you. He isn't being directed to sit or stand in place, only to back off so you can do what you need to do without his participation.

Ensuring that everyone in your household imparts the same meaning to the words they use is only fair. When this doesn't happen, no one should be surprised when a dog ignores what they say.

THANK YOU!

If you are looking for a good way to be verbal with your dogs, this is it! When any or all of my dogs stop a behavior at my direction, and when they drop the energy behind that behavior to a much lower level, I always respond with a soft "thank you." I consider this very, very important! Why? Because if all you do when you correct a dog is reprimand him, your dog will respond no different than you would if all you got were corrections.

Imagine for the moment that you just got reprimanded. How are you feeling right now? Are you happy? Are you relaxed? Of course not! You are probably a little on edge. But what if, after your actions were corrected, your mentor thanked you for doing a really good job at something else. Now think about your body language. Would you still feel as tense and coiled up inside? Would you still feel as unhappy? Probably not. For dogs – who live in the moment and don't hold grudges and don't make excuses for their behavior – giving them that "thank you" or "n-i-c-e" or "good decision" (two other softly spoken atta-boys I often use), or even a great big smile, changes everything...and the sun is shining again!

Really! You need to let your dogs know when you are proud of them as much as, if not a lot more than, you need to remind them when they have crossed a line. When your dogs respond to a correction and they stop what they are doing, and when they drop their energy level way down so they become quiet and watchful instead, always say a soft "thank you." I guarantee your dogs will respond to you better when they get quiet, positive reinforcement for their quick and continued response to your correction, and they will be much less apt to go back to the behavior that you didn't want.

Ending things on a good note also helps you! It lets you let go of any tension that the dog's unwanted behavior created, so you can carry on with the rest of your day in a better frame of mind.

TRY THIS EXERCISE: Try spending time with your dogs without a word spoken. Rely on your smiles, the quality of your energy and your movement (plus a few hand-wags, if you would like) to communicate. Nonverbal communication gets better with practice, and it can make your well-chosen verbal communication more effective. (You will learn more about using movement in Chapter 15.)

TAKE IT A STEP FURTHER: Whenever your dogs follow through on a command <u>and</u> drop any excited energy behind their actions, give them a soft, well-timed "thank you." Enjoy how it defuses the tension!

JUST LET ME KNOW
WHAT YOU WANT

*It is up to the artist to use language that can be understood,
not hide it in some private code.*
Robert A. Heinlein

CHAPTER 12
BEING CLEAR

What does being clear mean? It means following the rules discussed in Chapter 3, especially Golden Rules #1 and #2. It means calmly following through, every time, to get the behavior you want, so you can walk away with a smile. Being clear with our dogs also means being clear with ourselves, both in mind and in body, about the effects our energy and our state of mind has upon them.

To demonstrate how keenly your dogs are attuned to your energy level, try this: At a time when your dogs are lounging around the house, start jogging in place in a central location (your kitchen or living room, for example). Don't speak. Don't call attention to yourself in any way. Just jog in place. Then watch what your dogs do in response to your higher energy.

When I did this exercise this morning, as part of a personal 'stay in shape' effort, Skyy the Min-Pin mix, Pork Chop the Maltese mix and Katie the Labrador all rose from their slumber in three different rooms to trot into the kitchen to watch. Hiker appeared at my side, ready to join me should I move forward. Even Kent, the deaf Pug and Jobe the eye-less Shih Tzu wandered into the room with tails wagging. I didn't have to say a word. My increased energy alone caught their attention.

An awareness of energy (both quantity and quality) is routed in the survival mechanisms of the canine species. Even dogs that exhibit the weakest of survival instincts can sense when the quality of our energy and our actions aren't in sync. They will avoid it (or try to correct it).

For this reason, taking a matter-of-fact approach to much of what we do with our dogs has great value. Matter-of-fact simply means not too much of anything: not too emotional, not too loud, not too energetic and not too rough. Not too lackadaisical, either. In other words: allowing our personal state of mind to reflect calmness and clarity. Calmness and clarity, in turn, evoke security, the feeling that all is well in the moment. And security is something any dog can relate to. It is something any dog will follow.

LEADING BY EXAMPLE

Speaking of what dogs follow, being clear with them includes being willing to show by example. If you want a dog to be relaxed in any given situation, it really helps to be relaxed yourself.

Service Dogs are the epitome of calm under pressure, the perfect combination of excellent DNA, thorough socialization and calm, calculated experience and training. When first exposed to hectic situations such as events and transport centers, they echo the calm, confident energy of their handlers so this becomes their go-to energy, their default behavior given similar situations in the future.

Hiker and I have been together for six years now, and it still amazes me how well he walks through crowds at busy air terminals and train stations. He *heels*, *comes*, *downs* and *stands* on command at TSA checkpoints, as if he is the star in his own show. He navigates tarmacs, past moving planes with spinning propellers, to climb narrow steps up to jets at my direction, all in another day's work. He enters subways, trains and buses without hesitation.

He knows his job well, as my Vertigo Assistance Dog. He takes it seriously. As the human member of our team, I take my job seriously, too. That means that every time we encounter new situations, I lead the way by example. I demonstrate the same calm that I want back from him, given similar circumstances in the future. I have to, since every new situation we encounter is a chance to build good associations.

Chapter 5 illustrates my favorite and most-utilized way to show by example: introducing dogs to each other while walking. When we move forward (and continue to do so, no matter what the dogs at our side may try to do), we send the message to each and every individual, by example: everyone's job is to walk. Nothing more; nothing less. Peaceful, side-by-side coexistence is what the moment requires.

Contrast this with introducing dogs head-on, while hoping everyone will get along. Uh uh uh. We put our dogs – all of them – on the same team from the get-go, no questions asked.

LIVING IN THE MOMENT

An important element of being clear involves being willing to live in the moment. This means being willing to let small mistakes go, to see them simply as reminders to do things differently next time. Chapter 20 describes some practical tricks for doing this, techniques that can be used in many situations to ease tension and increase your presence in the moment.

A 'live in the moment' approach also helps when our dogs (even the best-behaved of them) have a "Have you lost your canine-mind?" moment. Dogs will be dogs (and puppies will most definitely be puppies), and the occasional challenge comes with the territory. Let me share one of Hiker's "Have you lost your mind?" moments, to illustrate:

> We were walking down a quiet street with four smaller dogs, when I tripped over a bump in the road and landed on my palms and knees. Did my super Service Dog come to my side, as he was trained to do, to help me up? Ha! Instead, he followed the lead of the other dogs (who thought this was all part of a game). In full Doberman play-mode, he pawed at my shoulder, knocking me further into the street. Granted, he was not wearing his service vest (his cue to behave accordingly), but still…he knew to do better! Much better, in fact.
>
> Getting my bearings back, I looked in both directions for cars, mortified and rather embarrassed. At that point, my training kicked in. (It had to, since Hiker's hadn't.)
>
> "*Back up*," I directed. "Game over." The dogs all backed up, dropping their collective energy.
>
> "*Stand*," I told Hiker. With a blink of an eye, he stood to help me up.

Now it was time to let the entire misadventure go. Sure, my palms were bleeding and I had gravel embedded in both knees, but anger or frustration wouldn't help me communicate what I wanted. The moment had happened. The same mixture of events with the same goofy little dogs wouldn't likely occur. And it would actually become a funny story to tell the following day.

It was time to pick the gravel out of my knees, smile to reward my dogs for their now-calm behavior, and continue with our walk.

What you decide to do in any given situation is going to vary with the particulars. Just be sure you don't respond to a dog's unwanted behaviors, heightened energy or unsettled states of mind with any of the same. Be willing to <u>let a bad moment go</u> and move on. Then smile to reward yourself for doing it.

MAINTAIN YOUR FOCUS

Being clear and leading the way both require an element of focus. For this reason, it is valuable to ask yourself where <u>your</u> focus is, especially when you expect great things from your dogs.

There is much in twenty-first century human culture that serves to narrow our focus. Just think of how many hours of each day we spend focused on computer monitors, television screens, and yes, even the printed page. Now consider all of the achy backs and necks, chair-driven postures and sedentary-life health issues that result.

Looking up from our devices, to expand our focus well beyond them, is good for our posture, our breathing, our general health and our circulation. It can even be argued that looking up and outward is vital to our personal growth and the preservation of our species. Just like our dogs, we have been born to observe and engage with our surroundings, not simply focus on inanimate objects eighteen inches from our noses.

Let your dogs help you to reengage! Put those monitors, screens (and yes, even this book) aside, and go for a walk with them. Look up and outward when you walk together, and reconnect with your environment.

TRY THIS EXERCISE: If you have mastered walking with your dogs at your side, find a walking trail where other dogs walk well next to their owners. Invite some of them to walk side-by-side with you for five to ten minutes, and then stop so the dogs can give each other a good sniff. Continue your walk after introductions have been made. The more you do this, the more you will master the art of dog introductions, and the more you can teach others to do the same.

WHEN THINGS AREN'T GOING SO WELL: When troubleshooting a dog's unwanted behavior, examine your responses. Is your demeanor calm and matter-of-fact, or do you exude emotion? Are you living in the moment and letting small bumps in the road pass? Where is your focus? Are you (or is your dog) leading the way? If asking yourself these questions doesn't lead to the answers you seek, keep the faith! More help is on the way!

CHAPTER 13
REPEAT, REPEAT, REPEAT

When you are a dog learning new things, practicing a skill five times over ten days leaves lots of time to forget what the lesson was. Practicing it ten times over five minutes is a much better way to learn! Simple repetitions help dogs form solid associations. They help dogs develop confidence, and they accelerate learning curves significantly. Here are some practical examples.

TEACHING GOOD WALKING MANNERS

My favorite place to teach polite walking manners is a set of gentle steps. The general idea is: my dog is allowed to 'claim a step' after I have claimed it, but not before. Starting with a loose leash and my dog at a solid level-one, I catch his attention just before each step with a point of my finger and a soft clicking of my tongue. When he stops next to me on the step (stopping completely, and not just pausing), he is rewarded with a big smile. Each step then becomes an opportunity to do things right!

Spend five minutes going up and down a set of steps with your dog, rewarding his focus on you with broad smiles. You will find it to be a rewarding exercise that your dog should pick up fast. You can then progress to doing the same thing at curbs, sidewalk transitions and doorways. You can also do it spontaneously, in the middle of sidewalks, roads and fields, the better to hone your dog's walking manners.

Have more than one dog? Let your other dogs watch. It is amazing what dogs will pick up, simply by observing each other!

INTRODUCING NEW SITUATIONS

We use repetitions to encourage calm responses to new situations at our shelter. For example, to desensitize our dogs to our videographer, we introduced her to the pack following our regular routine for new-person introductions (Chapter 5). We then had her follow me, camera in hand, back and forth in front of the dogs a dozen times. Back and forth, and back and forth, and back and forth, in a relaxed manner following the same path.

Were the dogs comfortable with this the first time we passed by? Some were, because they saw her actions didn't concern me, but others whined and a few alert-barked (see Chapter 24). By the time we passed for the third time, however, even the most reactive dog began to see our actions as predictable. Everyone then sat back to watch us in anticipation of the next step, their expressions conveying, "I get this! I now know what you humans are going to do, and I'm okay with it!"

We took the same approach when contractors arrived to erect the deck around our Center's pool. We introduced the men to our dogs (using our regular routine) before asking them to walk between the dogs' play-yard and the construction site and back again; back and forth eight times, until the dogs all walked away calmly, comfortable with the new routine.

Because our volunteers were there as calm role models for the dogs, offering relaxed smiles for each dog's quiet behavior, this process took but five minutes. It paid off every day over the next week, as the workmen came and went and constructed the deck within sight of the dogs, free from excited barking.

Simple repetition, when used to expand a dog's experience base, helps to make him into a calmer individual; one who is more comfortable with the world.

CAGES AND CRATES

When a dog is released to our facility by another shelter or his owner, we are often told, "He hates to be crated." But we don't worry when we hear that. We know that these situations come about when dogs have been pushed into crates many times over (their minds and bodies fighting the whole time) or they have been crated far too long without exercise or quality-of-life stimulation. Neither is going to happen at our Center.

How do we change a dog's negative association with crates, so he freely enters one at our request? We reach for:

❖ A large, roomy crate with a secure, soft pad.
❖ A leash.
❖ Some high-value treats.

We let our leashed dog get a whiff of the treats before tossing one into the crate to encourage him to enter willingly. The instant he eats the treat, we give him the command to leave. We don't let him linger. We want him to associate entering the crate with being rewarded (as opposed to being punished or cooped up) and to associate leaving the crate with a command from us (as opposed to bolting out after being locked in for extended periods of time).

Making a game of the process, we repeat this step six or seven times. At that point, we close and then open the door with the dog inside, waiting an extra few seconds before directing him out. This second step is repeated several times, extending the period that the door is kept closed by a few seconds each time. Building trust in carriers and crates takes repetition, which is why we use treats and make a game of it. It cannot be rushed or a dog will find reinforcement for his negative associations. This is something that we do over several days, several times each day. It complements another approach that we take to build comfort with crates, described in Chapter 18.

Additional positive reinforcement for crating comes naturally at our shelter, because all of our dogs are fed in their crate-condos, and an association with mealtime is one of the most powerful positive associations you can have! We highly recommend that our adopters feed their new dogs in their crates. It gives these dogs a sense of security and place (their personal den) while they eat.

LEASH-ON/LEASH-OFF

Offering lots of smiles, we play repetitive leash on/leash-off games to promote our dogs' comfort with slip-leads. With puppies and small dogs, we play this game with them in chest-level cage-condos, so we don't hover over them. With larger dogs, we sit at their side. We put our slip-lead on and take it off immediately. We then slip it back on and take it off another three to five times, using wide loops and the occasional "good job!" or biscuit offered in a way that encourages each dog to reach his head through the loop. That done, we then go for a walk. In no time at all, dogs that once avoided these leashes see them in a very positive light.

MUZZLE-ON/MUZZLE-OFF

We use similar on-off games to acclimate dogs to muzzles, when they are needed for nail-trims or behavioral modification. First, we use the muzzle to dispense treats, the better to encourage our dog to reach into it. We then put the muzzle on and take it off immediately. We put it on and take it off several more times, before clasping it around his neck. Lastly, we reward him with a treat when we take the muzzle off.

Contrast this experience with one that many dogs endure, when a muzzle is clamped around their nose at a time of high-anxiety, only to be followed by a scary or painful procedure. It is an all-too-common scenario, and one that is completely preventable using sixty seconds of playful repetition. If you have a dog that does better at a groomer or veterinary office when muzzled, purchase one and play the muzzle-game with him at home. Your next grooming or veterinary visit will be much more enjoyable.

SMALL DOG REACTIVITY

Small dogs that jump at the slightest movement and those that are skittish about being picked up or put down can benefit from repetitive exercises, too. When I handle a dog like this, I reposition his tail, if it is held tight to his abdomen (the better to communicate that a fearful state of mind isn't needed). Then, holding him in my arms, I lean to place him almost, but not quite on the floor (just so his toes touch). I then lift him back up in a calm and matter-of-fact way. Together, we repeat this simple down-and-up process six, ten, even twenty times over, however long it takes for him to relax and become comfortable with the movement. The next step is to lean left and straighten up, then lean right and straighten up, several times over. This further helps to acclimate him to my handling and movement.

HOW MANY REPETITIONS ARE ENOUGH?

How do we know when we have repeated an exercise enough? In the first case (teaching good walking manners), our goal is a dog who walks at our side on a loose leash. In the second case (introducing new situations), we want our dogs to ignore any new people or events, signaling their acceptance. In the third case (cages and crates), we aim for a dog's comfort in a closed crate, for increasing but always reasonable amounts of time, and we want him to walk into his crate with only a wave of our hand.

When building positive associations with items such as leashes and muzzles, we want our dog to reach his head toward the item. We want to be able to put it on and offer a three-minute massage before taking it off. And in the case of reactive small dogs, we want them to be less reactive. In some cases, they become so relaxed by our repetitive movement that they close their eyes and fall asleep!

Repetitive games help you to communicate clearly. They use time wisely, and they are a very good way to show your dogs the way.

REPETITIONS CAN HELP PEOPLE, TOO!

Just as repetitive exercises can build trust and confidence in dogs, they can do the same in people. One of my favorite exercises to do with people who are intimidated by over-reactive little dogs is: I have the person pass the dog back and forth with me, back-first and 'like a book.' After six or seven passes in this manner, both the dog and the person are a lot more relaxed with each other and each other's movements. That is the purpose of the exercise.

Why do I say 'like a book?' Because people are non-emotional about passing books back and forth. Most don't coddle their books. They aren't afraid of their books. They don't talk to them or stroke them if they think the book is nervous. Small dogs and puppies being passed between people need to experience that same degree of matter-of-fact confidence for them to develop good associations with the process.

Why do I say 'back-first?' Remember our canine social rules. Polite dogs don't introduce themselves eye-to-eye. Also, this position orients the dog toward someone who has already held him. His focus on that person helps him to feel safer.

SHOWING THE WAY

Whatever you choose to ask your dog to do, if you are clear about what you want, and calm and consistent in your approach, and if you provide repetition to allow him to make the right associations between your X and his Y, you and your dog will do pretty good as a team. The next step is to conduct your repetitions in new locations, the better to expand his horizons.

Moving in and out of crates and cages, walking back and forth through doorways politely, walking past strange objects confidently and calmly…anything that you want a dog to do well, feel free to make a game of it and do it over and over and over and over within a short period, until the little "Ah ha!" sign lights up in his eyes because he knows what is coming next and he is fine with it. Then reward his progress with lots of smiles!

It is a wonderful thing to be part of a dog's transformation in this way. No balanced individual enjoys living with apprehension or mistrust, and dogs develop a real sense of pride and purpose when they get the chance to move beyond them.

TRY THIS EXERCISE: Reflect upon your dogs' behaviors in each of the above situations. Do you see circumstances where repetitive exercises can help? Before you try any, reflect first upon your ability to lead your dogs in a calm, confident, matter-of-fact manner. Are you relaxed? Are you ready to smile? Do you have a picture of success in your mind?

CHAPTER 14
WILL WORK FOR SMILES!

Humans aren't the only species to define themselves by what they do best. Any Rottweiler, Chow or Doberman will tell you that being watchful is their specialty. Australian Shepherds and Shetland Sheepdogs live to herd (sheep, goats, children, their owner's ankles…it matters not). Breeds such as Huskies and Greyhounds are bred to cover ground, and terriers are bred to be tenacious. These traits are in their DNA, and they are central to their being.

This becomes an issue when people fall in love with a breed's appearance without much thought as to how that breed thrives. Considering adding a dog from the working, herding, terrier or sporting group to your household? Close your eyes and picture him doing what his breed does best. Picture yourself at his side, directing his actions and sharing his enjoyment of a job well done. If you are having trouble doing this, either because you don't know which traits lurk in his gene pool, or you can't appreciate the level of involvement needed, you may wish to rethink your next step. (See Chapter 27 for more about choosing the right dog.)

If you have already added a dog to your life without thinking the above through, don't despair. First, you have lots of human company in this regard. Second, there are ways to satisfy the DNA-driven needs of your dog that you probably haven't considered: exercises and events that will add focus and purpose to their lives while adding the same to your own.

If you have a non-working, non-sporting, non-terrier, non-herding dog, you are not off the hook. All dogs (yes, even Chihuahuas and Pekingese) excel when they have jobs to do.

THINGS TO DO, KIDS TO CORRAL

Giving a dog a job to do can be as simple as directing him to sit on a towel when you point to it (*place* is the command commonly used), releasing him* once a short time has gone by. It can consist of having him do tricks (such as *high-five* or *hop-up* and *hop-down*) on command, throughout the day. It can include teaching him to navigate cement ledges and small obstacles along your favorite walking path. Is this when you break out the biscuits? I don't, and it doesn't make me a treat-meanie. Rewarding my dogs with genuine smiles (and the occasional whispered "I love you!") connects us on a more personal level than treats ever could, and it better unites us as a team.

Want to increase an energized dog's concentration on the job at hand? Fit him with a comfortable backpack holding a few cans of tuna (or similar, size-appropriate item). Give him a cart to pull behind him on your walks, if pulling is in his blood.

Give your retrievers things to retrieve. (You know they will do it anyway.) Find a sheep-herding or treibball-playing** group in your area, if you have a herder who wants more than the local children to corral. Put a big pile of dirt at the farthest reaches of your backyard for your hound or terrier (or other natural digger) to dig in, and hide bones, chewies and treats for him to find at your direction. (Better that he dig in his dirt pile than smack in the middle of your yard!)

Dogs are problem-solvers by nature, and they love to follow their noses. A fun game that I have been playing with my own dogs uses several cardboard boxes, roughly shoebox-sized. I scatter them around a room before walking my leashed dog past them. He is urged to sniff each box, and he is rewarded for sitting next to the one containing his favorite chew-bone. Is this

---

* *Important: never force a dog to decide when he has stayed in place long enough. It sets him up for failure.*

** *Don't know what this is? Google it online, and then sit back to watch some really fun videos!*

the start of his training to be a tracking dog? Hardly! It is simply quality time spent together and another team-building exercise. It is a way to honor my dog's nature and have fun with it.

SHOW OFF!

Allowing your dog to demonstrate his best work occasionally helps to channel his best behavior when visiting public places. What we did with my land-shark Chihuahua friend, Ziggy (Chapter 3) illustrates this:

When taken to pet stores, walking trails and the beach, Ziggy's naturally mistrustful nature made him very reactive to strangers. (In his defense, their often hesitant, hovering nature would trigger the same response from many dogs.) Since we will never change how he perceives these people, and we can't always train strangers to approach him correctly, we gave Ziggy jobs to do, small tasks that directed him to behaviors that didn't include policing others. Directing him to sit on a facecloth placed in various locations, to carry or fetch items or hop up and down off of surfaces kept him occupied in ways that we could reward. Sometimes we rewarded him with a small treat; most often with a big smile and a soft "good job."

YELLOW-RIBBON DOGS

Ziggy was given an additional job. He served as a yellow-ribbon ambassador. Yellow ribbons tied to a dog's leash and the back of his collar – one hundred and eighty degrees from his tags – denote "give me extra space." (A ribbon in a horse's tail indicates the same.) Yellow ribbons don't necessarily indicate aggressive tendencies. Rather, a yellow-ribbon dog may have issues rooted in anxiety, or he may be dealing with health problems. He could be in training, or he might simply be a dog who behaves better without added distractions.

Instead of using actual ribbons (which wouldn't stand up to multiple uses), we used five-inch strips of yellow electrical tape, folded in half. This helped us keep well-meaning people back a few steps, without making anyone feel slighted. Whenever someone new approached, they were told, "Wait...Ziggy is a yellow-ribbon dog." We then placed Ziggy's facecloth on the ground, directing him to sit on it while we explained the purpose of yellow ribbons. In time, as soon as he heard us say "Wait," he sat and focused on us without his facecloth, secure in our control of the situation. This is teamwork at its best!

WORKING FOR YOUR GRUB

There is no better time to communicate what you want your dog to do than at mealtime. To illustrate, let me describe breakfast this morning at our shelter. Picture twelve dogs in roomy two-tier crate-condos, waiting for their meal and to go outside. When I enter the building, they watch me carefully: some sitting, some lying down and some standing. No one barks. No one whines. No one fusses. How can this be? (After all, this is an animal shelter, and some of these dogs are new arrivals who came to us without a day's training. Ever.)

The dogs all remain quiet because that is the job they've been given since day-one/meal-one.

being calm and quiet → dinner is served
barking, whining or fussing → no food is offered
dancing around, drooling or hovering → no food is offered
staring at your food in anticipation → no signal to eat
waiting calmly for the signal to eat → another handful of
food may be added to what lies in front of you

Any dog at our shelter longer than one day has had the opportunity to watch these rules being applied to other dogs (a powerful motivator). Even the wiggliest, most excitable dog gets with the program quickly.

Don't let your dogs' mealtime become a mindless task to get done! Offer food in multiple handfuls to reward your dog's politest behavior. (More about this in Chapter 19.)

FOOD PUZZLES

Do you have a food-guzzler or a dog who loves rooting around? Kibble-puzzles turn mealtime into an event for dogs like this. Several varieties can be found online. The super-simple ones that our shelter uses were constructed by our volunteers.

They cut six-inch sections of one-inch-diameter PVC pipe for our small dogs, six-inch sections of one-and-a-half-inch pipe for our medium-sized dogs and eight to ten-inch sections of heavy-duty two-inch pipe for our larger dogs. They then drilled four to six half-inch holes in each tube (scattered holes just large enough for kibbles to pass, given some nosing by the dogs). Removable PVC caps were then added to both ends. Ta da! Our dogs now have kibble-puzzles to enjoy when they go into their cage-condos for the night.

DOGS HELPING OTHER DOGS

Like children, our dogs are always looking to connect with us and each other, and this is something that we can use to our benefit. It is a big reason why I love working with more than one dog at a time. My dogs love the social aspect inherent in helping other dogs, and they take pride in the process. To illustrate:

Butch is your classic bug-eyed, wiggly, mildly obstinate, fun-loving Pug. In response to his growing reluctance to come indoors when the other dogs come trotting at my call, I got into the habit of calling *special invitation!* to urge him along. Okay, so it started with me asking, *"Does His Highness require a special invitation?"* Nonetheless, this quickly became a routine, one in which Butch would turn his back to me when I called everyone inside, ears pivoted in my direction, waiting to receive his "special" invitation. That was one routine I didn't want to pass onto the other dogs!

I knew not to approach the situation with excitement or extra conversation, and I was not going to play a game of "come and get me," when Butch declined to *come* on command. In the first case, my message would get lost in emotion or chatter. In the second case, he would have trained <u>me</u> to come to <u>him</u>.

Reaching for a handful of biscuits, to reward the behavior I wanted, was not an option. At the time, I was fostering one way-too-mouthy-for-his-own-good Boxer and a Shih Tzu on a special diet. Biscuits wouldn't work well for either of them. I reached out to one of my other dogs for help. For several days, I tied Butch to Sherry (one of my most well-trained, come-when-you-are-called dogs) using an eight-foot leash. She ensured that Butch came with the others when everyone was called. No more *special invitations* for him!

Another way that dogs can help each other succeed is through "competitive *sit*" and "competitive *down*" games. With small treats in hand, direct your dogs to *sit* or *down* (using the chosen command only once). Anyone plopping their heinie (or belly) down quickly gets a treat. Anyone slow to follow through gets ignored. Spontaneous games like this are fun for the dogs, and it doesn't take long before friendly competition takes over and dog-butts and bellies are hitting the floor like metal dropped on magnets.

WHAT POSITION DOES YOUR DOG WANT TO PLAY?

I have already mentioned how most dogs are born to be followers. This aspect of their DNA makes them very good members of a group. Put into any natural pack, they are comfortable in the middle: some days a step ahead of their friends and some days a step behind. (The middle of any pack is playfully fluid.) A much smaller percentage of dogs, however, possess traits from birth that place them at the very front of a given pack. Their DNA drives them to be leaders and leaders-in-training.

Why is knowing this important? Because dogs that fall into the front-of-the-pack category are not going to be happy any place else. As long as they are physically capable, they will strive to be the first through any doorway, the first at any food bowl, and the first to jump in and correct another. These dogs are not going to wiggle toward you on their backs, begging for a belly rub. They will be more inclined to convey "You and what army are going to make me do X, if I decide I don't want to do X," given commands that don't suit their purposes. Their self-appointed job is to make decisions in cases where a more secure leader hasn't set the course. This is where you <u>have</u> to be that more secure leader.

If you suspect that your dog is a true front-of-the-pack dog, one of the tests used in Chapter 27 will help you determine if this is the case. Recognizing his calling in life will help you to understand the motivation behind his actions. It may help you channel those actions into more productive and acceptable behaviors, allowing him to demonstrate his abilities while still acknowledging that ultimately, <u>you</u> are top dog.

In sharp contrast to front-of-the-pack dogs, back-of-the-pack dogs hang back and look back, as a rule, the better to warn their pack of danger at their flanks. Dogs that fall into the back-of-the-pack category tend to be more vocal in nature. Their self-appointed job is to alert their pack to things that other dogs simply observe. While this trait may be tolerated in some households, it causes great stress in others. (Chapter 24 discusses how limiting alert-barks through counting allows these back-of-the-pack dogs to do their job, just not at the cost of neighborhood peace).

DISCOVERING NEW DELIGHTS

Your dog holds a key that will open new worlds for you. Do an Internet search on "fun with a dog" and you will find links to sites on agility, treibball (my favorite for herding breeds), obedience, get-in-shape boot camps (think large groups of people exercising with their dogs), dog-friendly travel ideas, therapy dog training (great for lapdogs and senior snugglebugs), bikejoring (for dogs that enjoy pulling), Canine Good Citizen (CGC) training, tracking…even search and rescue training events. The list goes on and on. Let these sites get you excited to the possibilities, even if your dog isn't ready to jump in just yet. Your local non-puppy-mill-supporting pet store may be able to recommend regional walking groups, too. Visit events in your area (without your dog, initially) to see if the activity and the people involved may be a good match for you.

Dog people are, for the most part, outgoing. Yes, you may run into some opinionated personalities (and you will learn to avoid those that don't have the facts or experience to back up their opinions), but with such a wide assortment of opportunities, the chance of finding a niche that combines learning, entertainment and socialization is good.

Dogs really love having jobs to do, and that is what these opportunities provide. Good for them, and good for us, too, because there are few things more gratifying than watching a dedicated dog follow a good handler or a gleeful dog follow the dictates of his DNA.

TRY THIS EXERCISE: Consider what each of your dogs have been bred to do. Do some of their behaviors reflect this? Can some of those behaviors be channeled more productively? Search online to see if any of the activities mentioned would be a good fit for you.

TAKE IT A STEP FURTHER: Give your dogs small jobs to do sporadically throughout their day. Reward them with a big smile each time they do their jobs well.

GET MOVING,
TO MOVE ON!

When people will not weed their own minds, they are
apt to be overrun by nettles.
Horace Walpole

CHAPTER 15
LET'S GET MOVING!

Does your dog squabble with other dogs or cause trouble at the local dog park? Does he lack confidence or piddle when he sees you? Does he refuse to enter his carrier, get reactive at the drop of a hat, or show fear of certain objects or events? The secret to addressing all of these problems isn't complex. It is forward movement! Why movement? Because a dog's instinct is to track movement and be moving a significant percentage of his day. He is a fluid beast who communicates through movement, and it is his nature to get moving when times are tough.

This chapter discusses the use of forward movement in these situations. Chapter 16 discusses circumstances where encouraging backward movement works best.

GET MOVING, TO GET ON THE SAME TEAM

Do some of your dogs tend to feud, or do they act unfriendly to neighborhood dogs? Remember: dogs that walk together get along much better together. Walking is a bonding experience, and when it is done alongside or just behind a calm, confident person, every dog is put into the role of follower.

Dogs can't push each other around when walking at a vibrant pace, the way they can when they simply share space. A good, long working walk exercises dogs, and it puts them on the same track psychologically. Focused forward movement gives them a sense of <u>common purpose</u>.

Shy dogs blossom when walking with others. Rowdy dogs, however immature or untrained, benefit from lessons taught while walking. And walking is pivotal to the rehabilitation of aggressive dogs (as you will discover in Chapter 23). In all of these cases, outdoor walks and indoor treadmilling can be utilized equally to help dogs be their best. There is no better way to get them on the same team.

This is where someone will invariably say, "No way! There is no universe in which I will ever get Georgie and Jeffrey to walk politely side-by-side." And, as long as that is the conclusion they envision, they may be correct. I love meeting the Georgies and Jeffreys of the world, because each and every occasion represents a chance to put a more positive image in their owners' minds. If Georgie and Jeffrey sound like two dogs you know, let me offer this picture:

Imagine two people walking down a road in the same direction. Walking side-by-side but with ten feet between them (similar to the wings of a plane; no one in front of the other), both are relaxed, and they remain forwardly-focused and calmly directive despite the dogs on their far side bouncing and pulling toward each other.

dog - person - - - - - - - - - - - - - person - dog

It is Georgie and Jeffrey, and even though they were well-exercised individually for an hour, they are now acting their worst! Consider this to be their starting point, and allow yourself to mentally move beyond it.

Because both dogs are wearing well-positioned tools appropriate for their size and strength (head collars, Pack Leader collars or chest-ring harnesses, for example), and because any upward or lateral movement they make gets channeled into forward movement that doesn't stop, no matter what they do, they can only perpetuate their hyperactive hopping for so long.

Now picture both dogs settling down at their handlers' sides, focused more on the task at hand than each other. Over the next five minutes, their handlers gravitate toward each other, a foot or two at a time.

Ten minutes later, everyone is walking side-by-side.

dog – person – person – dog

Ten minutes after that, Georgie and Jeffrey are ready to progress to the next step:

person – dog – person – dog

Given ten more minutes, they are walking like this:

person– dog – dog – person

When working with the rowdiest of dogs, or people without a lot of walking strength, we use a variation on this theme. We tie the dogs to the back of golf carts or adult trikes. Using a golf cart or trike helps to give the dogs direction, and it prevents easily frustrated handlers from projecting tension down their leashes.

It saddens me to hear of households and neighborhoods divided to keep dogs away from each other. Especially if the dogs can see, but not interact with one another, this promotes a 'me vs. him' mentality. It creates two or more territories, patrolled by two or more watchdogs, and it fosters turf disputes. (More about this in Chapter 23.) Walking dogs together or (if it works better) bicycling or golf-carting them side-by-side turns canine division into canine equality.

KEEP MOVING, TO PUSH THROUGH LIMITS

Limitations are often placed upon dogs when people carry them around or pick them up to climb steps or hop into cars. This is most true with smaller dogs and puppies, and some of them can get quite neurotic as a result.

When a dog balks at moving into a new situation, only to be picked up and carried into it, the message he receives is: waiting to be carried is the behavior expected of him. If, on the other hand, he is guided onward by someone moving in the same direction, the message he gets is: it is okay to take the next step unassisted.

Aid your older, arthritic or injured dogs where indicated, most certainly. With the others, don't limit their abilities by helping them too much. Urge them forward by moving forward yourself. Healthy dogs love challenges, given the chance!

GET MOVING, TO ENTER HAND-HELD CARRIERS

In Chapter 13, I discussed how repetitive games using treats can encourage a dog to trot into a crate willingly. When it comes to small dogs entering hand-held carriers, our goal is the same: we point to a carrier's opening and he enters willingly; no pushing or extra prompting required.

Pushing a dog into (or, for that matter, tugging him out of) a carrier encourages his mind and body to fight you automatically, and the result is an association with carriers opposite of what you want. Remember how any dog's instinct is to move away from tension. Pushing him only strengthens his resolve to push back.

If you don't want to remove a carrier's cover, given a shorty who balks at entering despite the offering of treats, you can use a technique that exploits his placing reflex.* A dog's placing reflex tells him to advance his front legs, pads down, whenever his body is tilted butt-up or to the side.

To take this no-push approach, place your dog in front of his carrier. Then gently tip him so his hind legs leave the ground. This encourages his forelegs to engage and the rest of his body to follow, and most dogs get the idea quickly. Even in the case of the most stubborn or shutdown dog, less than a minute of patient tilting (nothing else) pays off.

The beauty of using this technique is threefold:

❖ It doesn't create or reinforce negative associations with carriers.
❖ It doesn't force your dog to do something. It encourages him to do it under his own power.
❖ Dogs usually stay inside a crate until they are urged out, having entered it in this way.

KEEP MOVING, TO ADDRESS SUBMISSIVE URINATION

Puppies will piddle to show submission to other pack members, and some individuals are slow to mature out of this behavior. Certain breeds (e.g., Dachshunds and Cocker Spaniels) are more prone to it than others. Owners of these dogs are usually told to ignore the behavior, and with time it will go away. Ignoring a dog that submissively pees is helpful because

---

* *Reflexes are automatic responses that occur without thought. They occur due to neurologic feedback loops that don't require the participation of our brains. This is what makes them so fast.*

it doesn't perpetuate his excited state of mind. Doing anything else, especially if you become vocal, just adds to his excitement.

Getting frustrated with the behavior hurts more than it helps, because frustrated energy projects tension. Piddle, piddle, piddle. Don't reach out to, hesitate near or hover over these dogs, and don't look directly at them when you put their leashes on or pick them up. That kind of body language puts them in a submissive state of mind.

Teaching piddlers to move forward into a slip-lead is helpful, especially when they require leashing to go outside. We do this with a simple two-part repetitive exercise:

Part 1: While walking our leashed dog at a relaxed pace at our side, we slip an extra slip-lead over his head and take it off again. We look up and outward, and we don't stop or hesitate when we do this. We put the slip-lead on and take it off ten to twenty times, until he ignores the approach of the slip-lead altogether. (Most dogs start to extend their neck, to make the exercise easier.) We do this exercise outside and then inside, walking up and down long hallways, and it is a good one to do while he is on a treadmill.

Part 2: Sitting across from our leashed dog (after he has had sufficient time to empty his bladder completely), we slip a slip-lead over his head and take it off, ten to twenty times. We then do this from a standing position across from him, to reinforce that approaching hands holding leashes aren't reason to squat and pee.

When we need to pick up a submissive piddler, we always do so on the fly, to keep our sneakers dry. While walking the dog at our side, we reach down and pick him up <u>without stopping</u> and without looking backward. Because 'moving forward' and 'submitting' aren't parallel paths in the canine brain, dogs picked up in this way are much less apt to piddle!

Of course, draining a piddler's extra energy using lots of forward-focused activities that boost his confidence and give him good pack identity is also very helpful. Treadmilling and working walks conducted in multiple locations work well.

GET MOVING, TO CALM REACTIVE INDIVIDUALS

Just as movement can have a calming effect on a crying infant, movement can also help to calm a reactive dog. When we have hyper-responsive little dogs in our arms, we start moving to give their minds something to think about other than whatever got them in a tizzy in the first place. Similarly, when we have larger, leashed dogs about to blow up in any which way, we redirect their energy by moving. We never stand still! Our calm, purposeful movement gives them something else to do, and it helps them to move on, both physically and psychologically.

People often talk to their dogs when they do this, but it is their movement and not their vocal energy that best defuses an unstable moment, welcoming in a new one.

KEEP MOVING, TO IGNORE FEAR-PROVOKING STIMULI

Forward movement can also be used to desensitize dogs to alarming stimuli. Because it is difficult for dogs to multitask, when objects, sounds and events are introduced at a <u>low</u> level of intensity at the same time a dog's brain is thinking "forward" and his four legs are confidently following, he learns to ignore things that would otherwise cause him to retreat or react.

We are asking the canine brain to prioritize, and we are helping to show the way. First, <u>we</u> are not reacting to the stimuli. Second, everyone is walking <u>forward</u> at a calm and steady pace, one that doesn't stop, hesitate or speed up when the stimulus gets repeated or gradually increased in intensity. By our own behavior, we are telling our dog "your job is to walk," not "your job is to react to this."

Playing low-level tape recordings of auditory stimuli (back-firing cars, appliance buzzers, firecrackers, even bombs from local military bases, for example) while walking Thundershirt-wearing dogs next to calm canine mentors* is one example. Playing the same kind of recordings while slowly treadmilling these dogs alongside more experienced dogs is another successful technique. The key to success is <u>calm directed movement</u>, so reactive dogs can form matter-of-fact associations and move on to a more relaxed state of mind.

*_The combination of a Thundershirt and a calm canine mentor is powerful!_

All three of these elements (calmness, direction and movement next to mentors) must be present because the goal is to relax our dog and help him to gain confidence, <u>not</u> to flood him with stimuli until he submits or shuts down! The difference is huge. For this reason, this kind of specialized rehabilitation is best left to the most experienced, empathetic and aware. Develop excellent leadership skills first. Acquire a working knowledge of all of the principles discussed in this book. Observe and learn from balanced dogs so they can refine your capabilities, sensitivities and empathy. Gain your dog's trust in all other matters. Learn how to introduce dogs of many sizes and aptitudes to treadmills. Work alongside and observe as many good canine handlers as possible (and learn to recognize what works and what doesn't work and why that is). Only then expand to specialized rehabilitation.

GET THE MOST OUT OF A DOG PARK

Shifting to a topic dear to the hearts of many dog owners, dog parks can be an exercise in irony. People visit them because they want to see their dogs move around, but so many then sit on a bench with their cell phone or friends and completely disengage from their dogs!

When you get up and move around a park, you encourage your dogs to do more than simply wander, and not a word needs to be spoken. As they sniff the ground, meet new dogs and find things to explore, they are made to keep an awareness of your location. Your movement leads them to move more (and burn more calories), one of the biggest reasons you brought them to the park in the first place! In other words: when you visit a dog park, do so with the intention of moving around!

LET'S GET MOVING!

Just as moving forward empowers a dog and helps him to move on to better things, physically and psychologically, it can do the same for us. The journey, as they say, begins with the next step.

With the invention of step-counting gadgets, our culture is becoming more aware of how many steps we take. This isn't such a bad thing. Consider your dog another ally in your pursuit of good physical fitness, one step at a time. Consider him to be even more, when it comes to your best mental fitness. Chapter 31 was written with this thought in mind.

TRY THIS EXERCISE: Notice how your dogs track your movement around your home. Consider how this characteristic can help you to communicate with them.

TAKE IT A STEP FURTHER: Should any of your dogs exhibit some of the issues discussed in this chapter (with the exception of desensitizing them to certain stimuli, which is best handled by professionals), give some of my recommendations a try.

CHAPTER 16
WHEN TO BACK UP

While there is a lot to be said for forward momentum, there are times when backing up is best! In Chapter 9, I mentioned one example: returning hand-held dogs to their play-groups, butt-first. Four other situations are:

❖ When we want to guide dogs closer.
❖ When we teach our dogs to sit.
❖ At thresholds, when a door opens.
❖ At mealtimes.

GUIDING DOGS CLOSER

Movement can be used to catch a dog's attention and guide him in a particular direction. This can be a hand movement, the movement of your entire body or the movement of an object, such as a toy or a treat. Movement is body language in action, and it works much better than words.

Teaching a dog to *come* is a good example of this. When I first ask a dog to *come*, I will step or jog a few steps <u>backward</u> to catch his attention and direct him to a spot in front of me. To urge him even closer, I will simultaneously draw my hands toward my abdomen, and then up to my chin.

By stepping backward, I am giving him extra room to move closer. Why is this important? First, because dogs don't readily jog up to immobile objects (unless they are looking to scale them). Second, because respectful dogs honor the concept of personal space. They may stop a step or two away from you for this reason. When I am teaching dogs to come at my call, I want them to come closer than that.

When I want small dogs or puppies to come closer, so I can reach <u>straight down</u> to pick them up, I use the movement of my softly clapping hands to guide them toward my feet as I half-turn and back away. Following the movement of my hands and my body puts these dogs at ease. It gives them something to follow, so they feel comfortable about approaching.

Inviting dogs in, using movement, is better than reaching out to them.

TEACHING A DOG TO SIT

Those of you who have taken or watched obedience classes have seen instructors move a treat from the nose of a dog back over his head, to encourage him to look up, track the treat backwards and then sit. Later, many of these dogs recognize a simple hand signal directing them backwards as the nonverbal command to *sit*.

WHEN A DOOR OPENS

Dogs who politely take a step backward when a door or gate opens in front of them are rewarded with a broad smile at our facility. They then receive a soft "<u>good</u> decision" when they calmly yield the space in front of them, waiting for their person to pass. Contrast this with dogs that shove you aside, with their noses against the door as you reach for the doorknob. Not in my house!

door opening = step back, to let the person pass first

This behavior is taught via a simple repetitive exercise done at various thresholds, both inside and outside. With my leashed dog at my side, I use my foot, as a third hand, to gently direct him to take a step back as I open each door (or gate). The purpose of using my foot is to keep my posture upright and my leash loose. When my dog backs up, he is rewarded with soft praise. I then close and open each door, several times, before walking through it in a relaxed manner.

This is another one of those simple practices that is easy to do with multiple dogs, as one dog's rewarded response encourages the others to follow suit.

MEALTIME

Dogs that wait patiently for their food are a pleasure to be around, and a dog who respectfully waits for his handler's cue to start eating without undue excitement is a delight. Never reward any extra energy or forward movement from your dogs at mealtime. Calmly wait for their level-one, relaxed energy. Wait for their pupils to get smaller, if they are dilated. Wait for their bodies to back up. Give quiet dogs a big smile and wait a few more seconds. Then reward those good manners with a calm signal to eat.

When picking up a dog's food bowl, we never pull it toward us. Doing that would only encourage him to track and fixate on his bowl. It could encourage food-guarding. If we need to retrieve a bowl when a dog's nose is in it (for example, when a dog has mistakenly received another dog's food), we always pick the bowl <u>straight up</u>. This directs his body backward and his focus politely upward.

Joey's story illustrates another approach that rewards polite backward movement:

Joey is a teacup Chihuahua who came to our Center suffering from a serious concussion believed to have come from an aggravated, irritated owner tired of how he grabbed at his food. Emaciated when he first arrived, Joey was a pup who became frantic and very mouthy at the mere sight of a kibble! To the uninformed, he was a nasty, biting little dog. We knew him, however, to be a desperately hungry youngster who needed feeding three times a day and a few courses in good canine manners.

As part of his rehab and retraining, Joey was taught to back up from any hand putting food in his crate. His job (remember, even Chihuahuas need jobs to do!) was to back up, sit quietly and watch us. We then added more kibbles to the pile sitting in front of him. The more he sat patiently, with his focus on us, the bigger his pile of kibbles got.

He picked this ritual up quickly, but he still had the tendency to dive into his food whenever the signal was given to eat. We addressed that by giving him the occasional bigger job to do: clean up kibbles spread across fifty square feet of floor.

A third exercise also helped to fine-tune his manners: we instructed him to sit, and we offered him individual kibbles placed under his chest, between his front legs. This strengthened his trust in us, and it further served to back up his focus, creating a new muscle memory for mealtimes. As a result, his diving into his dinner greatly diminished. Good boy, Joey!

TRY THIS EXERCISE: Reward your dogs with a big smile when they back up politely at mealtimes and at thresholds. Wait to see that their energy is calm and without anticipation before you take your next step, with energy that reflects the same element of relaxation.

CHAPTER 17
FUN WITH TREADMILLS

Although their use should never take the place of good working walks, treadmills can provide excellent exercise for active dogs, especially when weather or other circumstances preclude outdoor activities. From three-pound Chihuahuas to ninety-three pound Doberman-Dane mixes, the dogs at our Center have enjoyed treadmilling for years.

Walking on our eight treadmills is something they look forward to each morning. It is a social occasion for them. It builds upon their natural instinct to move forward and in groups, and dogs that treadmill well together form a common identity. They form a more cohesive pack. Treadmilling also burns off their extra energy (which decreases tension and unwanted behaviors), and it teaches our dogs a skill that makes them more adoptable.

At speeds ranging from 0.5 to 1.3 m.p.h. (depending upon size) our dogs walk at a leisurely rate with their pace varied periodically to spice things up. This is not cardio-conditioning! Let me emphasize that. We are not working the dogs at fast speeds!

First, our dogs gather to treadmill not too long after eating their breakfast. That is not the time to go jogging!

Second, we are asking for mindful, pleasurable movement, not rip-roaring self-preservation. Our dogs <u>think</u> more when they are not concerned about catching up.

Third, slower speeds – varied up and down in 0.1 to 0.2 m.p.h. increments – transfer to a more relaxed natural gait when we walk our dogs outside.

DREADMILLING ISN'T FUN!

In contrast to pleasurable treadmilling, let me describe dread-milling. Dread-milling is where a dog treadmills alone at an unchanging monotonous pace. It is not fun! It is simply a task to get done.

So how do you ensure your dog's treadmilling experience doesn't turn into dread-milling? Any of the following will help:

❖ Utilize two or more treadmills placed side-by-side, so your dogs (or you and your dog; or your dog and his neighborhood buddy) can treadmill together.

❖ Treadmill smaller dogs side-by-side on the same belt, if the width of your treadmill allows. Four Chihuahuas routinely share one of the larger treadmills at our Center, like a team of miniature Clydesdales (two in front and two in the back), and they wouldn't have it any other way!

❖ Vary the treadmill speed up or down every five to ten minutes.

❖ Let your dog use his treadmill when you are in the same room, doing something else. Your company means a lot to him!

❖ Place your treadmill by a window, to provide dogs with a little visual scenery. Never do this with prey-driven dogs, however, because it can increase their prey drive should they see other animals (or in some cases, people) passing by.

TREADMILLING TO ADDRESS BEHAVIORAL ISSUES

Anxiety, aggression and hyperactivity are all fueled by excess energy and stress. Remove both, and it is much easier to address these issues. For this reason, we always teach our more unsettled dogs to treadmill! Treadmilling helps to turn unruly individuals into well-behaved ones, unfocused individuals into more focused ones and mistrustful individuals into trusting ones. Thundershirts and backpacks can be worn while dogs are treadmilling, to promote calm and increase focus.

The calm, positive feedback that dogs get from us as they treadmill helps to strengthen the bonds we have. When smiles, hand-wags and massages are part of the treadmilling experience, the dogs soak them up like sunshine!

Our volunteers come to see dogs that can treadmill as capable individuals, and that helps them leave the traumas and dramas of the dogs' pasts behind. They also come to see these dogs as distinct personalities and not just another red Dachshund mix or another Beagle mix or yet another black Lab, as they help each one take his own path toward learning this new skill.

It is worth emphasizing that not every person has the skill set required to use this tool! Empathy, patience and an awareness of a dog's state of mind and body language are vitally important. So, too, is putting a positive picture in your mind. Most dogs go through a short period of being unsure when a treadmill is first turned on and the ground moves beneath them. Given a confident handler that supports them through this period, they gain confidence quickly. Given an unsure handler, they become concerned, and this sets them up for failure.

LAYING THE GROUNDWORK

Laying good groundwork is vital when teaching a dog to treadmill. If you rush a dog's introduction, you can create harmful associations that can be hard to overcome. You can't go too slow. You can very definitely go too fast. When in doubt, repeat a step several times before going on to the next one. When in doubt, treadmill your dog for less time, and not more, until he demonstrates both a comfort with the process and an enjoyment of it.

When teaching treadmilling, we frequently reach for small treats or canned food. They help us to engage a dog's nose, which stops his brain from overanalyzing what his legs are doing. We will also be more verbal with our praise. Treadmilling is an active pursuit, and here we don't mind a little extra energy in the air because the treadmills help to keep it focused.

Some dogs take to treadmilling like horses to hay. (Terriers, especially.) They love the forward momentum involved, and they are happy to follow your lead as you urge them on. Other dogs will progress toward confident treadmilling only in stages. How long that takes depends completely upon the dog.

Before you start, gauge the following:

❖ Are you feeling patient? (Any element of impatience or frustration will work against you.)

❖ Are you distraction-free? (Things might take longer than you think.)

❖ Are you ready and willing to start a series of small steps which could take several days, or do you want things to progress pretty quickly? (Be willing to take slow steps.)

❖ Are you feeling confident? If you aren't confident, don't expect your dog to be!

❖ Do you know how to use a fine touch on a leash when needed, and how to release tension when your dog is doing well? (This is mandatory, as tense leashes make dogs tense!)

Teaching a dog to treadmill requires a patient, positive state of mind. It requires all the leadership characteristics that I have discussed. And it requires the ability to make split-second up-and-down adjustments on a leash, the better to guide dogs through short periods of trial and error. Developing positive associations is the name of the game, and directing energy is the means.

While it is acceptable for a dog to hop up on a treadmill with eagerness and enthusiasm, it is important that he leave it using good manners. It is equally vital that he is moving <u>forward</u> when his treadmill gets turned off. A dog that is moving forward, when his treadmill is turned off, will be ready to move forward when it is turned on again. By the same token, a dog that is pulling back or to the side, when his treadmill is turned off, will tend to pull back or to the side the next time it is turned on.

Learning how to treadmill is a skill, and like any skill, it is easier for dogs to grasp when they aren't too hyper. Enthusiastic? Yes. Engaged? Most definitely. Hyper? Go outside for some ball-catching or similar energy-draining activity first.

TEACHING A CONFIDENT DOG TO TREADMILL

Many dogs pick up the talent of treadmilling the first time they try it. Others require progressive steps ending on a positive note, spread over a day or two. And some progress to confident treadmilling only after three days of patient, progressive increments toward that goal.

Please read through this entire chapter several times before following the next steps, the better to give your dog the help he needs along the way.

Step 1: Allow your dog to lie quietly for ten minutes within sight and the sound of a running treadmill. Feel free to use a crate, if it suits your purpose. Offer him the occasional small treat. If your dog can watch others being rewarded while they treadmill, even better.

Step 2: With the treadmill turned off, place your dog on its belt, as if it is a grooming table. Brush him for a little while, making sure not to reinforce any signs of insecurity or anxiety. Matter-of-factly reposition his tail to a neutral position, if it tends to clamp between his legs. Smile whenever he relaxes.

Place treats in front of him that he needs to <u>step forward</u> to retrieve. The treats will encourage him to use his nose, the better to let his legs do what comes naturally.

Take him off the treadmill at some point, making sure that he is relaxed at the time. Go for a short walk, and then repeat this step for as many times as it takes for him to be completely relaxed, both standing on the treadmill and taking a step or two forward to retrieve treats.

For the most insecure dogs, this step may need repeating several times a day for several days. Remember: you cannot go too slow when introducing a dog to a treadmill; only too fast.

Step 3: With the treadmill still turned off, place a line of tiny treats or kibbles up the center of the treadmill belt and encourage your dog (leashed) to climb onto the treadmill to eat them <u>without any tugging on his leash.</u> (Remember: pulling a dog forward only encourages him to pull in the opposite direction.) Feel free to use lots of well-timed smiles and "good boys!" As soon as he finishes eating, guide him off the end of the treadmill (not the side) using your leash and verbal cues. Repeat this step for as many times as it takes for your dog to hop onto the treadmill for a single treat (four to six repetitions is common).

Step 4: Once your dog walks onto a stationary treadmill at your direction, make a game out of the process. Jog around the room with him before jogging onto it to receive a treat. This helps him to associate the treadmill with moving forward (even when it is turned off). It may help to have a good helper standing on the other side of the treadmill, if it isn't positioned next to a wall, and a third good helper standing in front of it, dispensing additional treats. Jog up to and onto the treadmill seven or eight times.

Step 5: This step requires:
  ❖ A completely positive picture in your mind.
  ❖ Calmly directive energy.
  ❖ Split-second adjustments.

Have a helper turn the treadmill on (at a slow speed of 0.5 to 0.8 m.p.h., depending upon the size of your dog), while you jog around the room. As you jog your dog onto the now-moving belt, position yourself at his side with your leash held straight up (over his ears). Keep it loose whenever he walks centrally on the belt. Draw it upwards (never forward or back) if he moves off-center, and release all pressure the second he moves into place. In this manner, you can guide him through a short period of trial and error, one in which he tests his boundaries.

walking centrally = no tension on his leash
too far forward or back = slight upward tension
return to center = release of all tension

Dogs that hop off treadmills before succeeding will always see hopping off as a viable option. For this reason, it is better to support them through this period of trial and error than to let them hop off before they are successful.*

---

* *This is where good helpers – those with confident energy and a clear picture of success in their mind – are vital. If they step to the side, letting an unsure (but not at all panicky) dog step off the treadmill, they will send a message of failure, and not success, to him.*

Reward your dog (and yourself) with smiles and lots of verbal praise when he gets things right. Then choose a time when he is doing well to turn the treadmill off. Reward him with a little massage and then a walk outside, before repeating Step 5, the better to build upon your success.

With treadmilling, it is important to start and finish at a slow speed, with your dog facing forward. Doing this fosters good muscle memory. It also helps to stop his treadmilling session just before he wants to stop. You want him to be enjoying himself, so he will look forward to more of the same at a later date.

TEACHING INSECURE DOGS TO TREADMILL

Insecure dogs blossom when they learn to treadmill! Treadmilling helps them to develop confidence, and it burns off anxious energy.

That said, introducing insecure dogs to this tool requires good intuition, extra patience and, in many cases, a strong back and knees. Why a strong back and knees? Because insecure dogs tend to lag behind. They don't move forward readily, and they aren't apt to walk, let alone jog, onto a treadmill on their own (even with treats offered). They also tend to overthink things, and this hinders what their bodies would do naturally. When first placed on a treadmill, their front legs and back legs tend to go through separate learning curves. You may need to support their hind end a few inches off the belt for a little while (we call this "wheelbarrowing"), to encourage their front legs to move forward, their state of mind to relax, and their hind legs to catch up.

This doesn't mean these dogs won't take to and thoroughly enjoy treadmilling, given the right help. It only means that their initial approach requires finesse, because a dog that is lifted onto a treadmill is in a <u>stationary</u> state of mind, unlike a dog that is already moving forward. There is a fifty-fifty chance that instinct will lead him to pull back – as opposed to move forward – when you start the treadmill, more so if the speed is anything but extremely slow. What happens next, and how does one address it? To illustrate, let me describe Ella's introduction to a treadmill:

Ella is a puppy-mill Poodle who had been caged for long periods of time and bred twice a year for four years before being dumped at a municipal shelter. Sweet-natured, she has never seen a leash, let alone walked on one. To help improve her muscle tone, our goal is to slow-treadmill her for ten minutes a few times a day. Doing this will allow her to join our other dogs for group treadmilling, something that will inspire confidence and build bonds.

Our first step is to lift her onto a treadmill for a few episodes of grooming. This she enjoys more than the small treats we offer in the hope that she will walk onto a treadmill under her own power. (She refuses to do that, even when presented with canned food.)

When we determine she is ready to take the next step, a volunteer stands in front of the treadmill with small pieces of steak and chicken in hand (this, she loves). With Ella leashed and centered on the treadmill, we turn it to its lowest setting (0.5 m.p.h.). Her response is to pull back, with her legs locked in extension. I immediately lift her back legs off the belt, wheelbarrowing her. This eases all tension on her leash, and it encourages her front legs to move reflexively.

Are her hind legs ready to follow? Not yet. We have a little trial and error to go through first, and this is where I am glad she is a ten-pound Poodle and not an eighty-pound retriever. She needs her hind legs kept off the belt – with my supportive hand under her belly or between her back legs – until her canine brain stops overthinking what her legs are doing.

My helper reaches a piece of steak toward her, encouraging her to move forward to lick it, and then accept it. This goes a long way toward relaxing her. Ella's hind legs begin to reach for the treadmill belt, just toe-touching with her right side at first, and then her left. Her hips begin to sway, following the motion of her front legs. It is a good sign, but she still needs my support.

Twice more, she starts to overthink things, and her hind end freezes up. Each time, my helper offers her some more meat. As long as Ella thinks about the food, and not what her legs are doing, she does well.

Her trial-and-error learning curve takes about six or seven minutes, and because it is one that we cannot stop in the middle and restart without creating the wrong associations, it requires patience and that strong back and knees I mentioned. We continue to support her hind end and offer gentle encouragement, until her toe-touching progresses into a natural four-legged gait. We then let her walk a few minutes without assistance before turning the treadmill off.

Is it time to take her off the treadmill? No. It is time for a massage and some pieces of chicken offered in a way that requires her to move forward to receive them. (It is important that Ella link treadmilling with 'moving forward.') Only then do I lift her off the treadmill, letting her know how proud I am of her achievement.

Later that afternoon, we urge her to walk onto the treadmill to get some more steak and chicken, and she does so on her own! The following day, we do the same. This time, when her treadmill is turned on, her period of trial and error (with our wheelbarrowing support) passes quickly, and she slowly progresses to treadmilling at 0.6 m.p.h., a comfortable speed for her. Yea, Ella!

With other small dogs, we take a slightly different approach. We lower them onto slowly moving belts, and we let them toe-touch for a few seconds before lifting them up. We repeat this several times over, allowing them to gain confidence with each repetition. We then let them walk on the belt without assistance for a minute or two, if they appear ready to do it.

Both of these approaches work equally well, and the process is the same: support the dog's body until her four legs move forward naturally.

KEYS TO SUCCESS

The keys to any dog's successful introduction to treadmills are:

❖ Engaging his nose through treats, canned dog food, pieces of chicken (whatever goodie works!). The more a dog new to treadmilling follows his <u>nose</u>, the less he overthinks what his legs are doing.

❖ Approaching his period of trial and error in a confident and matter-of-fact way, using good leash-work and/or support.

❖ Ending things on a positive note (your dog calmly moving forward). Ending things this way promotes good associations, so dogs look forward to their next treadmill session.

The key to keeping treadmilling fun is to never let it devolve into dread-milling!

BAD TO THE BONE

Imagine a little kid sent to a corner for a time-out, fussing and fighting and complaining the whole time: "You can't make me! It's not my fault! I hate you!" (Or the classic, "You're not my _real_ mother!") Now picture a dog on a treadmill, pulling the same routine. Since we work with a lot of Chihuahuas and small terriers at our facility, we occasionally see these five- and ten-pound prize-fighters. They are skilled at manipulating the people around them through fear, perseverance and good old-fashioned guilt. When they bark, we are supposed to come running, right? When they pull back on their leash, we are supposed to turn around and pick them up, right? I don't think so!

When treadmilling these dogs, remember Golden Rules #1 and #2. (Reward what you want, and stop rewarding what you don't want.) Allow them a little time for self-correction, since any micromanaging on your part will be seen as the attention they seek.

These bad-to-the-bone boys and girls will pull back on a treadmill's crossties. They will chew at them. They will walk forward a few steps and then purposely pull back, glaring at you as if you are the meanest human in the world. Hogwash! They aren't scared, and they aren't intimidated by the apparatus. They aren't being abused. They are simply being bratty, and treadmilling is an excellent way to stop their ill-mannered behavior and bring out their best.

As long as your dog isn't freezing up (that is, as long as _all four_ of his feet track normally between temper-tantrums), let him go through his spits n' spouts while watching from a distance to ensure he doesn't work himself into too much of a tizzy. (He probably won't.) After a few minutes, and a repeat performance or three (after all, this type of dog is very good at this kind of behavior), he will eventually settle down and walk forward naturally. When that happens, stop the treadmill and give him a small treat for giving you the better behavior you want. Then take him outside for a little while. The next time he is put on a treadmill, he will walk forward with less bratty behavior. He can deny it for only so long before admitting to himself that treadmilling can be fun.

GENERAL TIPS FOR TREADMILLS

Once a dog is comfortable walking on a treadmill, you may wish to tie him to it so you can supervise him from afar. In this case, cross-tying his collar from both the left and the right works better than attaching a single leash from above. It protects his nose from getting bumped repeatedly. Repurposing older leashes works well for this, and we have found the old-style metal chain leashes to be particularly good for puppies and fidgety adolescents who like to munch on their leads as they walk.

You can also attach a length of lightweight plastic chain across the front of the treadmill. (This inexpensive chain can be purchased by the foot at your local hardware store.) Hook one end of a large double-sided clip to a central link. Hook the other end to your dog's collar. Use two clips if you wish to treadmill smaller dogs in pairs. These clips are easy to move between links when adjustments are needed, and because they are of a good size, they are relatively easy for people with arthritis to use.

For dogs who enjoy tread-surfing, with two feet on the belt and two feet off (terriers often like to do things differently), a little creativity may be needed to keep them centered. In different circumstances, we have used cat carriers, boxes balanced between treadmills and foam pool noodles glued on either side of the belt to encourage these guys to avoid the edges. If you need to place something in front of a treadmill, to prevent a dog moving too far forward, use something that he can see through (such as a baby gate). Nobody likes walking up to walls.

Don't forget to regularly vary your dog's treadmill speed, to keep things from getting boring. After all, we want him to enjoy treadmilling, not endure dread-milling!

We set a one-hour time limit for each dog, and some of our treadmills have timers and automatic shutoffs to help us establish this. Older and less-able dogs treadmill for a shorter time. Bigger, bouncier dogs may want to come back for an additional half-hour on occasion, and that is fine, but we insist that they go outside to empty their bowels and bladders after sixty minutes, to keep them comfortable.

Just before turning off a treadmill, we tell our dogs *"Slo-o-ow down,"* as we decrease their speed a notch or two. It teaches them another command that can be helpful later on.

TREADMILL CARE

Dogs being dogs, motion on the outside sometimes gets motion going on the inside, and occasional accidents can occur. When this happens, you will find that treadmill belts rarely clean up well with a few wipes of a damp paper towel. A better approach uses a few drops of dish soap.

Remove any stool or urine puddles with a paper towel first, then use a dish brush to rub well-diluted dish soap onto the belt. Let things soak for a few seconds before placing a layer of paper towels over the soap. Since dish soap is formulated to raise dirt off of non-permeable surfaces so they can be rinsed clean, it raises the debris out of the cracks and crevices of the belt easily so it can be absorbed into the paper towel. One quick wipe of what is left, and the belt is back to looking good!

Treadmill cleaning is pretty simple beyond this. A weekly dusting, plus routine vacuuming of hair from under the treadmill (most have decks that fold up to allow for this), goes a long way.

Some treadmill belts require lubrication with silicone, but many do worse with silicone application. Read your manuals! They will tell you how to maintain and adjust your treadmills, to ensure that they operate properly and stand the test of time.

WHO, WHAT, WHEN AND WHERE

Who. When it comes to using tools to bring out the best in a dog, even the best of tools can be harmful when they are used incorrectly. It is worth repeating: people entrusted with treadmilling must be calm, confident, watchful and empathetic. They should know the power of a genuine smile, and be able to communicate with their dogs using delicate leash adjustments, the better to guarantee success.

What. Treadmills come in different lengths and with different features. Short ones are nice for smaller dogs, but larger dogs require longer decks. Dogs don't get excited about built-in fans or mp3 players, but it is nice to have timers, automatic shut-offs and cup holders (for treats, not water bottles). A variable incline is nice, too, for more active dogs.

Warning: some treadmills have a minimum speed of 1.0 m.p.h. That is too fast for many dogs under twenty-five pounds! (Remember: most dogs do their best between 0.5 and 1.3 m.p.h., depending upon their size.) Other models may start at a fast clip, requiring a quick downward adjustment each time. Dogs should ideally start (and end) each session at a slower, not faster pace.

When. Treadmilling can be done any time of day, but treadmilling in the morning encourages dogs to be restful for the rest of the day. Use common sense when doing this shortly after meals. A pleasant, leisurely walk should always be your goal.

Always let your dogs go outside to empty their tanks just before and just after treadmilling. Long walks with a big bladder or full colon aren't fun.

Where. We position our treadmills where we can keep an eye on them as we do other things. Multitasking is our goal. While our dogs treadmill, we prepare their food for the night. We do the laundry. We make phone calls. We work on our computers, and we catch up on housekeeping, all while keeping half an eye on the dogs.

If you use multiple treadmills, be sure to locate them next to one another! Why this configuration? Because it positions your dogs side-by-side, as partners and equals. This allows dogs with negative histories to become friends.

FAST-WALK MUSCLE MEMORY

Treadmilling done well is always positive, never negative. It should be done in a way that brings out the best in each dog. When handlers don't treadmill their dogs thoughtfully, so as not to dread-mill, a fast-walk muscle memory can ensue.

This is where a dog begins to walk mindlessly on walks, at a mechanical pace that doesn't reflect his handler's. Possible in dogs of all sizes, it is most commonly seen in larger dogs treadmilled at speeds over 1.2 m.p.h., especially when their treadmill speeds are insufficiently varied. To avoid this, don't forget: modify each dog's treadmill speed at least every ten minutes.

SPECIAL CIRCUMSTANCES

Dogs that have received injectable adulticides for heartworm should not treadmill before the eighteen-month anniversary of their treatment, regardless of what their blood test may say. Their bodies need a lot of time to resorb dead worms and heal! Too, don't treadmill dogs for ten days just after they have been spayed.

Chondrodysplastic breeds (e.g., Pekingese and Pugs) and those with mild heart murmurs frequently enjoy our treadmills, but in determining how long they walk, we use common sense. We treadmill them for fifteen to thirty minutes at a time (not a full hour), and we don't incline their treadmills.

Never underestimate what can happen when you have moving parts and creatures with the awareness of toddlers! We once had a very short dog with a very long tail who enjoyed walking backwards (the better to watch what we were doing, we suppose). Our lessons from him are two-fold. First, a short dog's tail can get caught in a belt's roller, given a number of otherwise unusual events occurring simultaneously. Second, never leave treadmilling dogs (especially if they like to walk backwards) unsupervised. We didn't, and this dog didn't lose but four hairs when his tail got snagged. Afterward, he was only allowed on the one treadmill that we have that has its rollers completely covered.

Whether you treadmill a dog for five minutes a day or an hour, make sure that the event is one that will leave him calm and happy and a better dog for the experience. We always reward calm endings to treadmill sessions with a gentle back scratch. Calmly rewarding good manners and an energy level of one leads to more… (I will let you finish the sentence.)

TRY THIS EXERCISE: There are many treadmilling videos on YouTube. Some of them show treadmilling done right, and others might as well be primers for how not to do things. View and evaluate some of them, the better to see things from the dogs' perspective, and the better to do things right, given the opportunity to treadmill your dogs.

HOW TO RESPOND
TO GET THE BEHAVIOR
YOU WANT

The great enemy of clear language is insincerity.
George Orwell

CHAPTER 18
HOW TO RESPOND
(TO SEND THE MESSAGE YOU WANT)

Few of us get the dogs of our dreams from the get-go. Most of us shape them and mold them over time, like well-written manuscripts. Add a few well-chosen words here. Remove others that get in the way. Review and reflect, and edit over time, to send the message we want.

Whether rewarding or correcting your dogs' behaviors, following eleven basic rules will help you to respond in ways that best shape their future behavior.

RESPONSE RULE #1: Calm behavior requires calm-reinforcing responses.

It pays to reward calmness (the better to get more of it), and it pays to reward it in a calm manner. Rewarding calmness with any amount of excitement only pops a dog out of the quiet behavior that you want to reward. Never forget how far you can go using only a genuine smile or the gentlest of hand-wags!

RESPONSE RULE #2: Timing is crucial.

To be successful with animals requires us to know not only what to do and how to do it, but also when to do it. If you want to develop productive new associations and stop unproductive ones from perpetuating, your response to X must be spot-on, practically split-second. X leads to Y. Period. No discussions. No delay. No "I'll get back to you about how I feel" when you are a dog. Dogs are marvelously uncomplicated.

People, on the other hand, are thinkers. We are reasoners. We enjoy talking things out, and many of us find it easier to hold grudges than to let go of what upsets us. As a result our timing may be more than a little off.

As you watch the energy that you project, watch your timing, too. Every action a dog takes doesn't require a reaction. Many do not. On the other hand, some behaviors are serious enough that responding when a dog first considers them is the best way to prevent calamity.

Scenario 1 (after the fact): JoJo chews on a shoe at ten in the morning, and you discover the damage at twelve noon. When this happens, responding to his behavior two hours after the fact is not the best way to preserve your shoes. It is too late to do much good, and there is a good chance that (although he knows that you are upset) he will misinterpret your disapproval since it didn't occur when he had your shoe in his mouth. Hand him an extra-large roasted knuckle-bone to chew, one that will keep him busy for many hours. Then vow to keep your shoes out of his reach.

Scenario 2 (in the midst of the action): Baxter has a history of hoarding toys – much to the dismay of your other dogs – and you see him begin to accumulate a pile on his bed. Calmly take all but two of the toys away and move them into another room. Then calmly stand between the rooms to send a matter-of-fact message to Baxter: his passing by to reclaim the toys is not worth the extra effort. Sensing your calm authority on the subject, he sighs and curls up on his bed, focusing on the toys at hand.

Scenario 3 (before things get worse): Yonnie's attention is grabbed by a cat running by. Before his excitement escalates, and before he begins to bark and jump around (catching the attention of the other dogs), you say his name once, followed by the command *watch!* Since Yonnie knows this command, it gives him an alternate choice of behavior (quietly observe the cat), and he knows it is one that gets rewarded with a calming "Good Yonnie, good *watch.*"

Scenario 4 (before things get worse): When standing with Kikko leashed at your side, you see her hackles go up when Jan (a person) and Lena (another leashed dog) approach. With a soft smile, you quietly turn to walk away from the newcomers, directing Kikko to follow. Over your shoulder, you then ask Jan and Lena to join you for a brief side-by-side walk, the better to convey to Kikko that everyone is on the same team.

With time and practice you can learn to identify when and how best to respond to a particular behavior. If you notice that your responses are a little off (and your dogs more than a little confused), know that your awareness of this is the first step toward getting the timing of your responses right.

RESPONSE RULE #3: You will get back what you put in.

Taking enough time to get a behavior perfected can be hard for some folks to do in this day and age of multitasking and instant everything. Waiting until a dog does exactly what you want or modifies a behavior that you don't want one hundred percent of the way before you reward him or walk away takes a little more time, but doing this pays off down the road. Please give that extra time to yourself and your dog so, when you move on (with a smile), he understands what you wanted and he does not go back to the behavior you were hoping to correct.

It is time for you to leave for work, and your new dog, Pine, sits next to the door, tail wagging furiously. Is this the energy and mind-set you want him to have in your absence? Of course not. You put your briefcase, coffee cup and lunch in your car, and then you return to your kitchen. There, you nonchalantly put a few dishes away. It is a mundane, quiet activity that doesn't support Pine's excited state of mind, so he walks over to his bed to chew on a bone. Is this when you leave? Maybe so; maybe not. What is his state of mind now? Is he ignoring you, or is he still watching every move you make? It may require an extra two minutes – or maybe even five minutes – but timing your calm, no-need-to-pay-attention-to-me exit with Pine's relaxed-and-about-to-sleep mindset will set him up for a quieter day alone.

When prolonged time is required to perfect a behavior, remember: a good book is a helpful tool to have! To illustrate:

Sonnet is a young Doberman who came to our facility from a nearby shelter, one day after she was spayed at their clinic. A natural follower by nature, she receives a score of five out of five on our basic behavior assessment (Chapter 27). Heartworm positive, and in need of some good nutrition, she is added to my home-pack so I can keep a close eye on her sutures.

She settles in quickly, but we hit a bump in the road when it comes time for dinner. She walks into a crate with slight urging, and she eats her dinner with great gusto. But as soon as she is finished with her food, she starts to whine and paw at her crate door. Letting her out is not an option. It would reward her whining and pawing, and it would set a precedent. Plus, six other dogs are quietly watching from their crates. I don't want to send the wrong message to them.

If Sonnet has crate issues, I need to help her to overcome them, to make her more adoptable. I tell her, "*Chicht!*" in the hope that a simple correction is all that is needed. No luck there. Her whines rise in intensity and she tries pushing her nose out the bottom of the door. Only the top of two latches is fastened, so I unemotionally reach to close the lower latch. I also reach for a good book, the better to turn my state of mind from one of annoyance to one of oh-well acceptance (and maybe a little better than that, since she just gave me an excuse to read another chapter).

To defuse any tension that Sonnet's fussing is bringing into the room, I smile at each of the other dogs resting quietly in their crates. I softly address each one: "Good job, Topeka. Good job, Porkchop. Good job, Hiker…" Sonnet stops fussing to listen, but she then returns to her fussing. She turns up her volume. She paws more at the door. She paws at the crate floor. She tries to get her nose under the door. She hasn't done anything to hurt herself or her sutures, and the small amount of anxiety that she projects isn't at the level of self-perpetuation, so I don't do anything more than stand calm and erect, six feet away. Her behavior gets worse before it gets better, but reading my book while maintaining my position allows me to keep my calm.

The phone rings in the next room, but I ignore it. I know if I walk away before I get the behavior I want, I will have <u>increased</u> the potential for more negative behavior in the future, and not decreased it. I take a relaxing breath and return to my book. Sonnet then stops her protests and pawing, choosing to glare at me instead. Though weary, she is determined not to lie down. Her message is clear: she aims to win this battle.

It is not going to work, because I have my book, and I am equally determined to prevail. More time passes, and I chuckle silently as I watch her head droop and her body fight to keep standing. It takes twenty-three minutes for her to give up. At that point, she circles twice and lies down. Excellent! Is it time to open her crate? Not yet, but I will after five quiet minutes have passed. I give her a big smile and a small wag of my hand, and I take a seat across the room.

Almost half-an-hour may seem like a ridiculous amount of time to go through a process like this (and these stand-offs rarely occur when we have nothing better to do), but they are what they are: excellent opportunities to clearly communicate to our dogs what we want.

The following evening Sonnet goes quietly into her crate, and her post-prandial fussing lasts but ten seconds. When she sees me reach for my book, the battle is over before it starts (and I am the victor). She sits back to see what happens if she waits patiently. I give her a big smile. Five minutes pass, and I let her out of her crate. The half-hour that we spent yesterday will not need repeating. To the contrary, it will save me hours of unnecessary aggravation in the days to come.

RESPONSE RULE #4: The best dog training honors the way dogs think and how they communicate.

Because dogs are pretty honest about their emotions, we can learn a lot by observing their responses to what we do. Have friends and family videotape you with your dogs. Then replay the videos, watching your dogs' body language. Studying their reactions to your directions, rewards and corrections will help you greatly with your learning curve.

You can also learn a lot by watching how and when a mother dog manages her brood! Mama's physical corrections can be subtle, or they can be quite sharp. Her verbal corrections can be low and rumbling, or strong and really to the point. No blood is drawn, but mama is good at getting her point across.

RESPONSE RULE #5: Aim for balanced behavior (not simply changed behavior).

Mama's goal is (and ours should also be) <u>balanced</u> behavior and not simply <u>changed</u> behavior. The former transforms a dog's conduct, energy and state of mind. The latter (changed conduct only) is often but a temporary fix, because it doesn't address the dog's energy or his state of mind. You have paused, but not really corrected, the situation.

Correcting a behavior, without addressing the extra energy that fuels it, leaves behind an element of tension, and this opens the door to a repeat of the behavior you didn't want.

Correcting a behavior, without changing the state of mind behind it, only teaches a dog to ignore your correction. This is equally true when you are correcting a single dog or a group of them.

Always follow through to get changed conduct, energy and state of mind. In other words, don't walk away until your dog does what you want calmly and with an accepting (as opposed to resisting) state of mind. At that point, you can walk away with a smile (and maybe a little hand-wag).

Let me use another crate-averse dog as an example:

Haiku is a six-year old Doberman-shepherd mix who isn't house-trained. We wonder how we are going to get her trained if we can't use a crate. Very thin, due to intestinal parasites, she isn't a high-energy dog. That is actually in our favor right now, because we will want to reward her choice of quiet energy and calm acceptance at every step of her training. She completely balks at walking into a crate, even with biscuits offered. Approaching the problem from another angle, we tie her leash to a spot just above the open door of a roomy crate, within sight of a volunteer's computer station. The location is chosen because it permits quiet monitoring for extended periods of time. We put a very comfortable dog bed inside the crate and a simple towel just outside it, and Haiku's food and water are placed at the very back of the crate. Arranging things this way offers her positive reinforcement for entering the crate, without a word spoken.

We have set her up for success, but do we leave the room now, without doing anything more? Absolutely not. What is her state of mind? Is she curling up next to the crate, ready for a nap? Or is she standing at the end of her leash, primed to pull the crate across the room, should we all walk down the hall? We absolutely cannot step away until her energy is completely calm and her state of mind is relaxed.

One-by-one, we exit the room, leaving one last volunteer working at his desk. Without watching Haiku directly, he keeps an eye on her posture, her pupil size, her focus and her respirations, the better to gauge how she is feeling. Typing at his keyboard, he smiles broadly when, given a little time, she chooses to sit on the towel outside of the crate. When she curls up and lies down, he drops his hand to his side for a little hand-wag; nothing more. He doesn't speak. He doesn't even look at her. His body language communicates enough.

After fifteen minutes have passed, he walks down the hall for a brief moment. He sits at his computer when he returns, only to get up and walk down the hall again, ever so briefly. He repeats this process a dozen times over the next half-hour so Haiku can experience short periods by her crate without company, but he is careful to do it only when she is in a <u>relaxed state of mind</u>.

Within the hour, Haiku ignores his comings and goings. By the end of the morning, she has eaten the food and drank some of the water at the back of her crate, and by the end of the day (after one of several refreshing walks) she has, on her own, decided that sleeping inside an open crate isn't such a bad thing after all. In a few days, we will close her crate door for gradually increasing times, but for now we have gotten the behavior we desired, the quiet energy we desired and the state of mind that we desired. Haiku can now be left tied to an open crate overnight, a big step toward her becoming house-trained!

RESPONSE RULE #6: Match the energy of your correction to the energy behind the offense.

When people who are having trouble communicating with their dogs approach me for help, it is often because their responses don't match their dog's behavior. Either their actions are way over the top, mistimed or telegraphed (and they have lost their dog's trust) or they tend to under-respond (and they have lost their dog's respect).

In the first case, I ask them to stop and imagine that they are correcting a second-grader in their care. That helps them to reflect upon and adjust their posture, their timing and the quality and quantity of the energy they project. In the second case, I ask them to imagine that they are ninth-grade teachers. It doesn't help anyone when the kids in their class are allowed to rule the roost.

When a member of my pack chooses a behavior that I don't want, I mentally triage the situation.

❖ Is this a lower-energy, non-perpetuating, non-threatening, self-terminating sort of behavior? (e.g., a single bark between two playful dogs). If so, I don't respond. It isn't needed. If I was to respond to every little thing, I would completely be at the mercy of my dogs, and I would lose authority. A good pack leader, just like a good teacher or perceptive parent, is calm and level-headed and not overly reactive.

❖ Is this a moderate-energy, non-threatening but possibly self-perpetuating behavior? (e.g., elevated barking associated with play). If so, I respond: "Jackie, *chicht!*" I then wait until Jackie's energy drops from a level-four down to a true level-one before turning my attention elsewhere. If I don't respond to his behavior, or if I don't follow through on my response to make sure he gets my message and changes the energy behind his behavior, the other dogs could pick up on his extra energy and their play could escalate into something not that playful. Waiting until Jackie's energy level drops completely (so I can tell him "thank you") might take ten seconds. It might even take a long minute. But I will not walk on until he follows through. His mother-dog would do the same.

❖ Is this a higher-energy, potentially injurious behavior? (e.g., a fifty-pound Catahoula pushing around an increasingly unhappy Maltese despite my presence a few feet away). If so, the Catahoula gets a corrective tap from me with his *chicht!* and I stand watch until his focus shifts away from the smaller dog. Obviously, I need to address this behavior clearly, because someone is going to get hurt if I don't. My energy is calm, but clear. My touch isn't over the top, and it absolutely isn't punitive or aggressive.

Let me expand upon that last sentence, because it is very important. Knowing when to respond (and when not to) and how to get the corrected behavior we want from our dogs, without emoting or projecting unnecessary or unhealthy energy, takes practice and a willingness to examine (and change) our own behavior. In the above three scenarios, the goal is the same: peaceful cohabitation between dogs. In each, the most important tools in my toolbox are patience and calm assertiveness (remember what that last word means: making a positive statement).

In the first case, only patience is needed. In the second case, my calm-but-assertive tone stops the misbehavior, and my patient follow-through ensures that it doesn't recur.

In the third case, even though I choose a higher-level correction (a corrective tap), my touch and the energy I project are matter-of-fact and calm. I don't reach for the Catahoula from afar. (Telegraphing my intentions could be interpreted as aggression. I also want an element of surprise.) I am not stabbing the troublemaker with my finger, either. Using extra force (a jab or a stab as opposed to a simple, well-timed re-booting tap or light poke) would be counterproductive, and it would reflect a lack of control. I am not bumping the dog, and I am not pushing him. I am also careful not to project extra emotion. (Anger, frustration, fear, retribution or extra verbosity would definitely not support my leadership role.) Let me use an analogy to illustrate:

> Imagine that you are a woman walking down the sidewalk with your sweetie. Unexpectedly, you catch him checking out the pretty women that walk by. What is a gal to do? It may not be the best of choices to call him on his behavior verbally. He would only tune you out or reply in a way that could elevate the situation into more than it needs to be. Instead you reach to give him a one-fingered nudge in the side, a sort of surprise 'gotcha' that gets the point across that he's been busted. He should be paying more attention to you!

That is the kind of reboot/rebalance touch I use with dogs needing more than my *chicht!* to correct their behavior. How does it feel? To find out, hold one hand up. Now poke your palm with one or two fingers of your other hand. That is all that I am doing when I give a dog a pointed touch to correct a high level of energy or some potentially threatening behavior. The purpose of my touch is simply to pop him out of what he is doing, so he can make better behavioral choices.

If you don't work with higher-energy or potentially volatile dogs on a daily basis, situations requiring a reboot/rebalance touch will likely be few and far between. If you do work with these kinds of dogs, know that a simple disapproving (never dominating), non-telegraphed tap can quickly correct escalating behavior before it spreads, behavior that if left unchecked in a group of dogs could result in someone getting seriously hurt. It doesn't matter if you are working with ten Poodles or ten Pointers. In cases like these, you need to be the calmly directive soul that everyone looks up to, and they need to behave in the manner you dictate, to keep them safe.

Always remember that your goal should be balanced behavior and balanced energy that you can reward with a smile, and not simply "changed" behavior. To achieve this, your responses need to be calm, appropriate for the offense and matter-of-fact. X equates to Y, with no added emotion. No X occurring means no Y will happen.

RESPONSE RULE #7: Be consistent.

Simply put, if you do something the same way twenty times out of twenty, you send a clear message to everyone around you. If you change your response but one time out of twenty, any dog (like any child) is going to notice it, and they may capitalize on it when you least want them to.

Let me use jumping dogs as an example. My apologies to those who think it is cute when dogs jump and paw at their legs. I have to disagree, even when it comes to little dogs. I empathize with toddlers, the elderly and people who don't enjoy dogs launching themselves in their direction. I also prefer to pick up and hug my dogs on my say-so, not because they demand my attention.

Beetle is a Schnauzer who has learned that jumping upon people gets her attention five times out of ten, and a fifty percent success rate works fine for her. She either gets picked up, or she gets petted. At very least, she gets talked to, and many people bend down her way, if only to push her aside (yes, she counts that as a win). Sometimes they ask her to sit (another win). After all, she demanded their attention, and she got it. They are focused on her now, and not what they were doing.

Beetle is zero-for-twenty when it comes to jumping on Todd, however. As a result, whenever he is around, she offers him tail-wagging friendliness from a distance of a few feet. Why is Beetle so polite with Todd? Because he is consistent in his response to her jumping. The first three times that Beetle jumped, he lifted his knee in a matter-of-fact manner, claiming the space around him in a nonverbal, matter-of-fact way. X (Beetle's jumping) led to Y (a leg lift), three times over. First three points to Todd.

Beetle then tried jumping on the backs of his legs. He simply lifted a heel backwards, claiming back his space. Again, X (Beetle's jumping) led to Y (a simple leg lift). Fourth point to Todd.

Beetle can take a hint, but she would have to surrender her Schnauzer membership card if she didn't try training him a few more times. When he next lifts his leg, Beetle bounces against it, pushing as best she can, given her fifteen pounds. He nonchalantly steps in her direction.

Stepping back from a jumping dog is almost instinctual, isn't it? Unfortunately, doing this rewards her with your space. A better approach is to step forward, into her space, to back her up. This equal-and-opposite response to what she is doing tells her that you are drawing a line in the sand, and your space is your own and not hers. Todd is always calm and unemotional when he does this. Using extra emotion, extra energy or aggression would be asking for the same in return, and it would be inappropriate for other reasons, not the least of which is: Beetle isn't being aggressive. She is being more assertive than is polite, so he remains calmly assertive in response. It is what another dog would do.

Point after point goes to Todd, and Beetle gets the message clearly:

- ❖ Todd's space is his own.
- ❖ Jumping on him will not result in conversation, added attention or extra handling.
- ❖ Repeated jumping doesn't change the result. Todd is consistent.

So Beetle tries something else. She wags her tail from a polite distance, something that Todd can reward with a big smile (and the occasional invitation to come closer).

RESPONSE RULE #8: Turn "don'ts" into "do's."

Correcting unwanted behaviors is an art as much as a science. What you decide to do in the moment is going to vary with the particulars.

❖ What a dog is doing.
❖ Which other dogs may be involved or watching.
❖ Which resources may be at your disposal.

An extra dollop of patience always helps when you work with adolescents, to turn their "don'ts" into "do's." These youngsters can be their own worst enemies, but they don't know any other way.

A case in point is Giovanni, a big dog with lots of energy. He is a ten-month old Doberman who is going through the dorky-dobie equivalent of the terrible-twos. His favorite activity is flinging his sixty-five-pound frame gleefully into other dogs. His second favorite activity is biting at the water in our big water bowls, replacing clean water with slick doggy drool while creating four-foot-diameter floods on the floor. Ah, canine adolescence!

As I walk a group of smaller dogs past his treadmill one afternoon, he finds another outlet for his energy. He starts to bark. This presents me with a catch-22 because, if I continue to walk on, he will see it as implied approval of his behavior. Like a two-year-old kid just learning the power of the word, "no," he will continue to bark, the canine equivalent of "no, no, no, no, no."

My responding vocally would risk adding tension to the room and energy to his own, so I opt not to do that, either. Gathering the leashes of the other dogs in one hand, I calmly and unemotionally reach toward the treadmill controls, to increase his speed a few notches.

This isn't a punishment. It is simply an "X leads to Y" response designed to create a new association, one in which Gio's unwanted bursts of energy are linked with better outlets for that energy. As he stretches his legs, I wait for him to refocus on the task at hand, letting the previous moment go. He fusses a little, but for less than a minute, before gradually transferring his attention from the smaller dogs to a spot in front of him. Before I leave, I want to reward his better behavior, and I do that with a very soft "Good job. Good decision, Giovanni." It takes the tension out of the air (both his and my own), while setting the stage for better things to come.

The following day, when I walk another group of dogs past Giovani on his treadmill, I make sure to reward his watchful, <u>pre-barking</u> behavior before he can contemplate getting vocal. As we walk by, I murmur, "Very good job, Giovanni." I want him to associate the appearance of the other dogs with the opportunity to get soft praise for relaxation, as opposed to the opportunity to vent his extra energy through barking. It is something that I will now do every day, to reinforce these good associations until his Doberman terrible-twos wane.

Another chance to defuse a situation and set a young dog up for better future behavior arises when Delia, a six-month-old Pit Bull mix, backs up and barks in alarm when one of our volunteers raises his arms over his head in an innocent stretch.

To desensitize her to similar movements and make her into a less reactive and more adoptable dog, I move her to a treadmill (giving her a job to do, an outlet for her extra energy and a way to move productively). Three volunteers then walk around the room, stretching their arms left, right, up and down, in a relaxed and enjoyable manner, an exercise that we will repeat daily for the next few weeks, rewarding Delia with big smiles and soft "good girls," plus the occasional biscuit when she accepts our actions with nonchalance.

To build upon this, I will umbilical-leash her when it comes time to do my evening stretches. This will introduce her to moving arms in another relaxed context and another location.

A third case in point is Argus, a two-year old shepherd mix. Argus approaches doorways politely, behind or at the side of his handlers. As soon as the door gets opened, however, he pulls his handlers inside before whipping around to face the door. Is he a rude and rowdy dog? Or might his actions reflect a prior association, one in which a door hit him in the butt on his way inside, and now he anticipates this happening again? Given this scenario, how many times might previous handlers responded in frustration – Stop it! Cut it out, Argus! – further reinforcing his negative association with doors? And how often might they have done nothing beyond step back in self-preservation, losing the opportunity to modify this behavior?

Now is the perfect time to invest five minutes (yes, simply five minutes of patient repetition) to guide Argus slowly back and forth through doorways, the better to teach him good manners and create a new association: one where we say "Go slo-o-o-ow, Argus" and he thoughtfully and mindfully puts his brakes on to receive a big smile (and maybe a short massage).

Recognize opportunities like this when they arise, and don't let them pass without capitalizing on them. In many cases, a few extra minutes of your time in response to behaviors that you don't want will help to guarantee better behaviors many times over in the future.

RESPONSE RULE #9: Beware micromanaging.

Micromanaging only creates stress for everyone, both the micromanagers and the micromanaged. Know that this can happen as we aim to shape our dog's behaviors.

The best way to avoid it, in my experience, is to watch large groups of basically balanced dogs at play. Watch how they self-regulate small issues as a group. Watch how quickly minor blow-ups blow over, and develop a sense for which issues need intervention and which do not. Doing this will also help you to appreciate dogs being dogs, and it will increase your awareness of canine body language (where a little goes a very long way).

RESPONSE RULE #10: Beware correcting the correctors.

A dog may be barking at another in play, or he may be barking in correction. Why is it important to know the difference? Because your response to these situations should be different.

In the first case, a quick "(Dog's name)… uh uh," followed by some calm follow-through can be enough to drop his energy level down a notch, so he continues his play quietly.

In the second case, one where Dog A is barking to correct Dog B's digging or her over-the-top rough-housing with Dog C, your correcting Dog A will just add tension to the situation.

His corrective barking will likely recur, because the instigating event has not been addressed. Address Dog B's digging or rough-housing, and Dog A's barking will stop.

RESPONSE RULE #11: Always end on a positive note.

When you choose to intervene, wait for the response you want, then reward your dogs in a calm-reinforcing manner for their modified behavior. (It is worth repeating: smiles, hand-wags and the occasional "thank you" go a long way toward removing any residual tension.) <u>Never leave things with just a correction</u>! If you do, you are not teaching your dogs what you want.

The coolness, calmness, sense of timing and awareness needed to respond with what works and works well is something that is developed over time, like your leadership skills. This is what separates people who have been exposed to canine psychology from those who know how to practice it instinctually, and I hope that practicing it instinctually will be your goal when you finish this book.

TRY THIS EXERCISE: Put these eleven rules of response in an order of your own, with the ones that strike a chord with you at the top of your list. Look for opportunities to follow them.

CHAPTER 19
WHO OWNS THIS STUFF?

Dogs don't accumulate, as a rule. They go through life lightly. Come what may, they are comfortable in their own skin. They don't waste time wishing they were a different dog, and they don't worry about keeping up with the dog next door. They are really very good at making do with what is in front of them.

Despite this blessing, canine hoarding can occur, and what is commonly called resource guarding arises in certain circumstances:

- ❖ When a dog has been teased (for example: with toys, treats or food).
- ❖ When a dog has been nutritionally deprived (so food guarding reflects an element of survival).
- ❖ When boundaries haven't been clearly and calmly delineated; rather, a dog's guarding has been ignored, or it has been condoned by others, either two-legged or four-legged.

What starts with the rude grabbing of treats can slide into increased assertion in other circumstances. And if this toggles into aggression, it can be quite scary to the people involved. The good news is: resource guarding is easier to address than most people think! The keys to doing it are:

❖ The right energy (a calm, confident, matter-of-fact demeanor).
❖ The right attitude (clear, dogged assertion, driven by a mental picture of success).
❖ Patience
❖ Proper posture and position (good body language)
❖ Knowledge of a few basic rules
❖ Making dogs work for their resources

Miss an important key, and you can make matters worse, and not better.

HOW DOGS CLAIM RESOURCES FROM EACH OTHER

To put the first four keys in perspective, consider how Willa, a Rottweiler-mix, claims a plush dog-bed that her Australian Shepherd friend, Rodanthe, is enjoying:

Willa stands over Rodanthe quietly, like a cloud. He groans in response and ducks his head, hoping it will send her on her way. It doesn't. She continues to hover over him. Her energy is calm, her demeanor assertive, and her message is clear: "I am not moving, no matter what, so you need to go."

He gives her a low growl. She doesn't buy into it. The fact that her persistence is getting his goat gives her one point to his zero. He gives her another low growl, but she couldn't care less. The score is now Willa-3, Rodanthe-0.

He shifts position to face his back to her. (Willa-3, Rodanthe-1.) She moves ninety degrees, the better to hover over his head. Although his eyes are closed in faux-sleep, he knows that she is there. He can't avoid her presence simply by closing his eyes.

Watching from afar, I know this is a pivotal moment; the winner of the dog-bed is going to be the dog with the most patience. The patience to stand one's ground, and the patience to ignore the other dog. A minute passes, and Willa's persistence wears Rodanthe down. He tries shifting position again. She does the same. He gives her one last half-hearted growl, but she knows his heart isn't into it. He then gets up and circles behind her as she claims the dog-bed. When it looks as if she isn't going to change her mind, he gives her his best canine harrumph before crossing the room to claim another one.

Dogs that live together claim resources from each other like this (in some cases, back and forth) all the time, each and every day. No harm; no foul, and peace reigns. They don't lose their composure. They don't show aggression, and they remain good friends.

In many situations, you can claim resources from your dogs using this same clear, patient, unruffled, assertive approach, and once a pattern has been established – one in which all resources ultimately are controlled by you – a simple *leave it* command is all that it will take for a dog to give you an item willingly and without fuss.

But don't try to imitate Willa just yet. It helps to know some basic rules.

DEAR DOGS: HERE ARE THE RULES

First, I will love and take care of you, but each food/treat/toy is my food/treat/toy until I decide to give it to you.

Second, when my hand approaches you, you can trust me and associate me with good things. (To earn my dogs' trust, I routinely offer meals in two or more handfuls. Each time my hand approaches, it is to add more food to a dog's bowl, and not take it away. That is very important!)

Third, to get a resource from me, you must look at me. Don't look away (I don't want your avoidance), and don't stare at the resource (it won't get you what you want). I will then reward your focus with a big smile (and a few extra kibbles, if it is dinnertime)!

Fourth, when taking a resource away (especially food bowls, full or empty), I will pick it straight up. I will never pull it away! (Picking an item straight up directs a dog's focus, body, and energy backward. Pulling a resource away directs his focus, body and energy forward, and that can be dangerous.)

WORKING FOR RESOURCES

When sharing resources with your dogs, much gets communicated when they are made to work for their share. Let me use Leonardo and Grande' to illustrate:

When Leonardo came to our facility at the age of two, he was a large-breed adolescent from a household that offered minimal guidance or training. He was hyperactive (his previous owners left him in the backyard to "self-exercise"). He knocked people over (never having been taught better behavior). And he tended to clash with other dogs (the result of his hyperactivity, more than anything else). He also tended to guard his food.

His rehabilitation began with lots of bicycling, treadmilling and walking in groups. He also learned our shelter's routine and rituals. This gave him the structure to shine, plus the social skills required of a good family member.

From day one/meal one he was fed only when he was sitting quietly, one to two feet back from a bowl set in a stand eighteen inches from the ground (so we didn't have to bend far to reach it). We placed a handful of kibbles in the bowl, saying "*Tssssssssssss.*" (Remember how this sound, and the energy it projects, tends to back dogs up.) When Leonardo remained sitting, with his focus on us (as opposed to the food), we rewarded him with a pleased smile before placing another handful of kibbles in his bowl using the same sound. Any leaning forward or focus on his food got him a stern *chicht!* but when he continued to sit, with his focus on us, another handful of kibbles was added. This practice was repeated a few more times before we pushed his bowl and stand toward him (further backing up his focus, body and energy) with the calm signal to eat (a soft *okay*). We then left him alone to enjoy his meal.

Leonardo quickly got with the program. Why shouldn't he? After all:

❖ Our energy was calm, confident and matter-of-fact (not in any way hesitant, aggressive or emotional).
❖ Our message was clear. The bowl belonged to us. The space around the bowl belonged to us. Our personal space belonged to us. And all of the food belonged to us, first and foremost.
❖ We maintained a relaxed, upright posture (no reaching or bending down).
❖ We offered a vital resource (his dinner).
❖ We were clear about our expectations (his focus on us, his calm energy, a respectful posture and a respectful distance offered to us).

❖ We offered numerous opportunities to be rewarded over the course of each meal (five to six handfuls, in most cases).

❖ We were consistent in our approach, allowing him to associate us with trustworthiness. He learned to associate eating with calmness, our hands approaching his bowl with <u>added</u> food, our presence in the room while he was eating with 'no big deal' and backing up politely with getting more food.

The single time that he reverted to mild food-guarding (an episode triggered by the sight of another dog during our filling-the-bowl ritual), we stopped the process to leash both dogs. Tying them roughly six feet apart, we brought out another food stand and bowl before continuing our feeding ritual "in stereo." Both dogs needed to back up their posture, energy and focus for them to get kibbles added to both bowls simultaneously, three times over; the same to receive the calm simultaneous direction to eat. This turned competition into teamwork, and it became a practice that was repeated over the next ten meals, to reinforce that the presence of other dogs wasn't adequate reason for food guarding.

Grande' (a Cocker-Shih Tzu mix) came to the Center at the age of three, with a history of guarding his favorite chewies. Fixing this problem wasn't difficult, using a three-pronged approach.

First, he was exposed to our usual routines and rituals, which included focused exercise and meals offered in multiple handfuls.

Second, he was taught the command, *leave it* (Chapter 24). This allowed him to associate giving up one resource with getting something better. We taught him the command using kibbles (first), then biscuits (second), followed by his chewy (third), and lastly, a few pieces of chicken.

Earning his respect in this way allowed us to then play Willa to his Grande.' All it took for him to surrender and walk away from his chewy was for us to stand calmly at his side and refuse to move on, no matter how much he tried to ignore our presence. The first time, this took two minutes. The next time, it took less than half of that. The third time, only a few seconds. To reward him for leaving his chewy behind, we occasionally gave him a better one, or we retrieved the original from where it got dropped, to give it back to him with a "good boy!"

Because our energy was equally calm and assertive, the message Grande' got was clear: his chewies, first and foremost, belonged to us, so guarding them was not a viable option.

We also made sure that an assortment of good chewies always existed, so there was less reason to covet any particular one.

TREATS AND BISCUITS

When offering treats, we do it palm-down with a closed fist, one piece at a time, and we reward a dog's <u>gentle</u> approach with our rotating and opening hand, together with a smile or a soft "<u>good</u> job" to reinforce that this is the kind of behavior we want. Dogs enjoy pleasing, and being acknowledged by, individuals that they respect. It is natural behavior, and resource guarding does not occur when this happens.

DOGS THAT GUARD SPACES

Prime real estate isn't just a concept understood by humans. Dogs know the value of a good spot, even when it may not be the most comfortable of spots.

Ducky came to us with a history of guarding passages. An arthritic older mix with hip dysplasia, he turned into a growly codger when other dogs tried to navigate past his favorite spot, smack in the middle of a busy hallway. Relocating him to more out-of-the-way locations boasting thick, comfy dog beds didn't work. He would ignore all of them to rest his ninety pounds, instead, on a wooden floor where everyone needed to step over him.

Numerous times we would peer down the hallway to find three or four smaller dogs waiting, afraid to walk by Mr. Grumpy-Duck. To reverse this, we slipped a leash on each of them for a half-dozen repetitions of walking back and forth past Ducky in a relaxed, ignore-him/he-has-no-say-in-this, no-nonsense manner. Because our demeanor was calm and matter-of-fact, all of the dogs, even Ducky, got the message, and the logjam of dogs at the end of the hallway stopped.

SHOULD YOU RISE TO THE OCCASION?

With this knowledge in hand, you may be ready to tackle your dog's resource guarding. On the other hand, you may not yet have the quality of energy or sense of body language needed, or you may need to do more to earn his respect in other ways. Know your strengths and weaknesses, and know not to try something if you are hesitant. Dogs don't trust hesitant people, and how they respond to their hesitation (with hesitation of their own, with avoidance, or with correction) depends upon the dog.

TESTS THAT AIM TO GAUGE RESOURCE GUARDING

Although developed with the best of intentions, behavioral assessments designed to gauge resource guarding at shelters can be misleading, misinterpreted and downright harmful. I absolutely hate when certain ones are used, since they have led to many good dogs being overlooked or put down. They also confuse a highly correctable symptom (resource guarding) with a problem (that which caused the resource guarding to occur). Remember: resource guarding can develop due to starvation or teasing. It can result from a lack of calm, confident leadership. Either way, it is not that hard to address!

The worst of these tests uses a rubber hand on a pole to pull food away from dogs. Aargh!! First, that is called teasing. Never put food in front of a dog and then pull it away. It's not playing fair. Don't. Do. It. Second, the people holding onto the fake hand often know little about how their posture (bending over slightly), energy (often hesitant) and position (reaching out) completely send the wrong message. Is there any wonder that dogs respond negatively?

There are better ways to gauge a dog's tendency to guard resources, methods that honor good canine psychology and encourage a dog to do his best (and not his worst). A description of them goes beyond the boundaries of this book, but it is worthwhile to know they exist.

TRUE CANINE HOARDERS

As I write this, I am watching Boss Hog, a goofy chocolate Chihuahua who also happens to be a canine hoarder. Sitting atop far more than his fair share of dog toys, chewies and bones, like a mother hen atop eggs, he isn't a happy fellow. Rather, he is one worried dude, concerned about protecting his stash. I genuinely feel sorry for the true hoarders of the canine world, since the psychology of their affliction is one from our species, and so unnatural to theirs. These dogs repeatedly focus on their "stuff," missing out on the freedom of <u>not</u> having stuff. Poor pups!

Although absolutely willing to surrender their hoards to me (in deference to my earned position as top dog), they waste not a second before re-accumulating any unclaimed items before another dog can get to them. They are what they are, and the best approach to them is simple management. I don't leave items of high value within their reach, and I don't leave them unsupervised where other dogs might step in to correct them. I give them lots of good exercise (the better to expand their horizons), and I give them little dog-jobs to do (the better for them to feel proud of their accomplishments).

DE-STRESS!

Don't mistake activity with achievement.
John Wooden

CHAPTER 20
TRULY LIVING IN THE MOMENT

When we seize the opportunity to really live with our dogs, we are given a unique gift. It is the gift of a benevolent, mostly forgiving reflection of our own behavior.

Dogs that share our homes, dogs that we meet on the street, and dogs that live with our friends and family: moment by moment, they can be excellent teachers, if we take the time to get their messages. Taking the time is key, since so much of the stuff that comes with being human can get in the way: day-to-day stuff, creeping-up-on-us stuff and do-it-yesterday stuff.

Most of us consider ourselves multitaskers. Many of us pride ourselves on being good planners. And a good number of us wake up in the morning with our minds in motion way before our bodies. (I feel your pain!) When I get up at sunrise to feed and let my dogs outside, I take a few minutes to acknowledge all the stuff on my day's calendar, and then I put it aside. I know that if I am low on energy, upset about something or feeling achy or distracted, I have got to leave it all behind before I greet my dogs. I don't want to bring poor energy to my pack!

The same thing applies to our Center's pack. Whether I stop to take a few cleansing breaths, or I take a short walk down the road and back, or I begin one of my favorite de-stressing techniques, I will not open the door to their building until I have let my stressors go. Sure, I do it for the dogs, but really, I am the one who benefits! I am the one who has just given herself a few hours of freedom from the day's hassles, if only for the time we are together. Easy to say, but perhaps not so easy to do, you say; and you are right. This is where the following five techniques can help:

- ❖ Build a mental tennis court.
- ❖ Pick a melody.
- ❖ Write yourself a note.
- ❖ Leave and come back.
- ❖ Picture success.

BUILD A MENTAL TENNIS COURT

Living in the moment is a lot like meditation, and one of the hardest things about learning to meditate for most people is keeping a clear head, unburdened by distractions. People put so much effort into keeping extraneous thoughts away that the entire act of being in the moment becomes an exercise in futile frustration. There is an irony for you!

Meditation doesn't mean an absence of awareness; rather it involves an awareness of each moment <u>without attachment</u>. So don't sweat all of the thoughts that pop into your head when you are trying to maintain an even emotional keel for your dogs. Just don't let them stay and develop legs, especially if they create stress. Picture your mind like a big tennis court. The thoughts come in like tennis balls, and if you do not want to deal with them in the moment, you can bop them out with one swat of your mental tennis racket.

thought in → bop → thought out.
thought in → bop → thought out.

This is a good technique to use when pesky little thoughts distract you from sharing time with your dogs. Should a thought come in bearing the label "FIRE," feel free to catch that one and deal with it. But for the little things that keep you from being present in the moment, use your mental tennis racket to clear your head. It works! Things will go smoother. Your dogs will be better behaved. And you will be better prepared for the rest of your day when it is time to move on.

PICK A MELODY

Repeating a certain song or melody is a trick many athletes use to get their best performance. It is hard for negative thoughts to crowd your head when you are humming a favorite tune. Pick songs that bring out the calm, effective, "together" you. Pick songs that put pep into your step. Pick songs that make you smile because, in smiling, your whole body relaxes.

There is no need to sing them out loud. Just enjoy them in your head as you go through your routines. Your dogs will pick up on your more relaxed energy, and you will find that they are much better behaved.

I often find myself channeling Tchaikovsky's Swan Lake and 1812 Overture, not my own favorite tunes but rather those of my late father. He enjoyed using these melodies in floor exercises as a gymnastics coach. The first time they popped into my head, I thought, "What the heck?" But then I had to smile, remembering how happy they made my Dad. To no surprise, my pack is happiest with me at these times!

WRITE YOURSELF A QUICK NOTE

We all write notes to remind ourselves to purchase items, call people and do things. Notes can also be of help when you need to let go of a particular frustration that is eating away at you. It may sound a little silly, but it works!

Picture this: You return home from work in a foul mood because Adam, a co-worker, has been dropping the ball. His behavior is irresponsible, and it has caused you such hassle that the thought of simply dismissing it seems unjust. You are right. He is in the wrong, and he is a total jerk to do what he has done.

The problem is: your dogs don't know what Adam has done. They don't understand how hurtful his actions are to you. They don't know that you now have a ton of work to do that someone else should be doing. They only know that your energy is way off. So grab a scrap piece of paper or a Post-it note. Heck, grab a crayon and a paper towel, if that is your only option. Then write, "Adam is a jerk!" Now put the note in your pocket and the thought out of your mind. (Don't worry; the note will still be there later, should you decide that you are ready to address what it says). Just put it in your pocket. Now watch what this does to the dogs around you.

This little technique works, and it is a gift that you can give to yourself for the time that you spend with your dogs. It is a gift of living in the moment, a moment in which Adam has no part.

LEAVE AND COME BACK

Sometimes you just have to do this. Leave for five minutes and come back. Ironically, you will probably save time, because if the alternative is to push through your day in a negative or a weak state of mind, your dogs will not behave as well and things will take longer in the long run.

PICTURE SUCCESS

I have mentioned this one before. If you doubt that you can do something, it probably isn't going to happen. Your hesitation will make that the case. Remember: dogs don't follow hesitant energy. Depending upon their temperament, they will override it (imagine a couch-peeing Pomeranian), or they will avoid it (envision a crouching Chihuahua). They might try to eliminate it (a few biting Bouviers come to mind).

Picturing success in your mind as you set out to do something is a good way to deal with that doubting Daniel in your unconscious. Picture success until that picture, and not one of doubt or weakness, becomes your reality.

Envision that you are someone else, if that works for you, someone inspiring who would have no trouble with your dogs. Channel your inner canine guru. Smile, and then pretend, for just a few minutes, that you are him or her.

If training personnel is something that you excel at, in other contexts, you might also imagine that you are training another person and your job is to demonstrate how things need to be done. It is a good technique for bringing out your most capable side.

PATIENCE

One of the best tools in your toolbox will always be patience. Patience with your dogs and a little patience with yourself as you work on getting things right. Now I am definitely not the most patient person around. When it comes to the School of Patience, I am one of those perpetual students who will never get her degree. But the neat thing about living with dogs is their patience with us! If we mess up one moment, there is always another moment to get things right.

One practice that you can use to bring a little more patience (and peace) into your life takes only five seconds at a time. That is easy for even the least patient of us to embrace!

❖ Wait an extra five seconds, with your dogs at your side, before starting your walk together. Use the time to look up and out, then smile and enjoy a relaxing breath. Use this time to relax your body and put a positive picture in your mind. (If this seems hard to do, go ahead and give yourself an extra five or ten seconds. Really…no one is counting.)

❖ As you walk, let yourself smile for five seconds whenever your dogs fall in step with you. It is a pleasant reward for everyone, and it helps to preempt sneaky little tensions before they become bigger ones, the better to prolong the healthy rhythm of the moment.

❖ Wait five seconds after your dog's successful response to a command (e.g., *sit*, *down* or *stay*) before moving on to something else. Use the time to give him a genuine smile.

❖ When you see your dogs relaxing around the house, stop what you are doing for five seconds and enjoy the moment with them. Giving yourself this small gift of time is a good step toward gaining inner peace, and it is through that peace that you can find the patience to get through the rough spots.

❖ Realize that dogs often give us their worst behavior just before they give us their best! It might last five seconds or it might last a minute and five seconds. Just don't get sucked into any unwanted energy or doggi-tude that is thrown your way. If you remain patient, the dogs can only throw it at you for so long!

And don't forget to allow your dogs to be dogs. Well-behaved dogs, most certainly, but dogs nonetheless.

PRACTICE, PRACTICE, PRACTICE

Get it wrong in one moment…oh well. Just move on to the next and get it right. We all learn lessons along the way, and this makes what happens first just part of the process, part of our achievement.

LOOK FOR REASONS TO SMILE

Aren't we a silly species? We forget to take the occasional deep breath, robbing our bodies of the most basic nutrient of all (oxygen) while collecting tension in our shoulders, arms and torso. We maintain positions for extended periods of time without stretching, and we routinely wear clothes that are too tight, dressing to impress as opposed to move comfortably. All of this may fool our fellow human beings, but our dogs recognize the rigidity that results.

Spontaneous, sincere, ear-to-ear smiles go a long way to undo this state, and they take minimal effort. They allow our bodies to shed accumulated tension without added input from our brains. Try smiling at times when you normally wouldn't, for example: in the midst of cooking dinner or while getting dressed in the morning. Allow yourself a soft smile when you wash your dishes, or when you glance out a window, surveying the mundane as much as the inspirational. Follow up each smile with a gentle wiggle or long stretch that relaxes your tensest group of muscles. The process is a telling one, and there are no downsides, only upsides.

There is no need to plot or plan the process. There is no need to set goals of X smiles per hour. Simply allow yourself these small freebies, with no strings attached, whenever the mood strikes. Just as adjusting the position of a dog's tail can adjust his state of mind, our smiles can help to adjust our own state of mind!

TRY THIS EXERCISE: Revisit the first two exercises from this book, if you haven't already made them part of your morning routine. First, make smiling the first thing you do every morning, even before opening your eyes. Regardless of what is going on around you or the thoughts that come up in the moment, enjoy a soft, genuine smile for a few seconds or more. Second, the first time you see your dogs each day, give them a quiet smile if they are calm and quiet, to reinforce this aspect of their personalities.

TAKE IT A STEP FURTHER: Did any of this chapter's simple de-stressing tricks resonate with you? Put them into practice where you see fit.

CHAPTER 21
DE-STRESSING YOUR DOGS

Dogs don't worry about image, style or ego. They project self-deprecating good cheer, and they don't take themselves too seriously. It would be nice to say that stress doesn't befall them, but that isn't the case. Hormones can create stress. Front-of-the-pack and back-of-the-pack DNA (Chapter 27) can also create stress. Living in a world where their much-beloved two-legged friends too infrequently understand their culture, their body language and their needs can be stressful, too.

The very best way to keep stress out of your dogs' day is to follow the principles and practices discussed to this point, particularly when it comes to associations (Chapter 4), energy (Chapters 6 and 7), movement (Chapter 15) and communication (Chapters 9, 10 and 11). Following the Golden Rules and canine social rules (Chapter 3) are important, and leading the way clearly (Chapter 12) is pivotal.

THE MOST IMPORTANT STUFF

Some dogs come to us mentally sound and well-socialized. Others come to us psychologically fragile, due to unstable events. In every case, it is important to give them a clean slate, every day. Every moment is a new one, and looking backward won't help them (or us) move forward.

Remember these basic premises:

Associations: How dogs view their environment depends upon the associations they make with its components: people, items and events. When we take the time to recognize existing associations, and when we work with our dogs to reinforce the best of them and form healthy new ones (ideally right from the start), issues that lead to stress are minimized, if not completely eliminated.

Leadership: Dogs become leaders by default. They rise to lead where there are leadership voids. When we rise to the occasion so there is no void, we allow our dogs to be happy four-legged followers, a more relaxed position for which they are better suited.

Social rules: Dogs are dogs. "Human" will never be their primary language. For this reason, honoring and following canine social protocols (as opposed to human social protocols) allows them to be more comfortable, especially when it comes to human-dog or dog-dog introductions.

Communication: Let your relaxed, genuine smiles and occasional hand-wags take you farther than any words can. Throw in a couple of butt-wiggles for fun!

Repetitions: Showing a dog a new skill is like planting a seed. Using repetitions to reinforce the new skill is watering that seed. It is a heck of a lot more apt to grow, and grow well.

Our energy: Being calm, confident and matter-of-fact (or calmly authoritative, where needed) is the name of the game. For us to help less-balanced dogs to relax and follow our lead, our personal energy must reflect these leadership traits.

Their energy: Be quick to smile when a dog exhibits his most relaxed, level-one side, to encourage more of the same.

Patience: We send the wrong message to our dogs when we leave them in a state of tension. On the other hand, when we patiently wait for their tension to dissipate, before we move on, we set them up for success in moments to come. Their energy and their state of mind is better, and our patience has earned their respect. Plus, this allows us to leave with a "thank you!" and a smile on our face!

HOUSING AND FENCING

A peaceful home serves to nurture health, happiness and safety for all, and attention to small details, particularly where they concern housing, fencing and routine, can mean the difference between peace and commotion, for your dogs and for your family.

Dogs kenneled, gated or fenced directly across from one another can find it hard to relax.* This shows in their posture and the positions they take. It shows in their activity and how much they vocalize. And it shows in the often-problematic way they relate to each other when the barriers are removed.

It upsets me to see books on training recommend placing baby gates between dogs that don't get along! This human-centric but not canine-centric, face-to-face approach only reinforces a "me vs. him" mentality. A much better approach is to take feuding dogs on regular, horizontally structured walks together, the better to give them a common job and get them on the same team. Should you still house your less-trustworthy dogs separately when you aren't there to supervise them? Most definitely, but do it in a way that prevents visual contact until the dogs have formed bonds.

I am a big fan of privacy fencing. It alleviates stress in a number of ways. It stops a significant amount of alert-barking. It helps to mitigate prey drive issues. And it keeps dogs, both large and small, safer. On the other hand, see-through fencing (e.g., chain-link) encourages dogs to have a heightened visual interest in what is on the other side. It promotes alert-barking and prey drive, and it encourages dogs to pace back and forth. (More about this in Chapters 23 and 24.)

GOOD ROUTINES AND RITUALS ARE VITAL

Just as your choice of housing and fencing can help you or hurt you, so can your choice of routines and rituals (Chapter 5). If your dogs don't act the way you wish they would, view your household routines and rituals as if you were an outsider, the better to critique and shape them into more effective ones. Are they stress-free and calming? Or are they hectic and arousing?

Look at your routines and rituals from the perspective of your dog. What kind of messages are they sending? What kind of associations are they creating and reinforcing? What kind of energy (quality and quantity) are they promoting? What kind of lessons are they teaching, and what kind of skills are they cultivating? Does what you do allow your dogs to show off

---

* Tour any boarding or daycare facility that you are considering, and keep this in mind. (More about this in Chapter 23.)

their capabilities? Dogs really aim to please, and the structure of good routines and clear, predictable rituals allows them to understand what is expected. This, in turn, minimizes stress.

EXERCISE AND ENRICHMENT

To de-stress stressed-out dogs, develop a good exercise plan with mindful outlets for their energy. If you don't already take regular working walks, this needs to be a top-tier goal. To add more mindful behavior to your dogs' day, give them small tasks to do. Find activities that honor their DNA (Chapter 14). Teach them commands that enrich their lives, as well as your own. Make up new ones when they suit your purposes! There is a never-ending number of things that you can teach dogs to do, simply by naming and rewarding behaviors as they do them (Chapter 11).

If you have more than one dog, allow them to observe each other responding to, and being rewarded for responding to, commands. Since dogs are pretty observant (and a little competitive) by nature, this is an excellent and easy way to teach several dogs commands at the same time!

Chewing is a beloved activity of dogs, as many a dog who has gotten reprimanded for chewing on the wrong things will tell you. It is also a good stress reliever. Providing dogs with multiple approved items to chew is a simple but important part of providing for their needs. In this regard, the more natural, the better. Man-made items shouldn't be the only choices!

BE PROACTIVE

Have a good plan to follow when human visitors refuse to honor good canine social protocol. We all know these people. They are either way too vocal or they move way too fast into a dog's personal space. Sometimes they project unhealthy, negative energies. To keep the peace, you might move your dogs to your backyard or leave them in another room with extra-large knuckle bones to chew on. Alternately, you might invite your visitors to take a short walk with you and your dogs, the better to get everyone facing the same direction to share a common, enjoyable goal.

Aunt Patsy and Cousin Monica are coming for the night, and you aim to be prepared. Rather than sequester your dogs with chew bones to keep them busy, you ask your relatives to call you when they are ten minutes away. It is your signal to leash up your dogs and begin a walk down your road.

Timing things well allows Patsy and Monica to join you and the dogs for a horizontally-oriented get-to-know-you walk around the block (Chapter 5) before everyone walks inside (Patsy and Monica first, then you, and then your dogs). At that point, your dogs have accepted them into your household, and peaceful co-existence and good manners prevail – no extra excitement, no alert-barking, and no pawing of clothing. This is leadership at its proactive best!

Being proactive also helps when it comes to veterinary visits, a stressful time for certain dogs and dog caretakers. If your dog acts nervous about visiting your veterinarian, a good question to ask is: How do you feel about taking him to the vet? If the answer is "I hate it, because of his behavior," here are some additional questions to ask, to identify the cause of his behavior:

- ❖ Does my dog get to enjoy car rides to places other than a veterinary clinic? (It builds good associations with the car.)
- ❖ Have I ever taken him to the clinic for no other reason than to give him a massage and some biscuits in the parking lot, before driving home? (This builds good associations with the location.)
- ❖ Do I walk through the door of the clinic first, or have I stepped back, confusing him in the process?
- ❖ What is my state of mind when I enter the clinic? (Am I anxious, annoyed, excited, sad or apprehensive? Or am I relaxed, in-the-moment, directive and matter-of-fact?)

If your dog is responding to issues at the clinic such as overpowering smells, the presence of fear pheromones, prior mishandling or the staff's poor body language, it is time to find a better veterinarian, but if he is responding to circumstances more under your control, you may find that changing what you do makes a world of difference.

Utilize the de-stressing techniques in Chapter 20 to get through tough times (we all have them), and learn how to let a bad moment (or even a bad day) go, so you can move on to better ones. Let the occasional smile help you reset your mindset. Your dogs will support you doing this, and the outcome will be better for everyone.

HORMONES AND STRESS

When it comes to stress, it is always more stressful to be an unneutered dog (male or female) than it is to be a neutered one. This is true health-wise and behavior-wise. Neutering your dogs is also less stressful on your pet food budget, since neutered dogs of both sexes need roughly one-third less food to maintain a healthy weight.

The following also applies:

- ❖ Neutered animals frequently have nicer coats, since hormones can wreak havoc on fur quality.
- ❖ Neutered animals feel less of a need to mark their territory with urine.
- ❖ Neutered animals tend to fight less.
- ❖ Neutered pets don't get reproductive infections, and their risk of certain cancers is significantly reduced.
- ❖ Neutered pets live an average of three years longer.
- ❖ Hormones perpetuate anxiety in dogs that have a tendency toward it.

For all of these reasons, neutered pets are much less likely to be relinquished to a shelter and possibly euthanized at taxpayer expense.

Unless you have a truly phenomenal representative of a breed, a dog with proven, healthy genetics going back several generations and an excellent temperament, spay-neutering is the way to go and a true kindness at that.

FOOD AND STRESS

Remember: overfeeding translates to additional energy and additional poop, both which can elevate a dog's stress level. Never trust a manufacturer's recommended feeding guidelines! They are usually way too high (in some cases, twice what is ideal). Your dog's waistline is the best guideline to follow, and it is best viewed from above. If you cannot see a defined waist behind his ribcage, it is time for a diet!

To help you feed the correct amount, feed your dog with his stomach size in mind, and not your own. Imagine how big his stomach is, in comparison to yours and in comparison to your other pets. Aim to fill it twice a day, but not more.

Want to prolong the fun of mealtime, without adding additional calories? Make some food puzzles for your dog (Chapter 14).

Food is a necessity, and mealtime is a bonding experience for our dogs, as much as it is for us. As I have mentioned, it is also a time when much can be communicated: the manners you expect; the level-one energy you expect, even who must defer to whom in multiple-dog households. Feeding order speaks volumes, without a word spoken. For this reason, I always feed my naturally lower-on-the-totem-pole dogs (the older ones, the timid ones and the infirmed) before those higher-on-the-pole. It helps to equalize everyone's position and keep the peace in situations where certain dogs tend to be too assertive and others too submissive by nature, and it is amazing how well it works.

CANINE ANXIETY

Canine anxiety is both energy-driven and corrosive. It self-perpetuates, layer upon layer. At its worst, it can elevate to the level of separation anxiety (discussed in detail in the next chapter). Rehabilitation of canine anxiety requires replacing each of these layers with psychologically healthier ones, and the process is like peeling off cold, wet clothing so you can don warm and cozy alternatives, but not quite that easy.

In situation after situation, time after time, patient redirection and a calm matter-of-factness about things and events are the keys to freeing dogs from this kind of mental hell.

The following principles apply:

❖ Dogs that have a calm and confident person to follow are going to be less anxious, more self-assured, quieter and happier, since it is always less stressful to be the follower of a good decision-maker than it is to be the decision-maker.

❖ Dogs that get calm, quiet rewards (such as smiles), when they are calm and quiet, are more likely to remain calm and quiet.

❖ Dogs that are well-exercised have less energy with which to feed their anxiety. This is especially true with herding, sporting and working breeds, bred to do a job (and by that, I do not mean office work!).

Where does one start? Start with long working walks, at least twice a day, since they will help you to achieve all of the above goals. Working walks put us in a position of leadership. They promote circumstances in which calm, quiet behavior can be rewarded in a calm and quiet manner. They exercise the dogs, and they help to build confidence. This helps anxious dogs (and their handlers) move on, both physically and mentally.

Take your walks away from distractions, initially. When you feel that you and your dog are ready for more public locations, use yellow ribbons (Chapter 14) to keep strangers from encroaching upon your dog's personal space, if needed.

Calm, matter-of-fact, nonverbal umbilical leashing can also help excited-anxious dogs drop their energy level and unsure-anxious dogs develop confidence. Recall how we use this technique to introduce dogs to new places and routines. By doing this, we prevent anxiety while promoting quiet watchfulness and good associations.

Remember the tale in Chapter 10 about tying the leash of an anxious dog to the collar of a more confident dog at the beach. Step aside once in a while to let a balanced dog umbilical-lead another dog through worrisome situations. As people, we can learn so much from watching the process!

Another technique that helps unsure and anxious dogs excel is called sandwiching. Sandwiching requires two confident and relaxed mentor dogs. To illustrate:

> Hadley is a large-breed mix who jumps into cars reluctantly. Not wanting to lift his eighty pounds, I reach instead for Cairo and Everest's help. Both dogs love car rides, and both will do anything for the smallest of biscuits. One dog at a time (using big smiles but no direct eye contact, excessive coaxing or conversation), I direct Cairo, and then Hadley, and then Everest into my car, with each dog getting a treat for his effort. The order chosen allows Hadley to be sandwiched by the more self-assured dogs, and this provides him with canine peer-pressure and good role models in a matter-of-fact way.

When treating anxiety, the goal is to promote calm relaxation in everything you do, normalizing a dog's response to his circumstances, whatever they may be. This is not the same as babying him through trial and error! Quite to the contrary. We want every event, every new thing and every new person to equate to 'no big deal.'

No matter what an anxious dog throws at you energy-wise, don't let yourself follow his lead by getting frustrated or anxious yourself. In any situation, you have two choices. You can get him moving, to move him on to a better state of mind, or you can leash him in place and wait out the behavior you don't want, to get to the behavior you want, so you can calmly walk away. Leaving a short leash on, twenty-four/seven, can be helpful in this regard. It allows you to <u>indirectly</u> reach for him when calm redirection is required.

When you need to correct misbehaviors in anxious dogs (leg-lifting on furniture or resource guarding, for example), minimize the energy that you project, as any beyond what is needed will only promote more anxiety. Again, the key is to be calm, clear and matter-of-fact. Channel your inner robot (Chapter 7), where need be.

When it comes to measuring your success, do so week-by-week, as opposed to day-by-day. In this way, progress will be easier to see: layers upon layers of anxiety peeling away over time, revealing the canine personality beneath.

TRY THIS EXERCISE: View your kenneling and fencing from the standpoint of your dogs. Might some changes bring more peace into their lives (and your own)?

TAKE IT A STEP FURTHER: To prevent stress in your dogs' lives, aim to perfect the principles mentioned at the beginning of this chapter.

CHAPTER 22
TACKLING SEPARATION ANXIETY

Separation anxiety warrants a chapter all its own, because it is so much easier to prevent than to treat once it occurs. To prevent it, and to address it, requires an understanding of canine psychology.

Dogs are pack-oriented. The nature of a dog is to follow his pack's leader, and dogs naturally gravitate to other pack members. For them, separation is not a natural state. Still, at some point in their lives, given the guidance of good mentors (initially their mother dog, and later their human caretakers), like kids going off to school, dogs learn to deal with varying degrees of it.

If you are a puppy, new to this world, you need your mom and/or littermates to stay within an intimate space of a few feet. Otherwise you are going to be one fussy, concerned little guy. If you were sleeping when Mom snuck off, you fuss and Mom comes back, and all is right with the world. This is normal. As you get older, your senses of sight and hearing improve, and you feel a lot better about Mom and the others being at a social distance (roughly three to twelve feet). Sometimes they initiate the space, and sometimes you create it, exploring. This is normal. But when the rest of the gang is more than twelve feet away, you are going to want to find them in all likelihood. You are not a big boy yet, and your feelings are normal.

If things go well for you, you get to stay with your mom and littermates for a minimum of eight (better yet, nine or ten) weeks, because Mom really does know best, and she introduces the concept of separation to you gradually, not all at once. From then on, your changing pack (with both four-legged and two-legged members) guides you calmly and confidently through trial and error, exploration and training, scary moments and minor disasters.

Along the way, you get healthy outlets for your energy every day. You get lots of exercise. And once you have been exercised, you are introduced to disciplines such as respectful leash walking, social skills in human public domains, social skills with animals outside your pack and talents such as resting quietly on your bed or in your crate for increasing (but always reasonable) amounts of time. You are not spoiled. You are first and foremost a dog, but since you had a good foundation from your dam and lots of exercise and then good training and calm emotional support from subsequent pack members, you have become a very valued member of a family.

But what if, along the way, you receive positive reinforcement whenever something makes you nervous? What if you receive cuddling and verbal soothing when something scares you, instead of being allowed to work your way through situations when you can? What if you don't get the chance to explore because your people hover over you? What if you don't get the exercise you need, or even worse, if when you are revved up and full of energy, you are stuck in a crate for more than just the time needed to cool your jets?

What if your human pack members give you what you need, or want, primarily when you are excited, and what if your calm side is rarely encouraged? What if they tend to leave you when you are in a state of exuberance *(Don't worry, baby; Mommy will be back soon!)*, as opposed to level-one calmness? And what if they greet you with a high level of excitement *(Hi there, sweetheart! Did you miss your Daddy? That's a GOOD girl!)*, as opposed to not making a big deal about their reappearance?

When nature and nurture collide like this, it can produce a dog that associates separation from his pack with excitement, an association that can slide into anxiety if there is any emotional support for it. And anxiety, being what it is, can build upon itself, creating layer after layer of increasing anxiety.

Treatment for separation anxiety needs to reverse this process, and it can be like peeling back multiple layers, one at a time. And time is what it is going to take.

When dogs come to our facility with anxiety, their DNA frequently reflects sporting, working or herding breeds, and they are often the product of all the wrong added ingredients:

- ❖ They were taken away from their dam and littermates before eight weeks of age.
- ❖ They went to households without calm canine mentors.
- ❖ They were often crated while in an excited state of mind and left that way for extended periods of time.
- ❖ They were under-exercised and roughly punished for their hyperactivity.
- ❖ They have had three (or more) homes (despite being only two to three years of age).

Since we can't change their past, there is really no use dwelling on it. Today is a new day and every moment a new one, and right now they need calm, confident leadership. Yes, they will need to modify some of their behaviors, but going back to the basics, it is their associations with certain human behaviors that we are going to have to change. And change is possible, because we aren't going to repeat the practices that encouraged their anxiety.

TODAY IS THE FIRST DAY OF THE REST OF YOUR LIFE

Your eyes are a bit dilated. Your respiration is elevated, and it is hard to control your excitement…you have fallen in love! After years of waiting for a Border Collie all your own, you finally have the time, the space, the lifestyle and the financial stability to add one to your home.

From the moment you see Tess's picture on Petfinder.com, you know that you were meant for each other. Her vibrant eyes and pink tongue call to you. Her glossy coat is gorgeous, and you can already picture her curled up on a big cushion next to your bed. Five years old, and already spayed, she is available for adoption at a shelter on the other side of the county. You grab a leash and your wallet, your keys and your cell phone, and you head to your car.

Arriving at the shelter, you are putty in Tess's paws the moment she leans into your leg, looking up at you. She appears healthy, and she is great with kids, cats and other dogs at the shelter. It is even reported that she treadmills! Yea! But her history isn't all kibbles and biscuits. You learn that she has been adopted out twice, and twice she has come back. It appears Tess gets unhappy if she can't be near her people. She barks. She chews on things. She paces, and she knocks things over.

For the first time since you saw her picture online, you start thinking with your head, instead of just your heart. You would really like to give her a chance, but you know that your union won't be in anyone's best interest if her anxiety over separation is not treatable. You walk outside, alone, for some quiet soul-searching.

Here are the questions you ponder:

- ❖ Can you provide several hours of mindful exercise every day for Tess's first week (and possibly longer)? She is going to need lots of it, to drain the energy reserves fueling her anxiety.
- ❖ Do you have helpers that you can count on: calm, confident, patient people capable of bringing out her best, without feeding into her worst?
- ❖ How is your leadership energy? To bring out Tess's best is going to require your best.
- ❖ Have you done your research? How much do you know about separation anxiety?

If you have got what it takes, then Tess is a lucky gal. If the answers to these questions leave you worried, then another dog may be a better fit for you. Sitting in your car, you grab your smart phone for a little online research. Twenty minutes later, you head back into the shelter. You are up for the challenge, and Tess is getting another chance!

So what do you do first? Do you head to your vet to pick up the latest sedative or anti-anxiety drug?* Not at all! The first thing you pick up is a Thundershirt. Thundershirts take the edge off a nervous dog's energy eight times out of ten, and they have absolutely no side effects. Dogs tolerate them well, and some love them so much that they seek them out prior to storms. Plus, they don't interfere with a dog's focus or abilities.

THE CORE PRINCIPLES

Reviewing some of the core principles that we have been discussing – association, communication, energy, repetitions and exercise – will help set Tess up for success.

---

* *Short-term medication may be something you investigate later, but only as an adjunct to the rest of your plan. The right medication, carefully dosed, can help some dogs avoid full-blown panic attacks.*

Association: Tess's association with her people leaving has been one of high anxiety (not calm matter-of-factness). New associations will need to be created that link periods of separation with peaceful acceptance.

Communication: Your nonverbal communication is pivotal, as extra vocal energy will just increase Tess's own. Relaxed smiles, aimed at nothing in particular, will put her more at ease than chatty banter. Soft music is okay. Anything loud or boisterous is not.

Energy: The energy of the people surrounding Tess must not feed into, nor fall victim to, her anxiety. It must be calm, no matter what she does, because only through this calmness will she find the role models she needs.

Lessons and repetitions: Separation from people is a discipline that Tess needs to learn and have reinforced. Other disciplines, such as learning the command *place* (Chapter 5) and achieving level-one energy at feeding times, breaks-in-play time and at doors and other thresholds, will also need to be learned and reinforced over time, through repetition. Building Tess's skill set will give her a sense of accomplishment and direction.

Exercise: Of course, Tess's lessons will need to be taught when she is in a relaxed (or at least relatively tired) state of mind, since no dog is in the best frame of mind to learn if she is full of pent-up energy. A tired dog has less energy with which to be anxious and destructive.

THE NEXT STEPS

You get on the phone to enlist the help of your good friend and fellow Border Collie enthusiast, Jennifer. Before Tess enters your home, your plan is to:

- ❖ Exercise her with some bicycling, using the two-leash method described in Chapter 8.
- ❖ Follow your bicycling with a long working walk for an hour or two.
- ❖ Give Tess a short break, and then exercise her with some ball-throwing.
- ❖ Give Tess a second short break before treadmilling her at Jennifer's house for fifteen minutes (since she is familiar with a treadmill). Because her herding dog DNA yearns for a job to do, you put a light pack on her back the whole time.

Jennifer's involvement will be pivotal over the next few weeks, since one of your goals is for Tess to have multiple role models. You want her to concentrate on the task at hand, not forming choke-hold bonds with one and only one person.

Wow! That is a lot of exercise for her and work for you. But it is all necessary and absolutely vital right now. Why? Because your next step is to walk her across the threshold of her new home. You want her to start her life there in a calm, thoroughly tired and unapprehensive frame of mind. This will help to form the following associations:

this home = a place of peace
default energy of this home = restful

Entering your home, you quietly umbilical-leash Tess from room to room, so she can get a good sniff. Offering calm smiles, you don't say a word that might pop her out of her level-one calm. This done, you tie her next to a comfortable dog bed (where a large chew-bone awaits). Curling up with a good book, you then wait for her to curl up, too, something that takes only a few minutes, since she has been well-exercised.

Excellent! You have one more step to take before calling it a day. Wordlessly, you walk outside and back inside through your front door twenty times, gradually increasing the time that you remain out of sight from ten seconds to five minutes. Each time you return, you perform a mundane household task, ignoring Tess completely (something quiet that does not involve noise, a lot of movement or food preparation). These repetitions done, you then wait for her to ignore you, before untying her in a matter-of-fact manner. Your goal is the following association:

your leaving/returning = no big deal

This is a practice that you will repeat every day for the next week. And with each successive day, as good exercise drops her energy reserves and she is exposed to calm, confident energy that supports her calmer, more confident side, Tess will be more able to trust that when you do anything (even when you leave her) it is okay.

CRATING

When Tess is tired, she is naturally looking to recharge her batteries and rest. This is a good time to introduce the concept of eating (or drinking water, if that appeals to her) in a crate. If she strongly associates crates with being locked up for extended periods of time (true of most separation anxiety dogs), playing quiet into-the-crate and out-of-the-crate games with biscuit pieces as rewards works well. (Refer back to Chapter 13. The alternate approach mentioned in Chapter 18 also works well.)

The length of time that she is asked to stay in her crate may be seconds at first, and then several minutes, and then more. To further promote her independence from you, when it is time to leave her crated for longer periods of time, let her have a special high-value, crate-only item that she can chew on, one that she can have only when she is in her crate (or on her bed or in a similar location that is not within sight of you). Extra-large roasted cow hip-bones (not the long bones) and Stuffed Kongs work well, but squeaker toys aren't recommended, since they tend to perpetuate excitement.

PACING

Many dogs with anxiety pace, and Tess is true-to-form. Back and forth; back and forth; back and forth and up and down the hall, and it starts the minute she finishes eating her breakfast. Is this when you crate her? No. The timing would be counterproductive, and it wouldn't teach her new skills. Should you try to talk her out of pacing? No. Getting verbal just adds energy to the situation.

Is this when you should reach for medication? Not at all. Examine the psychology of what she is doing before exploring psychiatry. Tess's pacing after breakfast is a <u>routine</u> that she has established for herself, as an antidote for her anxiety. Unfortunately, it is a self-perpetuating phenomenon, and she is caught in a loop. Simple, calm rebooting to a better routine may be all that she needs. Nothing verbal. Certainly nothing emotional. Simply a new Y to her X after meals.

How do you do that? The best tools in your toolbox are your calm-assertive energy, Tess's leash, a comfortable dog bed, your patient follow-through and your smile. The moment she finishes eating, you calmly and nonverbally attach the leash to her collar. You then walk her over to a cabinet, or a sturdy chair, within sight of an area where you will be for a while, and you tie her to it. Pointing to the dog bed that you have lying in wait, you calmly say *"place"* just once, and you stand still and composed (without touching her) until she finally steps onto the bed and curls up with a sigh. The entire process may take several minutes, as she mentally toggles between her old routine (pacing) and the alternative you propose. (You might even want to grab a paperback, to help you pass the time needed to wait her out.) Nonetheless, she will eventually come to the decision to lie down, on her own.

Give her a big smile when this happens. Let another half-minute go by, to ensure that she stays in place, and then reward her with another smile before returning to what you were doing. Your smiles (and the peaceful energy they project) are calm rewards for her calm behavior, and they serve to take the stress out of the room for everyone. Now Tess can relax and take a nap.

Is she going to practice the new routine, without direction, right away? Unlikely. But with a little patience, good follow-through and consistency, you will see results within a few days.

Other well-scheduled routines for eating, voiding, playing, training and exercise will support her rehabilitation. Anxious dogs do well with, and really appreciate, consistency and structure.

COMING AND GOING: WHEN ROUTINES CAN HURT YOU

That said, the acts of leaving and returning home need to be anything but routine, to break Tess out of bad patterns! To take the edge off her concerns about separation, you continue your practice of leaving your house to walk a short distance and then return, without a word spoken, several times a day. You reenter your home only when she is quiet, never when she is whining (since you don't wish her to equate whining with getting attention). You walk through a few rooms before leaving the house again only to come back after a minute or two. In each case, you repeat this exercise for however long it takes for her to ignore your actions, and you do the same when she is treadmilling (since walking forward and getting anxious are hard to do simultaneously). This is time that is very well spent!

Five minutes before you leave the house for real, you give her an extra-large knucklebone or a stuffed Kong, to take her mind off your wordless, confident departure. This fosters the association:

human leaving = good things

You always return home in a calm, emotionless manner, and you ignore her for the first fifteen minutes (no verbal communication, no touching, no eye contact and no loud or fast-paced activities). You want her to associate your reappearance with 'no big deal.' If she gets excited, you give her no attention. When she finally settles down to a true level-one energy, you give her a broad smile before going back to what you were doing.

You switch around your coming and going routine some more. You pick up your car keys, and then sit on the sofa to watch television. You put on your coat, and then eat your lunch. You set your alarm for six a.m. on a Saturday, and then roll over and go back to sleep. You eat breakfast before you shower on some days, and reverse the order on other days. You put your work items in the car while you are still in your bathrobe. Overall, you make leaving your home as un-routine, unexciting and nonverbal as possible. You want Tess to associate each of these events with 'no big deal' as opposed to 'big crisis.'

Above all, you follow Mother Nature. Since a dog in the wild works for her food, then she eats and then she rests, you feed Tess only after exercise; never when you first get home, and never when she is excited. You choose a diet that has no corn, since some reports state ingestion of corn in large quantities can decrease the level of serotonin in the brain.

Some veterinarians swear by calming pheromone plug-ins and sprays. You may consider them in the future.

Play-dates with Jennifer are planned a few days a week, to take some pressure off of you and expand Tess's horizons beyond you. You also enlist the company of your next-door neighbor's mellow retriever, Ireland, to walk on a treadmill next to her.

Tess loves being around other dogs, but that isn't true of all dogs with separation anxiety. Remember: anxious dogs are in an unstable state of mind, and other dogs may avoid or may even try to eliminate that state. Handlers of anxious dogs should never commit to adding a second dog to their household until they see how both dogs do with other dogs in different situations.

LIVING IN THE MOMENT

Fixing separation anxiety takes grit, determination, a good sense of timing, and patience. Progress can be slow, and it is easy to get frustrated by a dog's seemingly irrational behavior and occasional setbacks. Since any frustrated energy she gets from you will only slow her recovery, you absolutely, positively have to live in the moment around her. Letting go of whatever the self-destructive furry knothead did so many minutes ago is important. If nothing else, consider it one of the few gifts she is capable of giving you: a reminder to live in the moment.

LAYING A GOOD FOUNDATION

Most discussions of separation anxiety begin with a long list of risk factors linked to separation anxiety. I am not even going to end my discussion with one. So many of the risk factors listed (e.g., adding a baby to the household, moving, divorce) are life events that stress people, and their stress gets mirrored in their dog. The good news is: whatever happened, it is in the dog's past, and there is no future for anyone there. Let it go, so she can move on.

Three fundamentals bear emphasizing, however, to prevent more dogs from suffering this way:

❖ Puppies need to stay with their dam and littermates for a minimum of eight weeks. Nine to ten weeks is even better. This allows their mothers to introduce the concept of separation gradually.

❖ Puppies need to interact with humans and other animals <u>with a calm dog at their side</u>. They should be exposed to loud noises and potentially troublesome events <u>with a calm dog at their side</u>, to better prepare them for the same, for life. Please don't interfere with the process!

❖ Dogs who default to a level-one energy know peace. Dogs that can't do this have to sleep to find peace, and canine anxiety can result. Don't encourage excitement at times when calm will better serve your dog. Wait out his excitement, to reinforce his calmer, more relaxed side.

TROUBLESHOOTING UNWANTED BEHAVIORS

Even the worst of dogs has something to teach us.

CHAPTER 23
AGGRESSION: DECODING
THE "BAD" DOG

Aggression isn't aggression isn't aggression. If you want to take the fang out of "Fang," you must correctly identify two things: the underlying issue and his state of mind. Are his actions defensive (as in fear aggression), offensive (as in dominance aggression), an element of his DNA (prey drive) or simply a response to his circumstances (situation-generated aggression, the most common and most easily addressed type of aggression)? Is his mind 'in the moment,' or are his actions rooted in prior associations? Misinterpret the underlying issue or his state of mind, and your response can increase his aggression and not decrease it!

Hormones are the wild card. Because they cause so much stress and strife all by themselves, and because a dog's brain goes out the window at the first whiff of estrogen or testosterone, all bets are off until they are gone. For the purpose of this chapter on aggression, you should assume that they have been taken out of the equation. In the same way, you can assume that any medical conditions have been properly identified and addressed.

DOMINANCE AGGRESSION

"Dominant" and "dominance" are widely misapplied terms, and dog owners often blame unruly behaviors on dominance, when dominance isn't a factor in their dogs' actions at all. For this reason, a few definitions are worth review.

Meriam-Webster's Online Dictionary (2016) defines dominant as: *"commanding, controlling, or prevailing over all others; very important, powerful, or successful;* and *overlooking and commanding from a superior position."* Contrast this with a definition for dominance going back to ape researchers at the beginning of the twentieth century, a definition commonly used by veterinary behaviorists: *"a relationship between individual animals that is established by force/aggression and submission, to determine who has priority access to multiple resources such as food, preferred resting spots, and mates."* I argue strongly that the first, less emotionally supercharged and more universal definition should be used when canine dominance is discussed, and it is the definition I use throughout this book.

All of that said, dominance aggression is about who calls the shots in a given situation, and it doesn't arise where there is already a well-defined chain of command. Rather it occurs where there is a <u>leadership vacuum</u>.

Beehives have their queen bee; horse herds have their matriarchal mare, chicken coops have their dominant rooster and dog packs have dogs that consistently rise to lead the rest. In every case, the health of the hive, herd, coop or pack depends upon these individuals, and in every case, they must be <u>emotionally</u> strong, not just physically capable of the position.

Weaken a leader emotionally or physically, or remove him, and other individuals will move to fill the leadership vacuum. Whether a fight breaks out over a vital resource (food, water or shelter) or something that two individuals don't really need but just want (a treat or a toy), without someone to dictate otherwise, you could have the shedding of blood. For that reason, there is an emphasis on us, and not our dogs, being the ones in charge.

How do you become the one your dogs look up to?
- ❖ Provide their vital necessities: food, water and shelter.
- ❖ Meet their sociological needs: good routines, clear rules and lines in the sand. Establish these elements and reinforce them.
- ❖ Watch over them. That is, recognize potential problems and mitigate issues before they escalate. What kinds of

issues are the most common? Lack of guided group activities (physical exercise); lack of focused tasks (mental exercise); resource guarding, and problematic posturing between dogs. Health concerns, hormones and parasites, too.

❖ Demonstrate leadership in your communication and what you do. Be consistent. Be aware of your surroundings, and project confidence when it is time to act. Use calm assertiveness to command the space around you and to direct behaviors.

❖ Be mindful of your personal energy. Recognize your off-energies when they occur, and correct them before approaching your dogs.

❖ Strive for balance in what you do. Seek and enforce peace and quiet. Avoid excessive emotion. Avoid drama.

❖ Redirect the heightened energy of rabble-rousers, and house your dogs in a way that doesn't promote visual engagement, when you aren't there to monitor things.

Even if your care is only temporary (at a shelter, veterinary clinic or boarding facility, for example), dogs will recognize you as someone to follow (as opposed to challenge) by your actions, and dominance aggression will not be an issue.

FEAR-BASED AGGRESSION

While the key to handling dominance aggression is leadership, the keys to handling fear-based aggression are time, trust and authority. Gaining a fearful dog's trust alone won't work if he is willing to be aggressive. Being a calm, confident authority figure alone won't work if you don't have his trust. And neither will be attainable if you rush things. The good news is: when the time is right, the best way to gain the rest is pretty simple... through working walks!

More walking? Yes, more walking! Why walking in this case (and for that matter, every kind of non-medical aggression imaginable)?

❖ Walking is a communal activity that is fundamentally natural. Being kenneled, chained or perpetually carried around isn't natural.

❖ Dogs aren't good multitaskers. It is harder for them to posture aggressively or bite when they are walking at a good pace.

- ❖ Leading dogs on a working walk establishes you as the top dog. It is the <u>best</u> thing you can do to establish authority and trust.
- ❖ Walking keeps a dog's state of mind in the present, and it develops good muscle memory. This is important because fear aggression is often rooted more in the past than in the present.
- ❖ Exercise takes the edge off of tension, and it peels away excess energy…energy that could fuel more aggression.
- ❖ Walking fearful dogs next to balanced dogs provides them with good role models, and it helps unsure dogs build confidence.

How one approaches a fear-aggressive dog with a leash is important. To help him overcome any concerns that he might have, I may leave a leash in his crate or carrier (with one end dangling outside) for a short time, so he can smell it. Recall how this was done with Ziggy in Chapter 3, <u>after</u> giving him several hours to adjust to his surroundings. Alternately, I might use my leash to massage the dog, if the opportunity arises. And, given the chance, I will leash him while standing at his side, not from a position in front of him.

This sensitivity to position, timing and a dog's need for security is really, really important when dealing with fearful animals. Every minute pays off, so be willing to step back for an hour or more (even overnight), if the timing doesn't seem right. Taking this extra time will help you to get your personal energy and body language right, too. The last thing a fearful, unsure dog needs is a fearful, hesitant person approaching him.

Jethro is a good example. Trapped after a week of dodging highway traffic, he is seventy-five pounds of emaciated, fearful, snapping Great Dane. The first thing we do, when we approach his trap, is cover it with a blanket. This minimizes both eye contact and visual stimulation. We then transfer it to our van, without a word spoken.

Back at our Center, we move the trap to a quiet corner of our clinic's treatment room. This will allow Jethro to watch us from afar. Sensitive to his poor condition, we place his trap atop another blanket so he isn't perched solely on wire and hard tile. Without looking at him, and without saying a word, I open the door of his trap just enough to slide bowls of water and food inside. We then leave him for the night. He needs time, and he needs space.

Jethro's response, when we enter the room the next morning, is to growl and withdraw, so we ignore him and go about our business. At a time when he is laying down quietly, I nonchalantly add more kibble to his bowl through the trap bars, pleased to see that he has eaten everything offered so far. I do the same thing when it comes to adding water to his water bowl. I ignore any fearful posturing, but when he watches my actions without withdrawing or growling, I smile without looking at him, and I whisper, "Good job."

Tying a slip-lead to one end of the trap, I let the rest dangle inside so Jethro can smell it. Over the next half-hour, several of us walk calm, relaxed dogs past him, using our peripheral vision to gauge his response. Fearful dogs often look to other dogs for direction, and for the first time, Jethro's state of mind becomes one of cautious curiosity, and not insecurity. Our movements are calm and matter-of-fact (never hesitant), and the picture in our minds is always one of complete success. This is vital!

Sensing that Jethro really needs to urinate, I approach the side of his trap with Gemini, a laid-back Pitbull mentor, next to me. My relaxed, silent body language sends a message of confidence and security. Gemini's tranquil body language sends a message of peace and welcome. Untying the slip-lead, I loop it wide, so it won't touch Jethro's ears. This really matters to a dog! It tells him that he can trust us, and a fearful response is not needed at this time.

With one hand, I open the trap door and securely hook it, so it cannot spring shut. With my other hand, I guide Gemini to stand butt-first in the opening, with just enough room for Jethro to stretch his head out of the trap in her direction. As he reaches to sniff her, I calmly and casually slide the slip-lead over his head. His response is to pull back reflexively, and I give him plenty of room to do so while holding on to the very end of the leash. (Any pulling on my part would send the wrong message and panic him.) Eric, one of our most intuitive volunteers, materializes at my side with Rocket, another calm mentor dog, and their appearance serves to switch Jethro's state of mind from one of retreat back to one of cautious curiosity.

At this point, we all turn and walk forward, as if we have been a team of five from birth. And as a team of five (three dogs and two people), we move outside, so the dogs can relieve themselves before enjoying a long working walk.

Time, trust and calm, confident authority. Can you see how taking these steps provided Jethro with each of these elements? And no muzzle, catch pole or, for that matter, heavy gloves were needed. From the moment he came out of his trap, there was no turning back. He knew he could trust us to lead the way, and fear aggression was never again an issue.*

With any fearful animal, it pays to be aware of the effect their pheromones can have on other animals. Just as fear can unbalance an individual, creating behaviors not in his own or anyone else's interest, powerful fear pheromones lingering in the air after a fearful episode can unsettle others long after the episode has passed. To keep the peace after a fear-provoking episode, thoroughly clean up any saliva, sweat, urine or anal gland secretions left by fearful dogs. (Fearful cats, too!) Scrupulously wash your hands and arms afterwards, and if you were holding the dog or cat when he went into his fear-derived freak-out, it wouldn't hurt to change your clothes before you handle other animals. Fear pheromones are very potent, and they send messages more powerful than basic body language.

Fear aggressive dogs fall into three basic categories: the air-biters, the skin-breakers and the self-fulfilling prophesies. The air-biters are the easiest to work with, since they tend to be more bluster than bloodsucker. They are acting in self-defense, but they would rather be lovers than fighters. In my experience, they are easily rehabilitated given time, personal space, good routines, positive experiences in new locations and good leadership. In some cases, all it takes is the well-timed crinkle of a biscuit package (the promise of better things to come) to switch their fearful state of mind to one of curious interest!

The skin-breakers (the true red-zoners) are much tougher nuts to crack, in part because they are willing to cause so much damage, and in part because some of them toggle between fear and dominance aggression. Some of them may grow to become

---

Fast forward six years: I just received my annual holiday photo from Jethro's adoptive family. Curled up next to two children and another family dog, he looks quite nice in his holiday scarf in front of a Christmas tree!

well-mannered and trustworthy individuals, given appropriate rehabilitation and handling, but this kind of dog is not for the beginner, nor for the general public.

The third category is fortunately the rarest. That is the dog who is stuck so far back in his past that he cannot relate to the present. Fear-driven as opposed to simply fearful, he just doesn't see what everyone around him sees. In his eyes, there is no room for new associations because the world really is out to get him. This kind of dog is so unbalanced that he creates his own self-fulfilling prophesy time after time, over quite a lot of time in multiple places with multiple people. Giving him a clean state, good leadership and calm canine mentors isn't near enough, and he can't be kept with any but the most tolerant of other dogs because he is the kind that they will kill pretty fast. He is that unbalanced, and he is truly his own worst enemy, and sadly I have no magic remedy for him. More times than not, dogs like this suffer from puppy-mill DNA on top of abuse, and bad DNA just isn't treatable.

SITUATION-GENERATED AGGRESSION

Situation-generated aggression is the most treatable category of aggressive behavior. But to treat it, one must recognize the situation for being the problem that it is. Ten oh-so-common situations involve:
- ❖ Tie-outs and see-through fencing.
- ❖ The wrong person holding the leash.
- ❖ Excited dogs.
- ❖ Dogs rewarded for aggressive actions.
- ❖ Other animals playing victim.
- ❖ Dogs who have been overcorrected by domineering owners.
- ❖ Jealousy.
- ❖ A need for more personal space.
- ❖ Cage sharks.
- ❖ Redirected aggression.

TIE-OUTS AND SEE-THROUGH FENCING

Lack of exercise, exclusion from the rest of their pack, face-to-face interaction with the world and an inability to smell passersby…is there any wonder why chained dogs act out in frustration and become aggressive?

Sadly, chain-link and other types of see-through fencing can lead to the same scenario, since dogs separated from one other in this way can't move around each other naturally. Unable to stick their noses in all the important places, they tend to relate to things visually, and they become vocal. Their stress level rises. Ratchet that frustration up another notch with repeat performances of people, vehicles and other animals passing by, and what results is a "me vs. the rest of the world" mentality!

Let me offer an example from the evening news, where a child had his leg mauled by a neighbor's dog. Did this behavior occur spontaneously? Or was it the culmination of events that had been going on for a while? Most likely the later. Picture what happened from the dog's perspective: Every day, he was tied out in his yard (or let into the yard, limited by a see-through fence). Every day, he got to watch a three-year-old child riding back and forth, and back and forth, and back and forth on a Big Wheel trike. Every day, he sat at a distance, watching those little legs pumping around and around and around and around, set to the tune of a Big Wheel on pavement that every parent knows well.

He had never been allowed to sniff this child (and his exposure to children had been limited as a general rule). He had never been given the chance to sniff the trike. All he could do was watch them go back and forth and back and forth and back and forth. At what point did he want to stop this sequence, and being a dog, what options did he have to make it all go away?

Scenarios like this are similar to the ones shown in defensive driving classes, where you are shown videos of automobile accidents and then asked who could have prevented them from occurring. You are not asked who is to blame, only <u>who could have stopped this</u> from occurring. The answer, each time, is that <u>everyone</u> involved could have done something to stop what happened next.

If the dog's owner had recognized her dog's view of the world, she could have brought him inside during the child's playtimes. She could have socialized him better with kids and desensitized him to the trike (both motionless and moving, with no child aboard), rewarding behaviors that didn't involve focusing on it. Ideally, she could have erected a privacy fence, to minimize her dog's visual stimulation.

If the child's parents had recognized the dangers inherent in their child's actions, they could have directed him to play someplace else. Allowing children to run or bicycle back and forth by tied or fenced dogs is a really bad idea from the start!

Responsible individuals identify and mitigate issues before they escalate.

Dogs in chain-link kennels and yards need to leave them every day to mingle with the world on the other side. Dogs separated by see-through fencing need to come together, every day, for calm interaction and exercise, if only for thirty-five minutes at a time. If aggressing between dogs on either side of a fence occurs, they should be kept out of each other's line of sight until they can enjoy long walks together, led by knowledgeable people. It will help to keep the peace, and it will greatly improve these dogs' lives.

Does your neighbor's dog bark at you from the other side of a fence? Make sure that your body language (Chapter 9) isn't creating issues, then offer to take him for a walk!

Do you board your dog when you travel? If you do, be aware that across-the-aisle kennels and side-by-side chain-link runs are sadly quite common. This kind of kennel orientation creates stress, and it can make certain situations quite dangerous. A dog that can't get at his tormentor might turn on his handler or his buddy in frustration. Not a good situation! Smart facilities don't face dogs directly across from one another, or if their kennels are oriented this way, they cover up the lower half of the doors and runs on one side of the aisle, so visiting dogs do not eye one another continuously.

At our Center, our dogs sleep in roomy, non-metal cage-condos with solid sides, all facing the same direction. I cannot emphasize enough how relaxed and quiet our dogs are, as a result. We utilize chain-link around our outdoor play-yards, certainly, but when we need to place dogs in adjacent yards (to separate individuals with different energy levels during times of limited supervision, or to sequester dogs that are on restricted diets), we bring them together for group playtime every morning, and we bring them back together for additional play every evening. This ensures pack cohesiveness, and it keeps the peace.

WHEN THE WRONG PERSON HOLDS THE LEASH

Picture two leashed dogs lunging at one another, or a leashed dog lunging at a person. These situations require immediate action, and they are ones where the handlers involved can make the circumstances all the more unstable if:

❖ They don't calmly redirect everyone to walk in the same direction. Standing in one place, especially face-to-face, only makes things worse!

❖ They lose their cool and start shouting. Dogs pull away from that kind of energy. They don't naturally follow it.

❖ They pull back on their dog's leash. Pulling straight back only makes dogs pull forward, harder.

In this situation, any continued bad behavior is the symptom. The handler's lack of calm confidence and good leash skills are the real problems.

EXCITED DOGS

Excitement can spark aggression when newly arrived dogs don't project calm. One minute, everyone at a dog park is playing peacefully in small groups. The next minute, snarling ensues as dogs pick up and reflect the heightened energy of a newcomer. Add a few excited people to the mix, and this aggression gets redirected to them. Not good.

Aggression is fueled by energy, so spread the word to your family and friends. Tell them to exercise their dogs with a good long working walk <u>before</u> going to a dog park, preferably a good long working walk with other dogs doing the same. All the other dog owners at the park will appreciate it!

DOGS REWARDED FOR AGGRESSIVE ACTIONS

"Now, now, baby (pat, pat). It isn't nice to bite the nice veterinarian (pat, pat). Won't you be a good boy for Mommy? (pat, pat.) Please?"

It is counterintuitive, but many owners actually give their dogs positive reinforcement for aggressive behavior! It is a good thing that dogs of all shapes and sizes live in the moment, and their associations can be changed, given good leadership.

How many times have you reached to soothe a growling dog? How many times have you picked up or petted a dog when you thought he was ready to snap, thinking it was the best response to the situation? Recognize now how counterproductive that was, and promise to do it no more.

Remember the Golden Rules:

❖ Reward the behavior you want.

❖ Stop rewarding behavior that you don't want.

Now add this one:

❖ Exercise, exercise, exercise, exercise (yes, even the smallest of Chihuahuas), and know how to get your dogs moving, to help them move on to better behavior.

WHEN ANOTHER ANIMAL PLAYS VICTIM

Those of us who work with and house many dogs together know that unstable energy can enter a pack in all shapes, sizes and unhealthy intensities. Victimhood projects very powerful negative energy, in addition to fear-derived pheromones, and when one animal (be it a small prey animal or a dog amongst others) plays the victim-card, the dogs around him will match his intensity, often with aggression. Dogs do not like victimhood. They want it removed from their midst. Sick, injured or frightened dogs can be killed by their own pack members as a result.

This is another reason why calm energy and peaceful states of mind should always be your goals, and why leadership skills are so important. It is another reason why we walk dogs side-by-side, to put them on equal footing psychologically as well as physically.

When a dog with a tendency to overreact to things with shrill barks (and, in some cases, a pattern of hysteria) comes to our shelter, we never, ever place him with or even near our pack, unsupervised. It could mean signing someone's death warrant if we do, because this dog might as well be a squeaker toy. His unbalanced energy will bring out the weaponry in otherwise sweet-natured dogs, both large and small. In nature, victims represent instabilities in the pack that need to be eliminated.

Never baby dogs when they act victimized. It rewards the wrong state of mind. Look for ways to build their confidence, and then reward that, to bring out more of the same.

DOGS WHO HAVE BEEN OVERCORRECTED BY OWNERS ACTING OUT THEIR "DOMINANCE"

This is a very sad situation, but people being people, there is a tendency to act before we understand all the concepts. In the martial arts, there is a saying: "Beware the yellow-belts." Those are the folks who have achieved recognition for the first step on their learning curve, and now they set out to show everyone just how much they know. Scary!

The yellow-belts of the dog-handling world think they know more than they do, but they aren't there yet and if they aren't careful, they can create serious problems for their dogs. Understanding canine psychology occurs in layers, with each layer building upon another after careful observation and consideration. Reading a dog's body language, energy and state of mind correctly also takes experience. No one learns everything the first time around, be their information from books, classes, television shows, internet training, conferences or hands-on experience.

Three different people have been most pivotal in shaping my knowledge of canine behavior, and my first exposure to each of them occurred via videotapes. Did I view each videotape once? Not at all! I viewed each one at least three times, over time. The first time to see <u>what</u> they were doing. The second time to understand <u>how</u> they did it. The third time to grasp <u>when</u> they did what they did and <u>why</u> they made the choices they made. I still go back to those tapes periodically, to test what I know intellectually and, more importantly, what I now do instinctually.

It is vital to get the whats, the hows, the whens and the whys correct when you work with dogs. When people haven't taken the time to understand the big picture, they confuse important concepts, such as being dominant (*having command; having control*) with being domineering (*ruling in an arrogant manner; being overbearing*). They confuse being assertive (*making a positive statement*) with being aggressive (*all negative*). They then confuse their dogs with behavior that can be damaging.

Remember: being assertive does not mean being aggressive, and leading is not about being domineering! To the contrary, leaders who take over through aggression or through arrogant rule always have to watch their backs. These are not balanced states, and the followers of these people are usually not happy individuals. Some bite back! True leaders are emotionally balanced, and they are good communicators. They have become the top dog in their households and facilities because they project the attributes of leaders mentioned in Chapter 7, and their followers, who respect them, are also very happy to follow them.

But the top dog is the dominant one, right? Absolutely! But there is a huge difference between being dominant and being domineering. "Dominant" <u>just is</u> – it is a relative position subject to change, and it is one that we can earn through good leadership and energy – whereas "domineering" is <u>trying to be</u>.

It forces the issue, and we absolutely, positively don't want to project energy like that because it is unbalanced. It simply asks to be challenged!

One way to ensure you haven't become a canine psychology "yellow-belt" is to have a friend videotape you working with your dogs. A review of these videos can help you spot issues with your posture, position and energy, plus it is very educational to watch the body language (especially the tail position) of the dogs around you. When in doubt, <u>trust what each dog's response says about you!</u>

JEALOUSY

Canine jealousy is similar to human jealousy in that it doesn't support our best side, and it is easier to prevent than address once it crops up. It is something we tend to see in dogs arriving at our facility in a nutritionally starved state.

> Raven is a perfect example. When he came to us, he was a forty-six pound Doberman, with bones protruding like half-submerged boats on a reef. For the first time in a long time, he got to enjoy a stable environment, proper nutrition, peace, security and good routines. His was a slow road to recovery, over which we understood the importance of living in his present, and not in his past. Nonetheless, it was hard not to fuss over him a little, and by the time he weighed eighty pounds (on his way to a normal weight of ninety-two pounds), he was showing signs of being possessive, with all the neuroses of a jealous lover. He clung to our sides, warning the other dogs off. He picked fights when he saw them getting small amounts of attention. His focus on us went beyond a healthy awareness.
>
> Fortunately, the change of scenery and exposure to new leaders, new dog-buddies and the new experiences that he got when he was adopted was the clean slate and jump-start he needed, just as new events and new people help to get jealous people out of their funk. One year post-adoption, he is both physically and mentally healthy, and canine jealousy isn't an issue.

To prevent jealousy between dogs in your household, be careful never to show favoritism. It doesn't serve your favorite dog, your least favorite dog or you, when imbalances like this exist.

To address jealousy, if it is already an issue:
- ❖ Exercise your dogs together, side-by-side, as often as possible.
- ❖ Smile at your dogs whenever you see them coexisting peacefully, to reward their peaceful state of mind.
- ❖ Calmly and nonverbally redirect any jealous posturing into forward-moving group activities (walking, bicycling, etc.). Remember to move your dogs together, to get them moving on!
- ❖ Never respond to jealousy with anger or frustration (it just adds tension to a tense situation). Keep your attitude and energy matter-of-fact.
- ❖ Know that crating one dog while leaving others uncrated nearby can create issues, because dogs are then left to interact face-to-face.
- ❖ Feed any low-in-the-pecking-order dogs first, followed immediately by the offering of food to any wannabe-top-dogs. This lets the dogs know that you (and not they) will establish order in this household, and it helps to promote an association between the "low" dog getting fed and the other dog getting what he wants, too.

NEED FOR MORE PERSONAL SPACE

Everyone needs a little personal space, and dogs – just like people – require varying amounts of it. (Refer back to my discussion of yellow-ribbon dogs in Chapter 14). While people have numerous ways of communicating this basic requirement, a dog's way of doing so is limited if he is leashed and unable to back away. More so if he is clutched to a person's chest, or he has someone look into his eyes from inches away, with well-meaning but misguided intensity.

If a dog is unwilling to submit to having his comfort zone challenged, his options are restricted to lip curls, growls, snaps, nips and bites. Other dogs would see these choices as simple, straight-forward communication. People, however, label them aggression.

Praise be to all the lip-curling, growling (and yes, even the air-snapping) canine curmudgeons who don't nip or bite in this situation! They could have chosen to communicate their need for space more severely! Human sensitivity training, and not dog training, is what is needed to stop this kind of situation-generated behavior.

Another sad, but all so common, way that dogs have their personal space invaded, and comfort challenged, is when their owners act like equals or challengers, as opposed to leaders, teachers and protectors. This occurs when owners rough-house with their dogs. Rough play isn't play. It is roughness, and it will confuse your dog and bruise your relationship with him. Aggression can then ignite.

CAGE SHARKS

Abby is a cage shark. An absolute sweetheart when she is outside of a cage, she will lunge at you with fangs flying if put into one. The face-to-face interaction with the world that being in a cage entails puts her into a fight-because-flight-isn't-an-option mind-set.

Covering her cage door with a towel works well to keep visual contact minimized when caging her is required, for example at her vet's office. There, the staff knows to stand with their back or side to her, engaging her nose, before they open her door to let her come out on her own, in her own time.* They never look directly at her when doing this, because dogs like Abby take doggie social protocol seriously. Minimal (if any) conversation, no reaching out, no hesitant energy and absolutely no direct eye contact, please.

The good news is: most cage sharks return to being pleasant pups the minute they come out of their cages, as if nothing that just occurred ever happened, and Abby does this willingly. She is the perfect patient when it comes to anything else, and she is a favorite at the clinic.

REDIRECTED AGGRESSION

Redirected aggression is just that, aggression meant for one individual that is turned upon another when the aggressor can't get at the first individual (or the second individual gets in the way). Nothing personal; you just got bit because you were in the wrong place at the wrong time. Cats are notorious for this behavior, but dogs do it, too, and canine handlers need to be aware of its potential.

Dogs that pace by windows and see-through fences, aggravated by events on the other side, can redirect aggression

* *Remember: noses don't bark and noses don't bite.*

to their buddies. For the sake of their housemates, you need to address this pacing behavior (and any other signs of anxiety) before it escalates, and you need to keep potential victims out of harm's way. If it is too late for that, use inanimate objects (not your body) to break up fights between animals, to keep yourself safe.

PREY DRIVE

Prey drive varies greatly between dogs. It may be low, nearly non-existent, as in a squeaker-toy-loving Cocker who wouldn't hop off the couch to track a chipmunk. It may be moderate, as in a Beagle who enjoys chasing squirrels but finds cats and goats worth only a passing sniff. It might be high, as in a Malamute who lunges at the necks of livestock.

When it comes to prey drive, what flips a dog's switch can vary greatly. Movement is often a key factor. When a dog tracks movement with his eyes, his calmer, more curious senses of hearing and smell get relegated to secondary roles. That is why dogs that get along with cats up close will still chase a cat on the run. Their eyes dilate and hone in, and the body follows instinctually. Consider all the dogs that can't be trusted with smaller dogs or with toddlers. It's nothing personal. It is not about the individual cat, the individual little dog or the individual kid. It is about following movement and following another's energy.

Always take visually-mediated prey drives seriously and never, ever lie to another handler about them! The lives of others are at stake. Never keep prey-driven dogs behind chain-link fencing adjacent to public areas. Dogs who view the world from only one side of a see-through fence are going to have their prey drive <u>intensified</u>! Solid privacy fences are mandatory in these cases.

Dogs that exhibit higher prey drives should only be matched with owners who demonstrate good leadership and calm, authoritative energy under stress. Gaining the respect and complete allegiance of these dogs is vital, and the best way to do that is through long working walks. Conduct your walks away from potential prey species initially, and be very aware of how you handle your leash.

Leash skills are important with all dogs, certainly, but they are essential when working with dogs that have high prey drives. These dogs must learn to walk alongside their person on a loose leash, <u>ceding the space before them to their person</u>, no matter what they see, because any amount of tension on their leash will increase their drive, should potential prey appear on the horizon. Working with a good trainer, with the goal of teaching the dog to watch you, as opposed to others, is recommended.

REDIRECTING PREY-DRIVEN AND TERRITORIAL DOGS

Calmly redirecting prey-driven dogs to non-aggressive behaviors, such as *watch* and *leave it,* works well for three reasons.

❖ It switches their predominant sense from <u>visual</u> to <u>auditory.</u>
❖ It shifts some of their focus to you.
❖ It drops their energy level.
❖ It reboots their state of mind.

Either of these commands, followed by calm praise ("good *watch*" or "good *leave it*") to reward calm, watchful, non-aggressive behavior around prey species (the better to form positive associations), can greatly mitigate the intensity associated with <u>lower-level</u> prey drives. Both commands also work well with territorial dogs, for many of the same reasons.

Of course, every prey-driven or territorial dog that you meet may not have been taught *watch* or *leave it.* At the risk of getting dozens of e-mails calling me crazy (let me point out that I am not necessarily recommending that you do what I did here), let me share another story to illustrate how calmly invoking a dog's sense of hearing can counter his visual stimulation. The dog in question was both territorial and highly prey-driven. (He was later put down after he killed a succession of ducks and a rather large, sweet-natured goat).

I was walking down the road with a friend of mine who had no love for dogs. An avid jogger, he had shared more than a few tales of being chased by them. As we pass around a curve, I see a flash of fur in the distance. Not good. It belongs to a shepherd normally kept in a large outdoor pen, and a quick glance at the pen reveals its gate is wide open. We have never met before, but I know him to be a dog once slated to be put down at a local veterinary clinic because of aggression. The property owner is a technician from that clinic who convinced his owners to sign him over to her.

Knowing my friend's propensity to run, my first thought is to keep him from doing so. Any movement will only trigger the dog's predatory side and put him in harm's way. Before he can see the charging dog, I grab his hand and pull him off-balance, making it impossible for him to bolt.

"Whatever happens, <u>do</u> <u>not</u> <u>run</u>," I hiss, through clenched teeth.

"Huh? What? Oh-no!" is his response, as he sees the dog for the first time. At that point, he collapses in the middle of the street, white-faced.

Good, I think. One less thing to worry about. Now the surgeon in me begins to worry about irreparable damage to body parts – my body parts. My hands have to be protected, and without my arms, my hands don't matter. I turn slightly to the side and continue walking, and I pat my thigh, since it keeps the dog's focus low.

"Come here, Mr. Shepherd," I say, using a modulated but friendly tone. "Just wait until I tell your Mother that you got out of your pen and you were looking for blood. Come to me. Come and sit right here, so I can put your rotten little bad-boy butt back in your pen."

Of course the dog doesn't have a clue as to what I am saying. I could be saying "potato pickle blue patella spaghetti" for all he knows. All he understands is the tone of my voice (soft, positive and authoritative), together with my energy (Oscar-deserving calm and confident), plus my redirection to a behavior that does not involve him attacking someone.

From forty feet away, his head rises slightly. His pace slows. At twenty feet, his hackles soften, and by the time he is within five strides, he has slowed to a happy trot which brings him to my side. Praying that a car won't come along before my friend can pick himself up from the street, I hook my fingers around the dog's collar and direct him back into his pen, my heart racing despite my outer calm.

In this case, the tools at hand are simple, but very effective:

❖ My calm-assertive/calm-authoritative energy.
❖ My voice-driven redirection to better behavior, to "turn off" the dog's eyes and trigger his ears.

Both bring out the follower in any dog, instead of the part willing to take charge, and without both, either my friend or I would have been seriously injured.

Another time that I was approached by aggressing dogs deserves mention, for contrast. In this case, there were two dogs, and their state of mind was purely territorial. There was nothing prey-driven about it.

It is a crisp autumn day, and I am walking eight dogs of various sizes, next to a volunteer walking six smaller dogs. Without warning, two unleashed Labrador mixes appear from behind a house. With their tails up at attention and shark-fin-tense, their heads low and their hackles up, their body language leaves no doubt as to their state of mind.

I hand the leashes of some of my dogs to my walking partner, and I direct him to keep walking. I would rather the Labs' attention be on me. This leaves me with four dogs, one on either side and two behind me. I drop two of the leashes, knowing that those dogs will remain in place, no matter what I do. I then face the Labs with my arms extended to the side, palms out and at hip-height. This serves to claim my personal space and the space around me.

The tools at my disposal are simple, but vital:
❖ My calm, assertive, matter-of-fact energy.
❖ My authoritative posture.
❖ Confidence, driven by a positive picture in my mind.

These are the tools one needs at a canine stand-off, and that is what we have. The Labs stop their approach roughly twenty feet away.

Peripherally, I note the body language of my dogs. They are calm, and their tails remain tension-free. Excellent. None of them feels the need to respond. I want that to be the message the Labs get, too, so I quietly and authoritatively stand my ground. I look in their general direction, but I am careful not to look at either dog directly, the better to signal an interest in peaceful resolution, as opposed to antagonism. I smile softly to myself, to shed tension and trigger relaxed breathing, and my hands remain palm-out at my side, continuing to claim my space.

One of the Labs moves a few steps to my right, to put himself and his partner at five and seven o'clock. I respond with a step in the same direction, and I keep my posture upright. My palm-out hands raise ever-so-slightly, and my disapproving tone (*chicht!*) directs him to go no farther. I know to never let an aggressing dog walk behind me!

He stops, and the canine stand-off continues. A minute goes by, and then another one. A local drunk watches from his doorstep, bag-wrapped bottle in hand. My partner and his dogs watch from afar. With each passing moment, the Labs communicate their property rights and, with each passing moment, I communicate my own, and all of our communication is nonverbal.

Slowly the tension goes out of their tails, and their tails lower by several inches. I give them a relaxed smile, and I wait to see more. It takes another minute, but they finally give me what I really want: their noses lifted for a sniff in my direction. I give them another smile, and I lower my palm-out hands. I raise my own nose in imitation, signaling that I come in peace. I don't move on, however. They must turn and walk away first.

That takes another minute or so. Do I move on at this point? No. I stand my ground peacefully for another half-minute, before walking away, and I do so with a keen awareness as to any movement behind me. Dogs in this situation often circle back, the better to get behind you, and that is exactly what the Labs do (forcing the neighborhood drunk to shout in excitement). In response, I quietly turn to face them again, my posture upright and my palm-out hands open at hip-height. The Labs get the message, and they retreat behind their house so my dogs and I can walk on.

If you have come to this part in this book knowing that you probably would have panicked, became verbal or excited, or attempted to run from these dogs, you probably know that any of those behaviors would have sent the wrong message, with very bad results. As aggressive as these dogs were willing to be, they were equally willing to accept a peaceful resolution. Never forget: dogs, by their nature, prefer balance to conflict.

SMALL DOG LOLLIPOPS

One of the fastest ways to get a prey-driven or territorial dog more excited about something is to pull it away and hold it up high while using an excited tone of voice. And yet that is exactly what owners of small dogs often do when they see a bigger dog approaching. They might as well be saying, "Here puppy, puppy! Come get this big, fat, furry lollipop that I'm trying to keep away from you!"

Should you find yourself challenged by an approaching dog while out walking another, stand tall and <u>leave your dog on the ground</u>. Step in front of him, and channel your inner Mama Bear. Claim the space around you and your dog (and quite a bit more) using a clear, calm and authoritative posture that leaves no doubt as to who is in charge. Whether you say it out loud or just to yourself, your matter-of-fact message needs to be: this is <u>my</u> space (and a good ten feet around me is also my space), and you are going to have to get through me to get to my four-legged friend!

For the majority of these aggressing dogs the rule is: <u>no victim means no victimizing</u>, so remember to keep your dog's leash loose. The alternative will only increase his tension and make him more vulnerable to attack.

Never be the first to walk away. Remain calm, and wait until the aggressor's tail drops and he starts using his nose. Wait until he walks away, ceding all space to you. At that point, you and your dog can move on, maintaining your awareness of the aggressor's location, to ensure that he doesn't circle back.

KEEPING VERY LOW PREY DRIVES LOW

Just as prey drive and territorial behavior can be intensified when dogs are kept behind chain-link, it can also be learned from, and intensified by, other dogs. For this reason, our facility has a policy whereby everyone must get along (dogs, cats, goats and birds). Dogs with moderate to high prey drives just aren't brought into our pack.

As mentioned in Chapter 8, we have stopped the mildly bullying conduct of dogs with very low prey drives from escalating into more intense, even dangerous behavior around our goats by walking both species together after the dogs have been well exercised to drop their extra energy. Because of this practice, I trust Hiker enough with both sheep and goats to reach for his help herding them back to where they belong whenever they turn up where they are not supposed to be. Would I trust him with them on his own? Most definitely not. With me there? Without a doubt.

Every few months, I take him for another walk with a few leashed goats, to reinforce my inclusion of them in our pack. And I have done the same thing with low-prey-drive-exhibiting dogs and horses, llamas and halter-broke cows.

All of this said, pack-walking different species together is not something for beginners to do, because if you don't have a calm dog, and if you don't know how to read his body language correctly, and if you don't have excellent leash skills, you can intensify a dog's prey drive. I include mention of it here for the sake of completion, so you can see what is possible with a dog capable of level-one energy who completely respects and aims to please his handler, together with a handler knowledgeable about animal nonverbal communication.

DOGS THAT BARK AT STRANGERS WHILE ON WALKS

A dog that barks at approaching people while walking with his handler isn't, in all likelihood, being aggressive as much as he is communicating "something isn't right." Under varying circumstances, he might be saying:

❖ The bright light behind this person (or his hat or his sunglasses) is making his features hard to see.

❖ This person is using all the wrong body language. (He is reaching out, speaking in an excited voice or looking directly into my eyes.)

❖ This person's energy (or the energy projected by his dog) is all wrong. It is tense, hesitant, excessive or suspicious.

❖ My handler's energy is all wrong. She is being hesitant, tense or too forceful, or she is letting me pull ahead and lead the way, instead of leading the way, herself.

To mitigate issues before they arise, whenever you walk your dog in public places, ensure that he is relaxed and at your side, and you are equally relaxed and feeling confident, <u>before taking your first step</u>. Then smile, look up and lead the way. If your dog tenses at a stranger's approach, address your own tension (with a relaxed breath), before redirecting his (by changing direction to walk side-by-side with the newcomer). Without a word spoken, you have put everyone on the same team. You have sent the message that approaching people can be walking buddies; they can be friends, and not foes.

I can't emphasize enough the importance of keeping unsure dogs moving at times like these. The alternative (standing still) will only encourage their concern. Moving helps dogs to move on, from one moment into the next, and it puts you in command of the situation.

If it isn't possible to keep moving, position yourself and your dog <u>so everyone is facing the same direction</u>, the better to follow canine social protocol (as opposed to human social protocol). Reposition your dog's tail neutrally, should it be higher than the situation dictates, to calmly and nonverbally let him know that heightened tension is not required. Don't let your dog step in front of you. That would put you into the position of his follower. Draw up (and not back) on his leash or, better yet, calmly use your foot, to return him to your side in a calm and matter-of-fact manner. Step in front of him, if need be, to claim back the space he claimed. A simple "Uh uh" or similar sound of disapproval, is also appropriate when uttered in a calm and confident voice.

Never forget to reward your dog's relaxed, quiet nature in public domains with a calm smile (and the occasional gentle massage). It solidifies you as a team, and you will get more of what you reward!

To build good associations with approaching people, some handlers ask known "strangers" to approach their dog carrying crinkly bags of biscuits (the better to trigger his ears and nose, as opposed to simply his eyes). You might try this technique if you think it will help, but know that it isn't a substitute for a person's good body language. To keep your dog from getting mouthy or excited when they appear, have these people give <u>you</u> any biscuits to give to him, and offer them only when he is calmly focused on you, at your side.

AGGRESSION BETWEEN DOGS

Any plan to prevent or treat aggression between dogs, first and foremost must include:

- ❖ Common routines.
- ❖ Common direction when walking, introducing or housing.
- ❖ Common treatment. No inequalities fostered by human behavior.
- ❖ Calm, confident leadership.
- ❖ Neutering. Don't let horror-mones sabotage all your good leadership!

❖ Adequate exercise, since dogs with energy to burn often burn it in negative ways.

Without any of these elements, inter-dog aggression will find its roots.

Dogs don't look to feud as a rule, especially when more cohesive behaviors are available to them. If you find this hard to believe, put taking a trip to San Diego's famous Dog Beach (or a similar wondrous place) on your "Do Before You Die" list. There, on any day, you will see a hundred dogs or more – most who have never met previously – all cavorting in the waves and playing on the beach. No fighting. No feuding. Just dogs being very, very happy dogs.

Whenever we have two dogs with a tendency to aggravate each other, we give them monitored exercise on treadmills side-by-side, offering lots of smiles and occasional soft praise when they walk well together. We take them on side-by-side working pack-walks and bike rides, too, using backpacks to help them focus on the task at hand. This changes any negative associations to very positive ones. They grow to associate each other with exercise and fun.

We house them using visual blockers. Positioning them in ways that allow face-offs (using baby gates or crates placed across from one another) would too easily undo our hard work. I've mentioned this before, but it deserves repeating: baby gates send the message that your household has not one, but two discordant packs. That is not the message you want to send! Separate dogs, as you see fit, during times of less monitoring. Just separate them in ways that don't leave them face-to-face.

At mealtimes, we feed our dogs low-dog (first) to high-dog (last) on the totem pole. This helps to put our dogs on equal footing, and it supports our leadership role.

When it comes to the rare skirmish, we replay our video surveillance feed, to review who did what to whom. Nothing is better, when it comes to determining what really went on, than a clear video, and we have often learned that the problem children weren't the ones we suspected! To figure out which dog is the instigator of the action, we look at three different things:

❖ The energy level of all the dogs.
❖ The position of their tails.
❖ The tension in each tail.

If the energy of the pack or the energy of one or more individuals goes up, the chance of a brawl might, too, given the right mix of dogs. Instigation is all about <u>energy</u>. No extra energy; no trouble. If any tails go up, we increase our awareness of the situation. We take tail position and tail tension very seriously. We need to, because our dogs do.

USING MUZZLES

Whenever we handle a dog that might be an actual threat to us, we use a muzzle so we can maintain our inner calm and relaxed, positive energy. The last thing an unsettled dog needs is an unsettled handler!

To introduce the muzzle in a non-threatening way, we might leave it in his crate for a short time, clipped to a leash. (One end of the leash hangs out of the crate, allowing for easy retrieval.) When it comes time to put it on, we stand at his side – never in front of him – and we make the experience into a pleasurable game. (See Chapter 13.) Alternately, we might rub whipped cheese, canned dog food or xylitol-free peanut butter on its end (the latter in cases where nut allergies aren't likely to be a factor), and we let him reach into it for a few licks before slipping it over his nose, leaving the clasp unbuckled. We then take the muzzle off with a soft "good boy" and a big smile. We put it on again and then remove it, several times over, with the same quiet praise, until he accepts the muzzle in a calm manner. At that point, we snap it behind his ears and give him a short massage. Now he sees his muzzle in a more positive light.

When people see muzzled dogs, they often project concern. Unfortunately, this sends the message to these dogs that there is cause to be concerned. For that reason, I love a product called Funny Muzzles for short-term use. (They can be found online.) Funny Muzzles make people smile, which sends a positive message to these dogs. In the rare case that a muzzle needs to be worn long enough for a dog to pant or require water, we switch to a basket-type muzzle, carefully fitted so as not to bump his nose.

DEFUSING OWNER-PROTECTIVE BEHAVIOR

Speaking of sending the right message to our dogs, let me share a technique used at good veterinary hospitals, shelters and boarding facilities. This is where knowledgeable personnel know all too well the dangers inherent in approaching owner-protective dogs. Complicating the natural wariness of these dogs is often the nervousness (and therefore the weakened energy) of their owners. Walking up to a pair like this head-on, even with a relaxed, erect and confident posture, is never the best idea. To illustrate:

> John brings his Chow, Vixen, to his vet's office for a nail trim. Vixen hovers at his side, warily watching Terri, the office technician. Terri recognizes Vixen's unsettled state of mind, and she doesn't come too close.
>
> She stops six feet away, welcoming John while calmly ignoring the Chow. She directs him to walk Vixen around her, stopping at her side, with Vixen between them and everyone facing the same direction.*
>
> John – Vixen – Terri
>
> This action adds John and Vixen to her team. Standing side-by-side for twenty seconds, they share a relaxed smile, and when Vixen relaxes between them, John quietly passes her leash to Terri. He waits a few more seconds before walking away with a smile. Vixen no longer feels the need to be a wary watchdog. At Terri's side, and in a better state of mind, she can now be guided into the grooming room for her pedicure. This is simple, directive body language at its best!

WRAPPING UP AGGRESSION

To treat canine aggression, one must separate the underlying problem from its symptoms. That said, the vast majority of problems will be situational and readily correctable.

The next two pages list some common situations in which aggression occurs, together with a few keys to their solutions. Regardless of the kind of aggression at hand, an awareness of the energy projected by the people involved is pivotal. Good handlers know to correct or redirect the off-energies and poor posture of others, so their dogs see no reason to respond aggressively. They know to respond to aggression only with the calm, directive and authoritative energy of a top-dog, and never the domineering energy of a wannabe.

They also know that focused exercise and long working walks (not wandering walks) are fundamental to the rehabilitation of aggressive dogs. A tired dog following a calm,

---

* *Alternately, she might ask him to join her in the parking lot for a very short side-by-side walk, one in which Vixen's leash gets passed to Terri mid-walk.*

confident person is not going to summon the intensity of energy needed to challenge others.

Lastly, to achieve success, they don't hesitate to reach for a comfortable muzzle. Well-fitted muzzles, used short-term, help to provide for everyone's safety, while helping those involved summon their best leadership energy.

TRY THIS EXERCISE: Without your dogs, visit places where dogs and people interact. (Dog parks are good for this). Watch this interaction from the standpoint of the dogs. How does their energy dictate their behavior? What does their body language say? What are they trying to communicate to their handlers? Identify owner-dog teams that are doing well. Could others do better?

SITUATION: Dominance aggression.
SOLUTION: Calm, confident, matter-of-fact authority and good leadership.

SITUATION: Fear aggression.
SOLUTION: Time, trust and calm, confident authority.

SITUATION: Dogs oriented in ways that promote visual attentiveness.
SOLUTION: Orient dogs side-by-side, and not across from one another. Always monitor dogs that watch the world from one side of a see-through fence.

SITUATION: Leashed dogs, out of control.
SOLUTION: Allow a more knowledgeable person to get them moving, so they can move on to better behaviors.

SITUATION: Aggression at dog parks.
SOLUTION: Take all dogs for a long, focused side-by-side walk prior to entering the dog park.

SITUATION: Dogs previously rewarded for aggressive behavior.
SOLUTION: Reward the behavior you want to see; not the behavior you don't want repeated.

SITUATION: Jealousy.
SOLUTION: Treat all dogs equally and walk them together, to build bonds. Offer food to the jealous dog just after the other(s), and only when everyone is in a calm and relaxed state of mind.

SITUATION: Dogs that need extra personal space.
SOLUTION: Use yellow ribbons in public areas, where they can help you to create more space. Correct the posture, energy and positions of approaching people, where you can.

SITUATION: Cage sharks.
SOLUTION: Cover their cages until you want to let them out, then let them exit on their own. Use good canine-centric body language when you need to approach these dogs.

SITUATION: Redirected aggression.
SOLUTION: Block off all aggression triggers; keep potential victims out of harm's way, and provide lots of exercise to drain energy reserves.

SITUATION: Prey drive.
SOLUTION: Use visual blocks, such as privacy fencing, to keep prey animals safe. Teach these dogs to focus on you, in a positive manner, regardless of prey on the horizon. Teach them the command *watch*, and use it in a calmly directive manner.

SITUATION: Inter-dog aggression.
SOLUTION: Walking, walking and more walking together, side-by-side, at your side. Never separate dogs using see-through fence, kennels or gates. When separation is needed, house dogs in ways that don't permit or promote visual cuing.

CHAPTER 24
A BARK IS NOT A BARK IS NOT A BARK

Barking is a very common complaint of dog owners, and the more undrained energy a dog has, the more barking you are going to get. This is yet another reason that all dogs, even the little ones, need adequate exercise.

The likelihood of barking is going to increase in certain situations. How we identify and respond to them can determine whether it takes the form of one bark or two, a three-dog discussion or a ten-dog, ten-minute canine chorus. Dogs bark for a number of reasons, and one response does not fit all.

ALERT-BARKING (WHEN NOT TO SAY "NO")

Alert-barking is built into the canine species. This doesn't mean that every dog will bark in every circumstance, but it does mean the behavior is instinctual, and it serves an important purpose. (It just isn't a purpose that is always appreciated.)

Consider a common scenario: the dog in your backyard is barking at a cat. Your options are to:

(a) Bring him inside.
(b) Tell him "no!" firmly, before walking away.
(c) Ignore him (and take your frustration out on others).
(d) Project calm disapproval to stop the behavior (a *chicht!*

or similar sound works well), and then give him a substitute command once he quiets. Praise him when he follows your command, and then relocate the cat.

Of these options, choice (a) is going to work against you in the long run. You don't want a dog to learn to bark, to come inside. Choice (b) is not the best option either, because although your dog correctly interprets your "no" as a sign of disapproval, his canine brain will choose to believe that what you disapprove of is the cat! After all, the cat is the interloper, while the dog is the true and brave and very valiant super watchdog, justified in raising the alarm! You may have a difference of opinion on the subject, but that is not going to stop your dog from being a dog.

Sure, you can ignore him (and you can take your frustration out on the people around you), but you are not addressing the problem when you ignore it (and your friends and family have ways to get even). This is where substitute commands (choice (d)) work well. But before tackling the topic of substitute commands, let me go back to choice (b) for a moment.

Here is an irony for you: the word "no," especially if uttered in an excited voice, is almost guaranteed to get excited dogs doing <u>more</u> of what you don't want. Dogs do not understand no, non, ju, ne, nu or yok (that is "no" in English, French, Albanian, Dutch, Romanian and Turkish, by the way) because what they are reading is your <u>body language</u>, which tells them only that you are upset at what they are seeing (or, in some cases, what they are hearing). That gets them more upset, which increases their energy, which gets you more upset. Can you see where this could potentially go?

"No" is an excellent word, but it conveys an incomplete message (or totally the wrong message) when used with dogs that alert-bark and dogs that display fence aggression or prey drive, all higher-energy and mostly visually-cued activities. Just saying "no" will leave dogs in a state of tension. Substitute commands work much better.

SUBSTITUTE COMMANDS

A substitute command is simply something a dog can do instead of what he is doing. It is something you can praise, and that is what makes using it so effective. Your "thank you" or "good job," for a job well done, reduces his energy level, and this influences his subsequent behavior. It puts him in the frame of mind to further please you. My favorite substitute commands are *watch* (watch quietly) and *leave it* (walk away).

Watch! Whenever I see one of my dogs quietly observing something (the goats, cats or new people, for example), I say his name and "<u>good</u> *watch*." Very quickly, he learns to associate his quiet observation with the term *watch*, and he associates it with a happy person and positive energy. Later, when I ask him to *watch* something (as opposed to bark at it), he knows exactly what I mean. *Watch* is so easy to teach, and it is an excellent substitute behavior for alert-barking.

Recognize and softly praise quiet watchful behavior whenever you see it. You will love the results, especially if you work with normally watchful breeds such as Rottweilers, Dobermans, shepherds and terriers. Softly praise dogs choosing to stay quiet when other dogs are barking, too. Barkers often stop their barking when they see other dogs getting praised for not barking!

Leave it! This command can be taught to any dog in five minutes, and it has so many applications! Leave the cat alone. Leave the steak on the barbeque. Avoid the neighbor's toddler. Along with *watch me*, it is often one of the first commands any obedience instructor teaches.

To teach it, sit in front of your dog with a few kibbles, some small biscuits, a special favorite treat and some small pieces of meat within easy reach. Place a kibble in front of him and cover it with your hand. Tell him to *leave it* when he reaches for it. It is okay to calmly repeat the command a few times at first, as your dog will invariably sniff all around your hand before sitting back, to look at you. As soon as he sits back and shifts his focus to you, tell him "<u>good</u> *leave it*" and offer him a small but very tasty dog biscuit.*

Repeat the exercise, this time covering a biscuit and using a more enticing treat (Hiker loves apple slices) as a reward for the three behaviors you want:

❖ His level-one energy.
❖ His backing away from the covered item, to sit.
❖ His quiet focus on you.

---

* *If you are astute, you may be saying, "Hold on…that sounds similar to Scenario 1 from Chapter 11." And you would be right. What makes teaching 'leave it' like this different is your calm approach to repeating the command, so tension doesn't occur.*

Don't reward dogs who back up but continue to stare at your hand. And remember to smile when you get the behavior you want!

Repeat the exercise again, covering the treat this time, and reward your dog with a piece of meat when he backs up, sits and looks at you, as soon as you say *leave it*. Now you have reached your goal!

Three commands that should not be used as substitute commands are *sit*, *stay* and *down*. Unfortunately, this happens frequently. Picture a person shouting *"Stay! Sit! Sit! Down! Stay!"* at a twisting terrier or a hopping hound, tugging on his leash. Aaargh! That is like asking a dog to go from sixty m.p.h. to zero in a matter of seconds. It is asking for failure. Good commands used in bad ways create bad associations, and dogs get very resentful when this happens.

COUNTING THE BARKS

To let a watchful dog know that I am on top of things when I hear him alert-barking, I might also count the barks for him.

"That's one. That's two. Okay, that's three." I then give the command *that's enough*. To finish, I reward his silence with a soft "thank you" or a quiet "good job." This approach helps to take his focus off of whatever he is <u>seeing</u>, to put it on what he is <u>hearing</u> (my counting). When a dog has been trained to limit his barking in this manner, it is a delight. He gets to be the super watchdog he wants to be, but I get to say when enough is enough.

"I WANT TO SNIFF YOU" BARKING

Friendly dogs often offer non-aggressive "Come meet me; I want to sniff you" barks to people and other animals passing by. The fastest and easiest way to stop this kind of barking from a dog that just wants to get to know you is to present your side to him (using good canine social protocol), so he can sniff you. Wait until he totally relaxes and turns or walks away. Giving him that extra thirty seconds to turn or walk away is important. It lets him reach a point of trust with you and demonstrate that he accepts you via his body language. Having met you, using his nose instead of just his eyes, he now has no reason to bark at you!

TERRITORIAL BARKING

Territorial barking takes alert-barking and elevates it a few notches. The difference is the level of intensity. Territorial barking <u>projects</u> energy with each bark. This dog is not telling others that you are here. He is telling you that <u>he</u> is there. If there is no vital reason to enter his territory, and if you are not a master of calm-confident energy and canine psychology, you should leave this one in peace.

INSTIGATED BARKING

When my pack gets rowdy in one of their play-yards – for example, when two dogs are playing and one is refereeing – it is one of those situations where barking (and the elevated energy behind it) can self-perpetuate. Before I respond, I listen carefully to distinguish the voices. When I know which dog started the ruckus (he will be the one with the loudest, fastest and most intense bark), I say his name sharply, just once (nothing more). Visitors are amazed that this is all that it takes to stop the barking of twenty to thirty dogs, immediately and without recurrence, but that is all that it takes nine times out of ten! It is true, even when I am halfway across the property, well out of the sight of the dogs.

This works for two reasons. First, I have correctly identified the instigator. If I mistakenly call out the wrong dog's name, the barking won't stop. The instigator will continue barking, inciting the others to join up again, and the pack will respond as if I am barking along with them. When you have multiple dogs barking like this, <u>you need to stop the instigator, for the others to follow suit</u>. Second, my voice reflects earned authority at our facility. I am the decision-maker, the pack leader,* the provider of sustenance, order and security. Your dogs would not respond to my voice in the same way. Why should they? I haven't earned any leadership points with them. It isn't enough to simply identify and correct the instigator when it comes to barking. <u>Your correction must be seen as coming from an authority figure</u> for the dogs to respond.

It is quite amazing how this practice works. But don't overuse it. You don't want your dogs to think that you are

---

* *One of the benefits of having earned this position is that corrections become minimal. Correcting instigated barking with just the call of the right dog's name is an example of this.*

barking with them, and they can easily learn to bark to get your attention. Use this approach when you need it, and take the time to identify the chorus leader correctly.

Of course, with new dogs entering our shelter pack and with dogs that have similar barks, it can be hard to identify an instigator from a distance. In those cases, I use my generic "buzzer," a short *"eh-h-h-h-h-h"* sound, similar to a loud alarm clock. The rest of the dogs know this means two things: First, I am not far away. Second, I am not happy with what is going on. Often their response is enough to get the message across to any new dogs.

Of course, once all of the dogs have quieted down and they have dropped their energy levels to match, I always respond with a soft "thank you." It takes any residual tension out of the air, which goes a long way toward keeping the peace!

"I BARK, YOU JUMP" and "I LOVE MY VOICE" BARKING

Two other types of barkers commonly encountered are:
❖ The "I bark, you jump" barkers.
❖ The "I LOVE my voice" barkers.

Although people often lump them under the general category of nuisance barkers, their motivation is different. The "I bark, you jump" barkers have learned that humans come running (or join in vocally) when they bark, and they will bark with determination until they get what they desire. Sometimes it is one bark and sometimes it is thirty-one, but who can blame a dog for using this little trick as often as he can? It has paid off so handsomely in the past!

The "I LOVE my voice" barkers (we call them the "sparks" at our shelter) are like self-perpetuating firecrackers. Bark, bark, bark, bark! These back-of-the-pack guys (defined in Chapter 14) simply live to bark. It is in their DNA. It reflects their nature as much as their nurture.

When either of these types of barkers lands at our facility, we know that we absolutely have to create a new association when it comes to barking. This is a case where we can't come running. Any response from us (verbal or nonverbal) will be one point for the dog and zip for us! Ignoring this kind of barker doesn't help, because he will aggravate the others. We can't risk them answering or taking steps on their own to keep the peace. Aaargh! What can we do?

This is when we might utilize a tool that responds to the misbehavior where we cannot. One that sets a STOP sign where it is needed, buying us time to approach the behavior from other angles. This is when we may calmly reach for a well-constructed, well-maintained, tested and proven bark collar.* If a dog wearing the collar doesn't bark, there are no corrections and life is good. If he chooses to bark, then something happens that is annoying, but not over the top. A good collar's timing is spot on. Human mistiming can't mess it up. Too, its multiple settings will keep its correction from being more than what is needed.

We then embark on a good exercise plan, since a pleasantly tired dog has less energy left for barking. The dog is exposed to our routines and rituals, and he learns lessons in manners from the other dogs. As time passes, we reach for his bark collar less often. But in the short-term, it is doing what we cannot do ourselves: stop the nuisance barking before it escalates.

Any dog will tell you: a dog who is in a barking whirlwind is not a happy dog. A dog who self-perpetuates excited behavior is not a happy dog. Believing otherwise is like saying anxiety is perfectly natural and acceptable when there is nothing to be anxious about. I have known many dogs that visibly relaxed when a bark collar was put on. It was as if these poor pups couldn't self-regulate and they needed help setting limits, and that was what this tool did. For that reason, I purposely remain calm when collaring one of them. I want X (his barking) to equal Y (the collar) without any anger, frustration or other emotion on my part. When I collar an "I LOVE my voice" or "I bark, you jump" dog proactively – that is, before he starts his barking – I do so with a warm smile and a rewarding touch. As a result, the majority of these dogs come jogging up to me as soon as they see the collar. No fear; no concerns. Their association with the collar is absolutely a good one!

* *To prevent misuse, always keep this kind of collar out of the hands of the impatient. Keep them out of the hands of the intolerant, the unempathetic or the ill-informed. Should you feel that this tool is indicated with your "I LOVE my voice" barker: (1) Research the quality control record of the brand that you are considering. (2) Monitor the collar's use closely until you know that you have a trustworthy one. (3) Never leave the collar on all day or when you aren't home. (4) Position the collar centrally before you close its buckle. (Rotating a collar into place after buckling will cause it to rotate back to the side).*

A case in point: A Chihuahua in one of our play-yards starts a tirade of barks when another dog bumps into him. Sensing movement across the road, he then directs his barking at a goat walking by. While his attention is diverted, his sister moves in to take his toy, so he leaves the goat and runs over to bark at her, engaging her and the other dogs in what has the potential to become a fourteen-dog bark-fest. It is just another moment in the life of little Ralphie Kramdon, the four-pound mouth-of-the-South at our shelter.

What is a person to do? Any verbal response is going to be seen by Ralphie as another individual joining the fray (and Ralphie, who is not the most balanced dog around, enjoys commotion). Any response from us that carries with it an element of frustration will just add energy and tension to what is already a high-energy scenario. Letting things pass and quiet down on their own might work with other dogs, in other situations, but this little dog (who treadmills an hour every day) is called Ralph Kramdon (a.k.a.: Ralph Kramdog) for a reason. He likes his voice, and he has earned his name in every sense.

This is when a volunteer appears, calmly and quietly. "Come here, Ralphie," she murmurs. "It looks like you need your STOP sign."

Ralphie, with his tail wagging, runs over to her with his neck outstretched. He doesn't fear the bark collar in her hands. Rather, he associates it with gentle handling and a scratch under the chin when he stands still for it to be put on and adjusted correctly. At that point, he trots happily back to the other dogs, being sure to grab his favorite toy along the way.

Peace and quiet reigns, and it is easier for everyone in the vicinity to smile as Ralphie enjoys playtime with the rest of the pack. Later, when our volunteers leave to run errands, he will be brought inside, and his collar will be taken off. We don't leave this kind of barker outside with the others when we aren't in the vicinity to supervise. The trouble that his sparky-bark could instigate could come back to hurt him in the end. We also don't leave this kind of collar on when we leave the facility.

STRESS-BARKING

Barking that arises purely out of stress carries with it an unsettled tone. It represents vented energy, similar to a pressure valve. It can be a short-term thing that arises when a dog feels his basic needs aren't being met (his need for exercise; his need for direction or his need for security, for example), or it can be longstanding and self-perpetuating, the way it occurs in canine anxiety.

The way to address short-term stress-barking is to address its cause. Provide more exercise, direction and quality of life stimulation. Address the dog's need to feel secure by answering the questions mentioned in Chapter 5 (Am I safe? Who can I trust? What is expected of me? Whose lead should I be following?)

A good way to address the less-common but more malignant, self-perpetuated stress-barking of anxious dogs may surprise you. It actually surprised us when we first tried it with dogs that had been given up by their owners because of mechanical, near-ceaseless, hours-on-end barking. Only after extended lengths of time would they curl up on a blanket and relax. To reverse this highly-damaging and demoralizing spiral of behavior, we realized that we had to stop these dogs from taking the first step on its wicked staircase. We had to stop their first bark, so others would not follow. We reached for a good bark collar.

Just like with the "I LOVE my voice" barkers, the collar acts as a STOP sign, so these dogs can find peace as the alternative to chaos. They then get to rediscover more normal, productive behaviors, such as playing with other dogs and enjoying long naps in the sun, all because the option of uninterrupted, self-perpetuated barking was taken away. Given lots of mindful exercise, good routines and good direction, their stress level drops; their desire to stress-bark diminishes, and the collar isn't needed in the long-term.

If you came to this point in this book with strong emotions about bark collar use, or if your only experience with them is seeing them misused, I ask that you read the last two sections again, to put the use of this tool in the proper context. Bark collars can get misused, and we don't want to be one of the individuals doing this, but since good quality ones can be used humanely, on a temporary basis, to bring peace into a dog's life (and the lives of dogs around him), it is good to know how (calmly and positively) and when (with "I bark, you jump" barking, "I LOVE my voice" barking and self-perpetuated stress-barking) and why (as one element of a bark-reduction plan) to use them.

WHEN IS A BARK NOT A BARK?

So we have established: barks are not created equal. Here is a canine riddle for you: when is a bark not necessarily a bark?

The answer is: when it is a howl! Think of dogs that howl at sirens. Now picture two dozen dogs responding to that siren all at once, creating a canine chorus with gleeful participants. Folks, there is nothing you can do to stop this train. Just sit back and count the cars, until the last one clears the crossing. If you get vocal with a howling pack, they will assume that you are joining them, so let it rip. It will peter, out on its own, in due time.

BARKING AND VIDEO SURVEILLANCE

Back to barking that is barking: Our shelter's play areas are monitored using video surveillance cameras, and they are a godsend. We may be two buildings away, but if we hear a bark, we can look up at the screen and decide if our intervention is needed or not. More than anything else, we watch our pack's body language. Yes, we can see who is barking. Yes, we can usually tell what started it. But it is the body language, the response of the other dogs, that tells us if this is something that will blow over quickly, on its own, or something that will escalate if one of us doesn't start walking in their direction.

Is one dog pushing another around roughly? Is someone's tail up and at attention? Is everyone gathered around a cowering individual or two dogs ready to face off? (Now they've got our attention!) Or is everyone simply facing a waddling duck or a cat sauntering by with a smug look on her face?

What is the energy level of the pack overall?

When it comes to working with groups of basically balanced dogs, <u>watch the other dogs' responses</u> before getting involved. Remember: groups of dogs are similar to groups of little kids. Many things have a way of working themselves out... even more so with dogs because, unlike humans and as a whole, they prefer balance to drama.

On a side note, it pays to play videos back once in a while to watch your own body language and the dogs' response to what you do. Do you consider yourself a good canine handler? Then put it to the test by putting it in front of a camera lens. Video sequences, like mirrors, can be marvelous self-teaching tools.

GOOD TIMING, LESS WHINING

Whining is a natural go-to behavior in growing puppies. They whine when they want attention. They whine as they test and push new boundaries. They whine as a means of being persistent. They wiggle, whine and piddle to show submission to bigger dogs, and they whine to vent pent-up energy.

Like fingernails on a chalkboard, whining can be hard to endure, and it often gets worse just before it gets better. Knowing that occasional whining is natural at this stage of their development can help you to have more patience with it. Just don't give in to it! Remember Golden Rules #1 and #2. Never reward whining, unless you want to get a lot more of it!

The best way to reduce whining (in dogs of any age), until it stops on its own because it is not being rewarded, is to:

- ❖ Drain the energy that feeds it. A pleasantly tired pup is not going to waste energy whining.
- ❖ Watch your timing. Never open a crate, enter a room, pet, talk to, feed or open a door when a dog is whining! Do so only after fifteen quiet seconds (or more) have passed.
- ❖ Teach better substitute behaviors. For example, rather than encourage a puppy to whine at the door when he needs to go outside, teach him to use his nose to ring a bell hanging off the doorknob. When you hear the bell chime, come running!
- ❖ Never get vocal with or attempt to punish a dog who is whining. Either will only increase his tension, which will lead to more whining.
- ❖ Watch for opportunities to reward his quiet (with calm, genuine smiles).

LIKE BARKS, GROWLS ARE NOT CREATED EQUAL

I mention this because good dogs sometimes get punished for reprimanding other dogs who need it. Watch an adult dog correct a juvenile or give warning to an equal (especially if that equal is a newcomer testing his boundaries), and watch the other dog's response. If the behavior isn't escalating, and the body language (especially the tail) doesn't indicate impending calamity, there is no need to intervene and no need to reprimand. A growl can be simple communication. It isn't always an invitation to fight, and it definitely isn't always a sign of aggression.

In general, avoid micromanaging. It just creates stress, and your dogs will wind up manipulating you.

TRY THIS EXERCISE: Now that you know that a bark isn't a bark isn't a bark, try differentiating one type of bark from another. Observe the dogs' tails as you do this.

TAKE IT A STEP FURTHER: Observe how other dogs respond when one dog decides to get vocal. Often their response (or non-response) will tell you whether the situation needs addressing or not.

CHAPTER 25
TROUBLESHOOTING MISBEHAVIORS

WHY DOES MY DOG DO THAT?

The best way to figure out why a dog does what he does, in any given situation, is to ask a few key questions:

- ❖ Has he been rewarded in the past for doing it?
- ❖ Might a prior negative association be a factor?
- ❖ Have you failed to show him alternate behaviors, or might he be following a routine that needs changing?
- ❖ Is he looking for an outlet for his pent-up energy?
- ❖ Could the reason be instinctual (after all, he is a dog)?
- ❖ Are you projecting tension to which he is responding?
- ❖ Do you carry a negative picture in your mind? (Your dog knows it.)
- ❖ Have you failed to follow through in the past? (Your dog knows it, and he is willing to capitalize on it).

Let me expand upon the first five questions, before addressing some of the things we do that get in our own (and our dogs') way.

First, if a dog gets rewarded for a behavior one time out of twenty, he will consider it an option given similar circumstances in the future. (Herein lies the problem with one family member permitting, or even encouraging, a behavior when other family members prefer that it not occur.)

Second, if a dog expects Y to happen because Y has often occurred after X, it will take time and consistent repetitions of X leading to Z (as opposed to Y) for him to form new associations. More so when he is home than when he is away. The good news is: any dog arriving at a new location is ready for new associations. Specifically, he is looking to make them! Long working walks and visits to new places take dogs out of their element, to places where new associations can be introduced and new skills can be taught. The secrets to success:

- ❖ Be willing to take the chance.
- ❖ Put a picture of success in your mind.
- ❖ Live in the moment.
- ❖ Be calm and consistent, and be willing to lead the way, so your dog can be an awesome follower.

Third, dogs often repeat behaviors simply because they have never been shown different ones (and some of these behaviors can expand into routines, when better ones aren't in place). A funny, but actually quite common example is how many dogs get social when their owners are sitting on a commode. Why shouldn't they do this? They have repeatedly been petted for it when a simple *back up* command would send them happily on their way.

Fourth, dogs that have energy to burn, and no job to do, often create their own jobs, and they tend to pick jobs we wouldn't choose. Tired dogs don't look for trash to sort. They don't tease other dogs. And they don't chew up their dog-beds. Rather, they are happy to curl up in companionship, having had their need for things to do satisfied.

Fifth, sometimes the answer to the question, "Why does my dog do that?" lies in the fact that he is a dog. Given dirt to dig in or crotches to sniff or squirrels to chase, dogs are going to delight in doing it.

Dogs, by their nature, don't set out to create issues. Yes, they are opportunists, and they love to solve puzzles in order to get what they want (especially when a reward is in sight or sniff). But they don't seek out, nor do they nourish, drama. Shown a clear path to happiness or a clear path to peacefulness, they will usually take it.

DON'T SET YOUR DOGS UP FOR FAILURE

Earlier I mentioned that part of being clear with our dogs involves being willing to lead the way. Leading the way entails many things, one of which is recognizing and avoiding situations where our dogs have little chance of success, because something inherent is getting in the way.

A few examples of this are:

❖ Crating or gating dogs that aren't comfortable with each other across from one another.

❖ Allowing one dog's excitement to trigger the same in others. Better to mitigate one dog's excitement than to be forced to address the excitement of many.

❖ Not addressing the excitement of people (visitors, for example) before it incites the same in your dogs. There are ways to do this in a tactful manner, and it helps to keep the peace. (Your visitors will then compliment your dogs for their calm behavior, never knowing that it occurred because you corrected theirs!)

❖ Expecting a dog to respond to commands that require an element of calm (such as *sit*) when he is highly excited. Help him to drop his heightened energy first.

❖ Expecting a dog to respond to a command when his focus isn't on you (one reason why *watch me* is often requested and then rewarded, before subsequent commands are given).

❖ Trying to teach dogs new skills before exercising them.

❖ Introducing dogs to each other face-to-face, without walking them side-by-side for five minutes first.

❖ Not rewarding calm dogs with relaxed smiles, so being calm is a choice they make more often.

❖ Not following through consistently.

❖ Approaching situations while expecting to fail, or with any amount of tension.

Breaking any of the rules mentioned in Chapters 3 and 9 will also set a dog up for failure. We may not mean to do it, but when we do, it doesn't help our dogs give us their best.

When these kind of things occur, embrace your personal learning curve. Allow yourself to learn from your dogs, moment by moment. If you mess up one moment, simply learn from it, and do things better next time. Chances are good, your dogs will forgive you!

PLAN FOR SUCCESS

Whenever troubled dogs come to our facility, they get a <u>clean slate</u>. When the sun rises on each new day, they get another clean slate. And when we travel together to a new location, they get yet another clean slate. We will not let what happened yesterday, or someplace else, stop things from being better today, or in a new setting. In this way, we don't thwart ourselves, nor do we hinder our dogs' psychological growth and training by expecting the worst. To be thinking about a dog's past, while we work with him in the present, would only rob him of his next step toward a better future.

Every dog gets sufficient <u>exercise</u>, before we work on his skills. We bond over a few long, focused walks. If pent-up energy prevents him from walking well at our side, we grab our bicycles, our in-line skates or our dog-modified ATV for a full-bore, wide-open run.

Every dog also receives <u>structure</u>. That is, he gets to enjoy good routines and well-thought-out rituals. If he has picked up unproductive routines previously, we recognize them, and we direct him to better ones in a calm and consistent way.

Every dog gets rewarded with big <u>smiles</u> for level-one energy every chance we get, and we play games, as needed, to develop positive new associations with crates and treadmills.

Every dog is taught polite threshold behavior, and every dog is exposed to new people and places such as the beach, pet store parking lots and quiet paths in the woods. Our energy is <u>calm and matter-of-fact</u> when we do this. We don't wish to associate new things with excitement or tension unnecessarily.

Lastly, knowing that one tool does not fit all, we experiment with different collars, head harnesses and chest-ring harnesses, to find the best tool for each individual. Most importantly, we position our choice correctly (no collars riding against a dog's lower neck).

PRACTICAL EMPOWERMENT

Approaching your dogs' behaviors (and misbehaviors) in this manner will empower you in ways that go well beyond the ability to use new skills. Understanding their psychology (as well as your own) will also help you to become more aware as a person.

❖ Aware of whether a given situation requires intervention or not.

❖ Aware of simple ways to direct the action, so problems don't arise in the first place.

❖ Aware of the many opportunities available to appreciate when things go right. (When we reward our dogs with smiles, we give ourselves an equal boost!)

Let me make that practical with a few examples.

No intervention needed: Skyy, a Miniature Pinscher, gives a low growl to her hound buddy, Reggie, when he hovers over her, wanting to claim her bed. Reggie ignores her protest. Refusing to leave, he shades her like a tree branch. You recognize this as a situation that calls for no response. None to Skyy, for her growling. None to Reggie, for his calm assertion that Skyy's bed now belongs to him. The dogs will work things out, with one's persistence gradually winning out over the other. You watch from afar, enjoying a good lesson in canine communication.

Choice of simple interventions available: You hear the sirens of emergency vehicles in the distance, and you mentally triage what can happen next. If you know that your dog-hating neighbor isn't home, you might let your dogs echo the sirens with a hearty group howl. The look of pure glee on their faces will add another smile to your day, and there is nothing (short of group walks and group meals) like a group howl to bond dogs together. But if that neighbor is home, or if Waldo, your new Beagle puppy, is outside, you may choose to head off the howling by redirecting your dogs to a different task. Sooner or later, Waldo is going to find his hound-voice, but you would rather it be later, since it gives you more opportunity to reward the times he chooses to be the quietest little Beagle known to mankind.

An opportunity to help others and keep the peace: A Pomeranian, walking her owner in your direction, begins to alert-bark frantically at you and your dog. The woman responds with multiple leash-pulls and shouts of "Stop it!" while simultaneously apologizing to you for her dog's behavior (which only gets worse). You know how to deal with this! You invite her to walk next to you for a little while, and you urge her into a brisk but comfortable pace oriented in a horizontal line (dog – person – person – dog) for as long as it takes her dog to relax and walk quietly (now: person – dog – dog – person). Given the option to do this, the Pomeranian quiets quickly. With everyone on the same team, she now sees you and your dog as friends and not foes. Her owner sees you as a hero, having been taught a much better response to her dog's barking, and what results is in everyone's best interest. After all, this world can always use more peace and less tension.

Separating the symptoms from the problems: Your new Pit Bull, Alfie, keeps shredding bits of paper claimed from your deskside trash bin. You recognize his behavior to be but a symptom of a deeper problem, which may be:

❖   Alfie needs a job to do, something that provides him with focus and a sense of achievement.
❖   He needs something more appropriate to chew on.
❖   He needs better outlets for his energy.

You plan a program of bicycling together for twenty minutes each workday morning, and you set aside forty-five minutes (or more) for the same each weekend morning, to drain his overcharged batteries and keep them drained. You offer him an extra-large roasted cow hipbone to chew on. And you umbilical-leash him while you do your yardwork, the better to give him a job to do (follow your lead) while you multitask. If you have a treadmill and Alfie is comfortable walking on one, you also add a half-hour of varied-speed walking to each day.

Forming better new associations: Your Shih Tzu mix, Charlie, growls whenever he sees your neighbor's Great Dane, Harvard. Harvard is a benevolent beast of one hundred and fifteen pounds, but his owner is a crabby curmudgeon when it comes to smaller dogs. Every time Charlie sees the pair, he associates Harvard with his owner's negative energy. Since your relationship with your neighbor is otherwise peaceful, you would like the relationship between the dogs to be the same. Recognizing that the fastest way to get them on the same page psychologically is to walk them side-by-side, you offer to take Harvard on some of Charlie's walks. Your neighbor agrees, not knowing that your ultimate plan is to have him join you and the dogs on some of these walks, the better for Charlie to see him (and not just Harvard) in a positive light.

<u>Redirection needed</u>: You see your dog pacing back and forth along your chain-link fence. Although you aren't sure what started his pacing, you recognize it as unsettled behavior, capable of getting worse. Two options quickly come to mind. You can calmly direct him to stop and *watch* if he knows this command, since it will allow you to both identify the trigger of his pacing and reward him for better behavior. Or you could calmly relocate him indoors, putting an end to his pacing and the heightened energy behind it. What you choose to do might vary with the circumstances, but either way you have defused a bad situation before it got worse. You then start budgeting for some privacy panels.

<u>Know when another dog can help</u>: Leeda, your new Australian Shepherd, seems overwhelmed with changes, both large and small. Rather than baby her through scary events when they occur, you reach for Pedro's help. Pedro, your cool and calm Sheltie mix, is an older dog who has seen it all, and he is unlikely to feed into Leeda's anxiety, insecurity or avoidance. Tying Leeda's leash securely to Pedro's collar, and holding Pedro's leash in hand, you lead the dogs around your home, up and down your driveway, and progressively, over a few days, to places away from home. Pedro is a wonderful mentor, and watching him lead Leeda while following you gives you a new appreciation for him!

<u>Allow your dogs to show you how smart they are</u>: Trisket, your terrier, has a tendency to pull ahead when you approach your home gate. Sure, you would prefer that she remain at your side in a picture-perfect heel until you open your gate, the way your other dogs do. But Trisket wants to please you in another way. She wants to show you that she knows what comes next. So rather than get tense and force her to heel up to the gate, you change your routine to stop fifteen feet away. From a calm sitting position, you then direct her to *go out*, which allows her to run up to and sit next to the gate, showing you that she knows where to go. It is a little compromise, training-wise, but it is one that suits Trisket more, and the end result is the same: a dog who is focused on you, waiting patiently at your gate.

 <u>Reward the calmest of energy levels</u>: Muggs is a young Boxer, an active fellow with two speeds: slow trot and warp-drive, together with lots of vertical lift. You want to bring out his calmer side as often as possible, the better to shape this goofy adolescent into a well-behaved adult. When it comes time to bring him indoors after some playtime outside, you:

  (a) Open the door, call his name and step back as he races inside.
  (b) Open the door and call his name, but block him before he can run into the house. You then give him the command to *sit*, which he does with enthusiasm. At that point, you say, "Good boy!" before backing away for him to enter at a trot.
  (c) Walk outside and nonchalantly slide a slip-lead over his head when he trots up to your side. You then stand quietly while he fidgets a bit, offering a smile and a gentle ear rub once he chooses to stand quietly. When he is at his quietest, you walk into your house together, with Muggs following you politely. Turning, you walk outside and back in again, just as calmly and quietly (remembering how repetitions accelerate a dog's learning curve).

Option (b) is a step in the right direction, but my recommendation is to try option (c). By putting in the extra time to calm Muggs's natural enthusiasm, you reward his choice to relax and you demonstrate the behavior you want: his walking (and not running) into the house. With time and some more repetitions, Muggs will learn that entering your home means entering it respectfully. At that point, calling him directly into the house can be done in a more mannerly fashion.

 Never forget: many bad behaviors are rooted in bad routines. Showing dogs a better routine, given similar circumstances, is often all the situation requires.

 Napoleon, the Neapolitan Mastiff, springs into action whenever someone knocks at the door. Jumping up, he digs his nails into the woodwork and barks. When he did this in his previous home, his previous owners got tense, and Napoleon knew to match their tension with lots of his own. (After all, he is a dog, and that is what dogs do).

 This is where teaching him a better routine can keep the peace. First, you use your smile and a few treats to teach him to curl up on his dog-bed whenever you say *"place."* Then, when you get an extra half-hour, you enlist the help of a patient friend who visits often (someone who agrees readily, since she is as tired of Napoleon's antics as you are). You ask her to knock at your back door (and later at your front door), while you calmly stand on the other side with him leashed. Before he can hop up and vocalize, you direct him to his bed and reward him with a treat. Waiting out any excitement, you then tie him in this location and direct him to *wait* while you matter-of-factly open and then close the door. You repeat this exercise seven or more times, the first few times to demonstrate the new routine you want, and the rest to reinforce it through repetitions. (One smart cookie, you deserve some bonus points. Your friend doesn't know it, but you are training her, too, when at last you direct her to enter your home calmly – using good canine social protocol – the better to match Napoleon's new-found tranquility.)

SURVEILLANCE

While getting a dog moving (especially via working walks or side-by-side bicycling) is the best thing that we can do to mitigate and address issues, observing his body language is the second best thing. Invest in video surveillance. If a picture is worth a thousand words, videos can be priceless. Up-to-the-minute information provided by cameras can help you identify and prevent problems. It can even save lives, since dogs in multi-dog households don't always show higher energy before aggressing! Higher tension, yes, but not always higher energy.

Monitoring and reviewing behaviors (both canine and human) via remote cameras will give you, not only peace of mind, but also a greater ability to learn from what you see. You can then make changes before small issues become big ones.

COPROPHAGIA (A.K.A. EATING POOP)

Most authors don't face the problem of deciding where in their book to discuss the problem of eating poop! But then, most don't live with a few dozen dogs at a time, many of them fostered.

Coprophagia is a peculiar issue, and it is one that offends and unsettles most human sensibilities. It is also one easier to prevent than to address. The reasons certain dogs consume feces – sometimes their own and sometimes that of others – have been argued for decades. Is this an innate behavior? Is it an acquired behavior? Is something missing in the dog's diet?

Is there a single reason for it, or might it be triggered by multiple factors? I suspect the problem often has more than one root. One thing for sure is: there is a lot less testing of pack leadership and <u>significantly</u> less poop-eating at our Center when we don't poop-scoop in front of our dogs! With multiple populations, time after time, this practice holds true. In the world of dogs, leaders simply do not stoop to pick up poop.

Is it because, when we remove piles of stool we encourage our dogs to do the same? Is it because when we do this, we eliminate scent markers that they have left behind? Do the hunched positions we assume when we stoop to scoop poop play a part? I really can't say.

If you are thinking, "Yea! I can now leave poop-scooping to someone else," I apologize. That is not my point. Rather, my point is: poop-scooping ideally should be done when the dogs are not watching. Am I a responsible dog owner who picks up after her dogs in public places? Most definitely, and I hope you are, too. Common courtesy must trump canine psychology here. On my home turf, however, all poop-scooping is done when my dogs are inside.

A WORD ABOUT PACK LEADERSHIP

Directing dogs (and people) toward better behavior is what pack leadership is all about. That said, building a trouble-free pack isn't simply a matter of bringing a bunch of dogs together. That would be called a play-group. Play-groups reflect <u>location</u> more than identity, whereas packs represent <u>identity</u> a lot more than location. Packs are living, breathing, free-moving organisms made up of smaller living, breathing, free-moving organisms, and a stable pack structure, with a good leader at the helm, serves to support each individual, as well as the whole. A healthy pack structure gives everyone the opportunity to be their best.

Never forget: dogs naturally like balance. Give them a good foundation. Give them clear rules that foster the behavior you want. Be the one who helps them to feel safe, and they will give you their best in return.

Prior to reading this book, you may not have thought much about how dogs relate to your energy, state of mind and behavior. Now you may see how an awareness of this changes everything. Maybe you never thought of yourself as a leader before, since "Leader" was a title that you didn't want at the time, like "Cubmaster" or "Commander" or "Coach." Your dogs will remind you that "leader" isn't a title as much as it is the quality of energy you project and the quality of energy you nurture.

In every instant, we need to be role models and pack leaders for our dogs, not only because that is what they need from us, but also because it is how we get the relaxed, well-behaved dogs we all enjoy.

WHEN YOU ARE UP AGAINST THE WORST

The behavior of troubled dogs, more often than not, reflects trouble in their environment or handling. This is actually good news, because both environments and handling are changeable. That said, congenital issues can exist, creating misbehaviors well beyond our means to correct. Recognizing affected individuals is a topic that I will expand upon in Chapter 27.

Try not to define a dog by his mistakes. (You would hate to be defined by your own.) Know that those mistakes are part of his learning curve (and yours), and be willing to move on, so he can, too.

An occasional review of some basic principles can be helpful. They are listed in Appendix 1. Apply them moment to moment to moment. Develop routines and rituals that support your dogs doing their best, under your leadership. Recognize what doesn't work and do things differently next time. It is all a process, and the goal is not to make it a stressful one. Some things will come naturally, but there will be a lot that you will need to un-learn first. Don't despair. The journey is worth it.

TRY THIS EXERCISE: Identify situations that set your dogs (or dogs handled by others) up for failure, as opposed to circumstances that promote success.

CHAPTER 26
CHOOSING PROFESSIONAL HELP

A little help from the right professional can make a huge difference, even when you have the basics down pat. But how do you find the right person, when so many options are available? To judge the energy, aptitude, state of mind, awareness and use of tools by people offering training and behavioral assistance, it can help to do the following:

❖ Observe their dogs. Are their own dogs quietly focused? Does a calm state of mind accompany their good behavior?

❖ Look for a relaxed, confident demeanor and a good use of movement and body language.

❖ Watch for a reliance on a particular tool. One-tool trainers miss the big picture when they fit dogs to tools more than pick the best tools for a given dog, group of dogs or situation.

❖ Know that high-pitched voices and a reliance on treats can work against you, especially when you wish to bring out your dog's calmer side.

Avoid people who build themselves up by knocking others down. Perceptive, well-rounded trainers able to recognize their own learning curves don't need to do that. Avoid people who aren't quick to smile. You can do better. Choose someone who is a good communicator, someone willing to use common-man terminology (out of the dictionary), and not 'behaviorist-speak' more fitting to primates than to canines. (This is commonly done with words like "dominant" and "dominance.")

Question trainers about their limitations. We all have them. Individual limitations may be important to you, or they may not matter. Either way, it helps to have this information. Recognize the limits of classroom obedience. For the majority of dogs, it can be productive and lots of fun. Other dogs may not be ready for its structure.

Look for a trainer who requires you to be part of the process. I know many a well-trained and obedient dog that didn't stand a chance of fulfilling his potential, because he lived with a household of disengaged, dysfunctional people. Good trainers will insist upon working with you (and not simply with your dog). This is not to say that a short stay with a good trainer isn't a good idea. (It can be an excellent opportunity for some.) It is to say, however: ninety percent of any dog training involves training the <u>handler</u>.

Be willing to be an engaged handler. Be willing to learn from your dogs, and in tandem with your dogs. Be willing to exercise your dogs, both physically and mentally. And because issues rooted in fear, trust and anxiety can take time to correct, be willing to let things progress over time, when extra time is indicated.

Just as one tool doesn't suit every dog, every handler or every situation, one approach to training does not fit all. Whatever the approach used, be sure that it reflects the way dogs think (and not just how us humans think).

Bonus points go to trainers that encourage you to name, and quietly reward, behaviors as a dog does them (not just when commanded), and those willing to "walk-and-train!" These approaches recognize the benefits of getting outside in the real world.

STARTING OFF ON
THE RIGHT FOOT

*In a world where Big Agriculture, Big Sugar, Big Pharma
and Big Oil do not see the Big Picture,
a good dog always will.*

CHAPTER 27
CHOOSING THE RIGHT DOG FOR YOU

When it comes to people and their dogs, so many truths are based in simplicity and common sense. One of them is: we want our dogs to be a good match for us. We don't purposely go looking for bad matches.

But bad matches occur, because we have a tendency to fall in love with a cute face and hope for the best. Or we find ourselves attracted to a young dog when we don't have the time or the skills needed to handle a youngster. We may forget to research breeds when taking on a four-legged family member, or we may "rescue" out of guilt, only to regret the decision, given a little time.

Fortunately, this disconnect from reality is not that hard to address when you ask yourself these questions:

❖ What are your expectations for this dog? Do you want a playmate for another dog, a companion, a jogging partner, a guard dog, a gift for someone*, a babysitter for the kids* or the means by which to teach your children responsibility*?

Please refer to the end of this chapter for more on these topics.

❖ What is the energy level of your household on a scale of one to ten? *(You will want to find a dog that doesn't overwhelm or underwhelm you.)*

❖ Do you like to walk outdoors, jog, bicycle, rollerblade or go mountain climbing? *(Running around a backyard is not enough exercise for many dogs, regardless of size.)*

❖ What have you learned about this breed or mix of breeds from your research? *(Many breeds have a predisposition toward certain medical issues, one of the most common of which is allergies that affect their skin and eyes.*)*

❖ Do you have appointments set up with your veterinarian and groomer? *(Reality check: have your credit card ready.)*

❖ What is the chance that you will face a major life change in the next ten years? Might someone in the household be getting pregnant in the next couple of years, necessitating the choice of a toddler-tolerant dog? *(And the need for a newborn and dog to be watched over at the same time.)* If you are in the military, might a family member deploy or be reassigned?

❖ Have you spent time with the adult version of the puppy you are considering?

At our Center, we get a lot of appreciation from new adopters. We also get heartfelt thanks from people (especially new parents) who go home without a dog because we helped them to see that our dog wasn't the right match for them. I say "especially new parents" because studies have shown that more dogs are returned after adoption by new parents than by single women or single men. When asked why, the answer is: the dog did not fulfill the expectations that the parents had for him. Yes, many of those expectations were self-serving or unrealistic. Nonetheless the dog gets returned.

MATCHING ENERGY TO ENERGY

Near the top of our shelter's adoption application is the question "On a scale of one to ten, what is the energy level of your household?" We consider this to be one of the most important questions to ask. Why? Because people should not adopt dogs with energy levels higher than that of their households. No one will be happy with the choice. Not the

Please refer to the end of this chapter for more on this topic.

adopters, who will end up with more work than they bargained for. And not the dogs, because their needs may not get met.

Investigate the natural energy of any dog that you might adopt. Learn about his DNA. What is his breed bred to do? Research his needs. How much exercise will he crave? Will he need jobs to do (and might he create his own jobs if you don't help him to make better choices)? News flash: working breeds need work to do!

At our shelter, we point out the parallels between looking for a pet and looking for a spouse. "Don't fall in love with someone just because they have a cute face," we say. "A good match with a pet can last more than fifteen years, and that is longer than many marriages!" People can well understand these analogies.

When we decline adoption applications because the dog and household energies are not well-matched, we take the time to explain why, and potential adopters really appreciate it! They understand that we aren't trying to keep them away from a certain dog because we are obstructionists at heart. Rather, they see that we want the best match for them, and we are both on the same side. This way, our dogs go home with adopters who have, not only the financial ability to provide for their medical needs, but (having done their homework) also the lifestyle that supports their physical and mental requirements.

Sadly, many dogs that come to us are looking for their third or fourth family, because their previous owners didn't research their needs before taking them home.

GETTING THE BIG PICTURE

When we choose a dog to be a part of our life, it helps to have as much information as possible. For this reason, in addition to assessing a dog's natural energy level, we look for his:

- ❖ Green-light traits. These are traits that we can improve upon through exercise, neutering, training and good routines.
- ❖ Yellow-light traits. These are traits that can be reshaped, managed or eliminated, if we are up to the challenge. For example, anxiety or a willingness to use aggression. Treatable injuries, allergies and medical issues also fall into this category.
- ❖ Red-light traits. These are the all-important characteristics that we will <u>not</u> be able to change; traits

that are rooted in a dog's DNA, his nature as opposed to his nurture. For example: prey drive, behaviors stemming from physical conformation (blindness and deafness, for example) and congenital issues (many times the result of indiscriminate breeding).

When you take responsibility for a new dog, it pays to acknowledge your limitations, be they physical (age, weight, health or strength), time (there are only so many hours in each day), training (where are you on your learning curve?), finances (will you need to budget for special diets or extra grooming?), space or the presence of other animals. Given these limitations, we serve our dogs the best when our abilities match the challenges we take on, and when the chance of good outcomes (happy dogs in happy households) is maximized.

BEHAVIORAL ASSESSMENTS

Behavioral assessments can help you learn more about individual dogs. The rather simple one used at our facility is one that I have been doing for forty years, well before I became a veterinarian and long before most common variations were developed. It is simple and straightforward, and it is relatively easy to teach. It is also quite predictive of future behavior when performed several times over a few weeks to evaluate growing puppies.

More than anything else, I use this test to identify:

❖ Issues that need to be addressed before a dog can be considered a good match for the average family.

❖ Issues that more knowledgeable people could handle, should those people be available and interested.

❖ Issues (e.g., prey drive) that might bring trouble into my pack.

It is important to use and interpret behavioral assessments responsibly, and it is important to understand what each is meant to evaluate. A common one used in shelters (one that I don't like, nor trust) was designed to test for aggressive tendencies in dogs six months of age or older. It would be incorrect to call it a general test of temperament. It is very different from my favorite assessment, which judges, instead: natural assertiveness, a willingness to take direction and suitability for purpose (e.g., service dogs; tactical dogs; general family members), in individuals as young as six weeks of age.

Always remember that these evaluations are similar to snapshots. They let you know where a dog is <u>at a given time in</u>

a given situation. The more pictures you get, the better your information will be when it comes to making decisions. We really like the repeatability of our assessment for this reason. We also appreciate its multi-functionality, since some of its steps reflect tasks (such as a physical exam) that we need to perform on every dog anyway.

The best assessments of any kind honor how dogs really think, and the best people to do these assessments take the time to get their technique right. For example, if you are unsure about opening a dog's mouth or encouraging a dog to roll over willingly, practice on a few Labrador puppies before doing it on an adult Lab.

Should you wish to try the five-to-six-point assessment that I use, know that you absolutely, positively must have your personal energy right. You must be calm and quick to smile. You must be confident. (This is not the time to be hesitant!) Depending upon the dog and the availability of assistants, you may wish to have a second calm, confident person quietly observing, the better to see things from a different angle.

If you have read all of the chapters preceding this one, you recognize the benefit of videotaping. Behavioral evaluation is another situation where it can be helpful.

Most of the time, you will want the dog leashed, although puppies and small dogs may not need leashes. The setting you choose must be free of distractions: no other animals, people or events going on. Having a clean tabletop (for smaller dogs and puppies) and a chair (so you can sit next to larger dogs) can also be helpful. In most cases, the best location is a quiet room indoors; however, I have assessed many dogs on outdoor benches on the quiet side of municipal shelters. Use your best judgment.

Feel free to perform the following tests more than once, to give each dog an extra chance to be his best! Evaluate your results in the context of all the other information available, knowing the history that you have been given may include erroneous information.

As important as it is to have the right person doing this in the right frame of mind, to do his best, a dog needs to be in the right frame of mind, too. Let him urinate and defecate first, especially if he has just come out of a crate or a kennel. Then take him for an enjoyable working walk to drop his energy level and get him focused. Urge him to sniff around your testing area, to become accustomed to his surroundings. Every extra minute you spend will pay off. Once he has shed a lot of his nervous or excited energy, then and only then should you start your assessment.

Our assessment evaluates a dog's comfort at being handled and his willingness to follow the direction of a calm and confident human (steps one, two and four), because the best of family pets show these traits. It checks for issues with other animals (steps five and six), because they matter to most people. It also looks for signs of natural assertiveness (steps three and four). Will the dog gravitate toward the front of his pack, the middle of his pack or the back of his pack? Remember that middle-of-the-pack dogs make the best pets for most households, while front-of-the-pack and back-of-the-pack dogs (the latter which we identify through experience, and not through specific tests) aren't for everyone. The natural assertiveness of a front-of-the-pack dog can present problems for many, and the heightened energy and hypervigilance of a typical back-of-the-pack dog requires more tolerance than a lot of people possess.

Used by many breeders to evaluate and compare growing puppies in a litter, our assessment is non-confrontational, and it honors canine psychology. It doesn't encourage adversative behaviors such as resource guarding (the way an assessment that uses a rubber hand on a pole does). Done well, it will build trust between a dog and his handler, not bruise it. That is very important to us!

Our assessment, taken as a whole, is not pass/fail, and the final score means less than the information collected by going through its steps. It is most valuable when used to compare dogs to one another – for instance, when multiple dogs are being considered for one spot in a household – and the behavior of growing pups from one week to the next. Each task done well earns a full point. Dogs not earning a full point may be given quarter-points or half-points. Tests 5 and 6 can be done before or after tests 1 through 4. It doesn't matter. This is what you do:

Test 1: Talking softly to the dog, confidently open and close his mouth with his nose pointing up toward the ceiling, as if you were administering an imaginary pill. As soon as his mouth is open all the way, close it (in other words, don't attempt to hold his mouth open; there is no reason to do that). The best technique to use, if you are right-handed, uses your left thumb to push his upper lip over his premolars (this pries his mouth open with minimal pressure).

The rest of your left hand cradles the top of his muzzle and/or head. Your right index finger can then slip between his lower canine teeth to further open his jaws. The keys to success are a calm, matter-of-fact demeanor and confidence.

Smile and stroke his throat when you are finished, to let him know that he is a good boy for letting you do this. If he lets you open and close his mouth without resistance, he gets a full point. If he tosses his head around and paws at your hand, and if this action is not due to hesitation on your part, facial confirmation (small noses and very big eyes) or dental disease, he should get at most a half-point. If he tightens his jaws, growls or wrinkles his nose or pulls back his lip at any point, stop! He loses this point in its entirety, and any subsequent steps, should you choose to do them, should only be done with him securely muzzled.

Unless you need to eliminate prey drive issues with cats (test 6) right away, there is value in doing this test first. Having calmly and confidently handled many thousands of dogs in this way, as the first step in a complete veterinary examination, I have found that there is something about opening and closing a dog's mouth that relaxes most of them. It is behavior that they don't expect, but when it is done without fanfare and with a gentle scratch for good behavior, it seems to ready them for the next test.

It is rare for a dog with healthy teeth and gums to completely lose this point, but if one does, I stop my assessment to focus on the next candidate. This dog is not going to do well at our facility, and I would rather choose a dog that can.

Test 2: Starting at the tip of the nose, channel your inner calm, confident, friendly veterinary professional and perform a thorough examination of the dog. Stroke everything from the face and ears (including inside the ears), down the neck, across the back, over the haunches and down the legs to his toes, along his tail and between his legs. This not only gives you the opportunity to examine him for parasites, masses, injuries and more, it also lets you see how he feels about different parts of his body being handled. Your touch should be gentle but self-assured, and thorough but non-stimulating. No pinching or prodding or holding onto his feet!

If he is happy to have all aspects of his body handled, he gets a full point. If his only areas of sensitivity reflect medical issues, note them, but don't take off partial points. Notice any guarding of body parts, mouthing from the dog to stop your progress or pulling away, and let his score reflect that he isn't comfortable with your actions.

All other things being equal, these first two tests allow good-natured dogs to shine.

Test 3: Ask the dog to sit quietly in front of you. Gently pick up one of his front legs, positioning your palm-up hand under it, just above his wrist. Speaking softly, so as not to call attention to what you are doing, gently rotate your hand to finish palm-down on top of his leg <u>without pressure</u>. What you have done subtly, via your body language, is move yourself from a submissive position to a more dominant one. If he doesn't pull back, chew on your hand or vocalize, give him the full point and a short massage.

This third test is an excellent test for natural assertiveness, and many Huskies, Malamutes, Akitas and Chows (to mention a few naturally assertive breeds) will not earn this point.

Test 4: This test is one that I always do with small dogs and puppies, and less often with larger dogs, unless I need to choose but one larger dog out of many available. It involves gently turning a dog belly-up in my arms (small dogs and pups) or coaxing him into a belly-up position for a belly rub, on the ground or on a secure tabletop (dogs too big to be hand-held). In both cases, I reposition the dog in a friendly, <u>non-forced</u> and non-confrontational manner. If a dog is willing to relax into this position without struggling, he gets the full point and a big smile.

I won't conduct this test if other steps in my assessment point to aggressive tendencies. After all, I have already seen them. I don't have to push my luck looking for more. Look at it as a way to learn more about a dog's comfort and confidence with strangers, and view it as a way to judge his natural assertiveness (as opposed to his natural submissiveness). It is a way to give an extra point where it is earned.

Test 5:   Walk the dog next to handlers paired with relaxed, friendly dogs for five to ten minutes, and then allow loose-leash introductions in the manner discussed in Chapter 5. Dogs that readily introduce to and get along with other dogs get this point.

Test 6:   Walk the dog past cats, first caged and then moving, while observing his pupils, ear position, tail position and arousal. A dog who remains totally unaroused gets this point. Calm, nose-driven, relaxed-tail curiosity is fine. Any visual cuing, overstimulation or tension, especially with moving cats, is not. Zero points given for that.

I always recommend that people assess multiple dogs before making adoption decisions. This helps them to pick sweet-tempered dogs (as opposed to individuals who look good only in pictures), good companions that will suit their lifestyle next year and in four years and in ten.

TRY THIS EXERCISE: If you are considering adding a dog to your household, or if you will be helping another to do the same, practice your calm, confident handling skills on a litter of puppies. Channel your most accomplished canine professional and project the calming energy of a good mama dog as you conduct each of the above steps. This will help you to bring out every pup's best. Compare and contrast the pups' scores, to differentiate individuals.

* _Regarding the gifting of pets to others_: _The best way to give a loved one a pet of any kind is to give them the gift of adventure! Imagine your friend or family member unwrapping a series of boxes. In one is a really nice food bowl. In another is a pretty collar or harness. And in a third is some high-quality pet food. Lastly (drumroll, please), they open an envelope containing a home-made gift certificate good for the adoption fee for the pet of their dreams! You haven't just given them a pet...you have given them an ongoing adventure! Now you can both run over to the computer and search online for the perfect match. This approach to gifting a friend or a family member with a pet honors their interest in playing a part in_

the decision-making process (while retaining the option to offer an opinion or two along the way).

Regarding dogs and children: As any parent now caring for "their child's" pet will tell you: it is the responsibility of the parents, and not the pets, to teach children responsibility. Pets, alone, don't teach children responsibility. They also don't make good babysitters. It is better to consider them another kid in the house, ultimately the responsibility of the parents.

Regarding allergies and food sensitivities: Veterinarians frequently see dogs suffering from itchy, oozy, smelly skin, the result of food sensitivities. While certain breeds are predisposed (Shih Tzus and Golden Retrievers, for example) any dog can have this problem. Experience at our shelter has led us to believe that another chronic, highly painful, often immune-mediated disease (common in Shih Tzus, Cockers, Maltese, Pugs, Lhasa Apsos, West Highland White Terriers and other breeds) can also be triggered by certain ingredients, together with environmental factors. Commonly called "dry eye," it is also known as KCS (keratoconjunctivitis sicca, at times part of a broader disease called Sjogren's Syndrome) This is why reading the ingredient panel (and not just the brand name or key ingredients) of every bag or can of dog food is vital. Our recommendations for these breeds: no poultry or poultry by-products of any kind (even if "hydrolyzed") and no soy, no corn and no food colorings, to start. Other ingredients may need to be excluded if these eliminations aren't sufficient.

PRACTICAL LIFE LESSONS, FROM THE DOGS

Thank you, sunshine.
Thank you, clouds.

CHAPTER 28
SEIZING LIFE LIKE A DOG

There are a lot of good reasons – and many good ways – to seize life like a dog. Dogs know how to get the best from each moment. When they encounter another's bad behavior, negativity or criticism, they don't harvest it to share with their peers later in the day. They readily leave it behind, and move on. Life's strange smells and mud bring out their inquisitive side, a lot more often than their opinionated side. Dogs are naturally forgiving, and they are naturally compassionate. They aim to be good company, and they don't compare themselves to others. They are full of so many inherently good qualities!

CONNECT (WITH THE WORLD) LIKE A DOG

Dogs travel through life lightly. They appreciate simple pleasures. They don't choose to complicate things, and this allows them to better connect with their surroundings. Can we connect more with the world around us, like our dogs? Can we find more to appreciate and more to celebrate, for a greater portion of each and every day? Of course we can, and in this, our dogs make excellent partners.

Hannah's Mastiff mix, Dynamite, helped her to discover a few wondrous things. She describes it in this manner:

"Dynamite loves to explore, and he uses all of his senses to the max. He watches intently. He listens with every fiber of his being. He is quick to touch things and equally happy to taste them. And when his nose gets a-working, it is as if nothing else in the world matters.

I got worried, one day, when I saw him chewing on some wild violets, but when I researched them online, I learned that they were not only edible; they were also delicious! I added a few to my next salad, and I tried the same with edible nasturtiums. That led me to try other new things, such as purple carrots and yellow beets (both delicious). The next thing I knew, I was decorating my home with wildflowers. You could say that Dynamite's whole-body, five-sense love of the world helped me to appreciate more of it!"

LIGHTEN UP LIKE A DOG

Dogs are good at shedding tension. They enjoy full-body wiggles and a good shake. They allow themselves relaxing yawns. They don't hold on to tension a minute more than is necessary. Whenever we can, it serves us to shed tension just as readily.

Let your smiles reach up to your eyes. Find genuine reasons to laugh. Live in the moment, and if it isn't a particularly good one, know that another moment is on the way. Doing this helps you to appreciate the truly great moments, find comfort in the mediocre ones and let the bad ones pass. It is powerful and freeing, at the same time.

Tension is sneaky. It creeps into our muscles and our joints, and before we know it, we are walking around like the Tin Man, even when we are supposed to be having fun.

Forty years ago, when I was a newbie-trainer competing for top-dog honors at obedience competitions (scores of 196, or more, out of 200 was the goal), I often entered the show ring stiff as a board. I now recognize the message this sent to my dogs and how it worked against me every time. Yes, my dogs performed well, and we usually got the points, but they were glad to go home at the end of the day.

Debbie (a.k.a. Debut's Debutante) was the first dog to make this clear. A brilliantly colored black and tan American Cocker Spaniel, she was one competition away from earning her Companion Dog degree. Together, we had just earned 194 points, and we were tied with another dog-and-handler team for top dog honors. Subsequently, we were asked to walk a simple pattern side-by-side with the other team, to see who would walk away with the big ribbon. Directing Debbie to *heel*, I walked to the far end of the ring and turned, only to see her still sitting where I started, with a look on her face and message that was ever-so-clear: 'We did this once. I don't want to do it again. You are so full of tension…why should I follow you? I want to go home.' Wow!

Debbie got a few chuckles from the people watching at ringside; the other team got the ribbon, and I learned an important lesson. The process of getting the points didn't count if my dogs weren't having fun. And as long as tension was keeping me from having fun, tension (and not pleasure) was the message my dogs were receiving.

Every day, our dogs will remind us to lighten up, and we can be happier individuals for listening.

BE POSITIVE LIKE A DOG

Never forget the power of a positive outlook, and the ability of a clear, positive picture in your mind to direct what follows. Both allow your body (and your energy) to respond in an instinctual manner, as opposed to an intellectual one. Why does this matter when we work with our dogs? Because dogs, first and foremost, respond to things instinctually, not intellectually or emotionally.

Our species, on the other hand, tends to think things through. We discuss things. And we set aside our thoughts for future analysis. While it is true that wonderful things result – much of the time – these same tendencies can trip us up when we think things through too much or discuss things to the point of rationalization, frustration or inaction. You will never see a dog doing this.

For us to have the best results with our dogs, we need to practice the concepts set forth in this book with a clear picture of success in our minds, until our actions reflect our instincts, more than our intellect. This is where "I'm trying" doesn't work. "I'm trying to walk with my head up…I'm trying not to talk too much…I'm trying to be aware of the positions I take…" When we are <u>trying</u> to do something, we are usually thinking it through. This leads us to hesitate, and we all know that that kind of vibe isn't going to get us far with our dogs!

For example, consider Veronica and Jim, two new volunteers at our shelter. When directed to bring six dogs from one yard into another (while requiring them to sit or stand calmly at a gate first), they have very different pictures in their minds.

As Veronica approaches the gate, she thinks:

- ❖ Everyone is watching me. I bet I am going to mess this up.
- ❖ I wonder what that Rottweiler's history is. I wonder if he has ever bitten anyone.
- ❖ How do I stop the dogs from crowding my legs? (I'll hold on to the gate, so they can't dart past me.)
- ❖ Four dogs are sitting or standing still. What do I do about the other two?
- ❖ This is taking a long time, and I am just standing here. Is it supposed to take this long?
- ❖ C'mon, dogs. I am ready to let you pass. Just stop moving for a few seconds, so I can wave you by.

Because Veronica doesn't have a clear positive picture in her mind, her posture is guarded. The energy that she projects is hesitant and tense. And the dogs respond in kind. Some of them disengage and walk away. Others try to dart between her legs, to get to the other side.

Jim approaches the situation differently. He doesn't worry that he is being watched. He doesn't concern himself with any of the dogs' histories. As he approaches the gate between the two yards, he puts a solid image in his mind. It is a picture of six dogs waiting quietly for his direction, two or more feet back from his toes.

He smiles to himself, ensuring that his posture is straight but relaxed, with his weight centered in his hips. The calm, self-assured energy that he projects, when he opens the gate, claims the space around him. He doesn't worry when a few dogs take their time getting into position. He enjoys a few relaxing breaths, and within one minute, all of the dogs are exactly where he wants them. Giving them a big smile, he tells them, "Let's go," as he directs them past the gate.

The picture in Jim's mind allowed him to possess and project confidence. It allowed him to direct the actions and energy of six large dogs, and to do so in a manner that didn't reflect emotion. It didn't get intellectual. Rather, it was a straightforward, positive experience. Never forget to picture success, to get success!

BE THANKFUL LIKE A DOG

Dreaming "big" is fine, but the ability to appreciate "small" is even more powerful. Appreciation is not only a gift we give to others. It is a gift we give to ourselves.

Vickie hasn't always been able to sit upright, reach out or down, or lift items without stiletto-sharp pain radiating up her spine. On and off, for the past three years, while recovering from injuries sustained in an automobile accident, she has relied upon her Service Dog, Dodge, to retrieve objects, turn the lights on and off, and open her door to allow cool breezes to enter. They are a team, and they bring out each other's best. Recently, a procedure done by her physical therapist freed Vickie from a significant amount of post-accident pain, allowing her to be more mobile and a lot more flexible. As a result, she and Dodge have been going on a lot more walks.

"I am so appreciative of the ability to reach for things and open doors unassisted, that I have to remind myself to ask Dodge to do this for me once in a while, to keep his training up. When he rolls onto his back to wiggle against the carpet, I find myself echoing his joy with some full-body stretches of my own. Honestly, stuff bigger than the sheer joy of moving means so little to me nowadays. I'm too busy appreciating the small stuff." The grin that she offers can't emphasize her point more.

I argue that it pays to be thankful for the little things, those aspects of life that are easy to take for granted. If you cannot be happy about the little things, it will take progressively larger things to fulfill you. Be thankful for simple comforts, the better to enjoy them in the moment. Be thankful for small blessings, to be a happier person. Be thankful for opportunities that arise, especially if you can share them with others. If you suspect that you have forgotten how to do this, let your dogs help.

GETTING 'IT'

While attending a class on meditation, I overheard another participant speak about getting 'it.'

"Everyone talks about getting 'it,' but what the heck is the 'it' that they are getting?" he asked.

Everyone was silent in response, pondering the answer. Was 'it' simply a sense of peace? Was 'it' feeling one hundred percent present in the moment, without great attachment to whatever tickled your senses? Was 'it' a combination of both?

"My dog gets 'it,'" one woman said, finally. When all eyes turned to her, she explained further. "Ever walk into the kitchen to find your dog, belly up in the sunshine, in front of the refrigerator, with his eyes closed and a look of pure bliss on his face?" Many people in the room could picture that.

"That's 'it'," she said. Her definition was apropos.

HONORING THE CULTURE OF "DOG"

Recognizing and honoring our dogs' unique culture can help us to appreciate some of the nuances of other cultures, both animal and human. Honoring our dogs' body language, their love of movement, and the way energy (both quality and quantity) directs their responses, creates an awareness like no other. Honoring the fact that they communicate differently than we do – sometimes one hundred and eighty degrees differently – allows us to better connect. Some simple rules to remember:

- ❖ To invite a dog closer, stop reaching for him.
- ❖ To gain a dog's trust, ignore him, so he can approach in his own time.
- ❖ To urge a dog forward, stop pulling him forward.
- ❖ To direct a dog back, stop pulling him back.
- ❖ Using the word "no" (if it projects tension) can lead to an increase, as opposed to a decrease, of a particular behavior.
- ❖ To show acceptance of a dog's behavior, walk away.

Life is full of interesting one-hundred-and-eighty-degree rules. A few more that come to mind are:

- ❖ To feel loved, offer love to another.
- ❖ To see things clearer, step away from them.
- ❖ To get more, be prepared to give.
- ❖ To better solve a problem, stop thinking about it for a little while.
- ❖ Take some of your life back, by letting go.

CHAPTER 29
TAKING BACK BY LETTING GO

Although all too human, I certainly don't claim to be an expert in human psychology. It is safe to say, after decades of living with large groups of dogs, that I am a better judge of their character, and a better person for the lessons they have taught, one of the most remarkable of which involves the sheer and profound power of letting go.

When events seem unjust; when life hits you low and hard; when our fellow human beings are mean-spirited (or worse), human psychologists encourage us to talk about it. Talking to your dog might make you feel better, but when you are finished, your dog still has a big lesson to teach you, and that is: it is okay to simply let go. It is okay if you want to take an entire rotten episode, a wrongful, undeserved, miserable moment in your life and deny it the right to be part of your next minute, your next hour, your next day or for that matter, the rest of your life.

Every life has its share of obstacles. Yes, even those born into richness and privilege have obstacles to overcome (two of which are that very same wealth and privilege). Some obstacles are completely unfair, and some are certainly bigger than others. But what makes us, or breaks us, as individuals is how we overcome them when we are powerless to change them.

As a rescuer and veterinarian, I have seen hundreds of animals survive horrific injuries, neglect and abuse. Although wiser for the experience, every one of them landed squarely on their feet psychologically. I have seen comatose cats, run over by cars, fight their way back into this world despite their only functional parts being a nose for food and a healthy gastrointestinal tract. I have rehabbed dozens of skeletal starvation cases so willing to forgive the hand that didn't feed them, that it would break your heart. And I have seen both cats and dogs that have been set on fire, thrown from moving vehicles, dipped into paint, and tied to rocks and tossed into ponds, survive such horror to trot happily down the hall of my veterinary clinic the following day.

Each and every one of them had something in common: they were capable of letting the past go. It had happened. It was not likely to happen again. They could not go back and change the course of what happened. Most of all, it didn't serve them to hold onto it. They left the past in the past...all of it.

Are we, as humans, capable of this? Some may argue no, but I argue yes, we are...to a greater degree than we believe possible. Not only are we capable of it, it is absolutely in our best interest to do so. It may require help from others, certainly. Physical injuries take time to heal and physical therapy goes a long way toward reducing physical scars. Too, neuromuscular memories created when one's body is forced into fight-or-flight tend to surface years later, like flotsam and jetsam long after a tsunami.

When it comes to emotional healing, however, what the dogs have taught me is the power of saying, "Enough is enough." Right now, right in this moment, what happened in the past (recent or long ago) is not going to get in my way. It is not going to hurt me again. I won't allow it. I don't have time for it. And it is not going to be bigger than me.

Will this kind of empowerment work for you, given your own circumstances? Maybe or maybe not. You won't know, unless you decide to try. The alternative, for some, is never-ending, self-perpetuated punishment.

There is a small homeless encampment, off the railroad tracks, in a nearby town. It serves as a home base for a small number of people, some of whom have dogs. For this reason, it caught my attention several years ago. When I stopped to ask if anyone needed help getting heartworm preventative for their dogs (the local mosquito population was horrible), one older gentleman really stood out from the rest. Paul didn't abuse drugs, and his liver hadn't been scarred by alcohol. He was kind and soft-spoken, and as our friendship grew, it was also apparent that he was a superbly talented artist. His sculptures would have sold for many thousands of dollars, had he ever been able to seize this aspect of his life. He was also an eloquent writer. This was one very talented individual!

I learned more about his life over the following months, when I stopped by with heartworm preventative for his shepherds. Sitting next to his tent in the woods, with the dogs curled up at our feet, I learned that he had been sold, as a tiny infant, for sixty dollars (he still carried his adoptive mother's receipt in his wallet, from a crooked attorney along the Mexican border). Although his adoptive mother was loving, she was subservient to his adoptive father, a politically connected man who was physically abusive. By the age of fourteen, Paul was pushing back and in trouble with the law.

His pleas for intervention fell on deaf ears, and his abusive father went unpunished. The juvenile detention system became his home, as his pain-driven behavior got worse. The next three decades were a blur of acts designed to hurt the man, but they hurt no one more than Paul. Paul hadn't seen him in twenty years, when he learned of the man's death in Bolivia (where he had fled, rather than face charges of abusing his niece). Justice, however needed, was not going to be served, and Paul's was a grief-filled, just-getting-by life that no one would have wanted.

Paul's natural talents kept him employed and moderately productive, but he didn't have the long work history and savings needed to provide for adequate health care or any sort of retirement. With the passing of the years, all of his previous acts and errors in judgment were coming back to haunt him. He injured his back, lost his job as a result, lost his apartment and moved into the woods with his dogs.

"Look at them," he said to me one evening. "I rescued them from a drug dealer who was beating them. They were so thin, and so racked by parasites, that their hides clung to their ribs. I saw that they and I had an abusive past in common. But what I didn't see, for a very, very long time, is how they had moved on. They didn't hold onto their hurt, however justified. They didn't allow their past, or the actions of others, to define them or dictate their actions, in the present or the future.

"I admire my dogs for their muscular strength. I admire their can-do attitude. But the biggest strength of theirs that I admire is their power to let things go, even the most horrible of things beyond their control. I spent my life trying to take back control of a life well beyond my control, and in doing so, I gave control of my life to my past. Dogs know to not do that. I wish I had figured it out sooner."

Paul died a year after that conversation, still living in the same encampment. But where he had spent decades of his life reflecting upon, talking about and acting in response to the horrors of his past, he spent his last year reaching out to young men following the same path.

"They don't want to listen to me," he often said. "They are so angry and so wrapped up in the need to take control and make somebody pay for the past, they don't realize how much they are hurting themselves. I keep hoping that the dogs can get through to them, like they got through to me. I now know, more than many, that there are few things more powerful than the ability to let go and move on."

MOVE ON, LIKE A DOG

Just as dogs don't hold onto big worries, they don't have the habit of holding on to little ones (making it harder, and not easier, to deal with them). This is another skill worth learning and practicing.

To allow yourself to move on, like a dog, and to get a substantial weight off your heart and shoulders, forgive yourself for small mistakes (everyone makes them). Let go of irrelevant internal chatter, that blah-blah-blah that gets you nowhere. Remember to thank someone – belatedly, if necessary – and remember to apologize when it is called for. You will feel so much lighter in spirit for it. Treat yourself to Dale Carnegie's oldie-but-goodie, "How to Stop Worrying and Start Living." Though written in the 1940s, its wisdom holds true to this day.

Moment by moment, our days become more enjoyable when we sort out, and refuse to be burdened by, past events. Doing this helps us to move on, just like our dogs.

ALLOW FOR PLAN "G"

Having well thought-out plans helps life go smoother, but building flexibility into our plans is what keeps tension at bay when problems arise. We learned this lesson, over and over, when we first set up our shelter. We started out humbly, with sixty-one acres of tree stumps, a pock-marked dirt logging road, well over twelve tons of accumulated trash and two post-Hurricane Isabelle trailers (donated only because they had been heavily damaged in the storm).

Many of our plans went awry when North Carolina's unpredictable weather interfered. Some derailed when pivotal contractors and volunteers moved away, or changed job schedules, becoming unavailable. Material prices went up and animal emergencies intervened. It was frustrating how often good plans for good people to do good work got thwarted. Every time we thought we had a firm handle on things, something (or several somethings) would get in the way.

The process of creating a safe place where homeless dogs could recuperate, learn skills, and above all, become physically and mentally healthy, was making us humans into physical and emotional wrecks! Were we living in the moment when this happened? Not at all. Were we relaxed, calm and confident that things would work out for the better? Not in the least.

Numerous Plan A's became Plan B's and then Plan C's. But then someone would think of an excellent Plan D, which sowed the seeds for an even better Plan E. Plan F was formed when somebody donated vital funds, supplies or talent, and at some point, we got to Plan G, God's plan for us. Not only was Plan G the best of all; the act of getting from Plan A to Plan G, many times over, taught us to have patience with the process.

Making plans is a good thing made better when we allow a certain fluidity. Dogs go through life with that same sense of fluidity, and when we need a reminder of its benefits, we can again, turn to them.

SERENITY

You may be familiar with the Serenity Prayer, of which the most commonly quoted lines are:

> *God grant me the serenity*
> *To accept the things I cannot change;*
> *Courage to change the things I can;*
> *And wisdom to know the difference.*

You may not know that the next three lines are:
> *Living one day at a time;*
> *Enjoying one moment at a time;*
> *Accepting hardships as the pathway to peace.*

I can't help but think our dogs would agree, although they might rewrite the first four lines to read:
> *God grant me the serenity*
> *To accept the owners I cannot train;*
> *Courage to train the owners I can;*
> *And wisdom to know the difference.*

CHAPTER 30
GLASSES HALF-EMPTY

Dogs know that dysfunction is dysfunctional. It isn't cute. It isn't something to aspire to. They step up to correct it or they avoid it, to the best of their ability. Dogs don't steep in negativity, either – their glasses are always half-full, as opposed to half-empty – but it is surprisingly easy for people to develop this habit.

Jillian's boyfriend, Evan, had a somewhat strained relationship with his father, a man in his sixties who lived one town over. One of the reasons frequently given was: his father approached life with a glass-half-empty attitude. Evan was a dutiful son, and he looked after the older man, but the two were far from best buddies. Evan often said that he didn't want to be like his father.

Evan's father wasn't the only person in the family who tended to see the cloudy side of life. Evan's own negativity peppered his days. Jillian knew that he didn't see it, so she tried a small experiment. At the start of a long car trip together (the beginning of a long-anticipated joint vacation), she pointed to a pretty roadside planting and asked Evan to remember it. She indicated a mile-marker next to the planting, and she promised to mention something specific about it later in the day.

With warm and sunny weather perfect for a car ride, they then traveled the New York State Thruway for one hundred and thirty miles. Evan spoke. Jillian, for the most part, listened. She kept a quiet count of drivers who shouldn't be on the road, problems with the towns they passed, worrisome things that occurred that week, complaints other people had filed and events Evan worried were about to happen. On the positive side, Evan spoke about his new job (which he actually liked), how excited he was about improvements to the neighborhood pool, and new books at the local library. When roughly two hours had passed, Jillian asked about his father, knowing he would shake his head and say something to the effect of, "He's never happy, that old man." Evan didn't disappoint.

"How about you?" she then asked.

Grinning, he emphasized that he couldn't be happier with his job, in his relationships with the people around him, and to be where he was, only a half-hour away from a long weekend in the Adirondack Mountains. You wouldn't have known it from listening to him.

"Remember those pretty flowers between Syracuse and Canastota?" Jillian asked.

Evan nodded.

"That was one hundred and thirty miles ago. You know how much you hate your father's negativity?"

"Uh huh," he replied, suspiciously.

"Would it surprise you to hear that, in the one hundred and thirty miles since we passed those flowers, you had something negative to say one hundred and twelve times?"

Evan wasn't really that surprised. Saddened by Jillian's statistics, yes, but not that surprised. He then stated that he wanted to change, and she offered to help. Hence began the twenty-five-cent challenge. Every time Evan said something negative that wasn't really necessary, he had to give her a quarter that was subsequently donated to a good cause.

He did well for the first two weeks, handing over a dollar here and a dollar there. They got a few laughs out of how often he got tongue-tied, barely stopping himself from saying negative things before she could hold her hand out (her body language for "pay up!"). By the third week, however, he was angling for a five-dollar pre-pay plan, or an I'll-buy-pizza-this-week plan, or even an I'll-give-you-an-hour-long-massage plan! Anything so he was free to be negative again!

The negativity habit is very hard to break. But the problems with it are many-fold:

❖ What you speak about reflects what you think about, and both affect how you hold your body.

❖ Negativity gets in the way of our being thankful for so many things. Weightless but still weighty, it can siphon the joy out of our days.

❖ People (and dogs) who can add positive energy to your life tend to avoid negative energy.

❖ Excess negativity gives power to negative things, allowing them to pass from one moment into the next, toll-free.

Gossip based more in fiction than in fact, negative media that shows others in their worst possible light and conclusions that assume the bleakest...we are as we think, and our dogs know it. Modern movies and television shows celebrate dysfunction, but what is funny on the screen is rarely so funny in real life.

Set your bar higher! When it comes to the thoughts you choose to possess, be selective. Don't allow negative feelings, opinions and beliefs to linger recreationally. Periodically clean out your mental junk box, the better to decrease unwarranted stress, unclench your jaws and shoulders, and increase a sense of inner peace and purpose.

SUBSTITUTE BEHAVIORS (FOR PEOPLE)

Any good dog trainer knows that it can be hard to change one behavior without replacing it with another. When training our dogs, we replace unwanted behaviors, states of mind and energy with ones that we can reward. Substitutions like this work well with people, too, and they can help you to break the negativity habit.

Should you find yourself orienting toward the negative, practice acknowledging and appreciating more of the positives around you. It may sound trite, but if you really want to let the negativity go, appreciating something as small as the fact that your pencil has a sharp point, or your favorite sweater is within reach on a chilly day, may be all that you need to shift your state of mind. To keep your thoughts in a better place, couple your change of focus with some movement (you know how this works with dogs). Walking to another room, or outside for a few minutes of gentle stretching, can keep the negativity at bay.

You might take a moment to appreciate the results of someone else's hard work, something that exists because someone else cared to do a good job. (In my eyes, that is always worth celebrating.)

Alternately, you might stop to recognize and be thankful for the truly spectacular, things much bigger than all of us combined.

> Whenever Davis finds himself getting unnecessarily negative, he spends a minute with one of the many posters and pictures of galactic nebulas decorating his home and office (even his car!). They display, in vivid color, the Veil Nebula, Crab Nebula, Cats Eye Nebula, Butterfly Nebula, Hourglass Nebula, Ant Nebula and Monkey's Head Nebula (to name a few). Appreciating the vast energy they represent helps him to find a reason to smile.
>
> "The simple act of smiling helps me to reboot my thought process," he explains. "And a quick minute spent appreciating some of the biggest of the big pictures our universe has to offer reenergizes me. It puts any issues that I am dealing with into perspective, so I can better deal with them, something that I was having trouble doing before nighttime walks with my dog, Royal, opened my eyes to the sky. (Thanks, Royal!) It is beautiful, invigorating, inspiring and humbling all at once, and it is what I need to put my best thoughts forward."

Dogs may not know much about the forces of nature, but they know the world is full of neat things to appreciate. As a result, they don't waste time on frivolous negativity, and they see no value and no reality in recreational dysfunction. In this, they can again be our teachers, and we would do well to follow their example.

CHAPTER 31
TEACHERS AND LIFE COACHES

There are many ways to view our dogs. They are our companions and, in some cases, our work partners. They are a source of good humor, pleasant distraction and comfort. As family members, they are the "cheap" kids. They never need sneakers, cell phones, college funds or the latest DVDs, and they never demand Saturday trips to the mall. You can crate them (for reasonable amounts of time) and you can neuter them, and they will kiss you when you haven't brushed your teeth. Consider them your teachers and your life coaches, too.

Dogs:
❖ Get everything they can out of a good walk.
❖ Naturally observe first and speak second.
❖ Are honest about their emotions.
❖ Take pleasure in the simplest of things.
❖ Avoid (or correct) drama.
❖ Naturally live in the moment, and they are willing to let the past go.
❖ Are patient, and they readily forgive.

They can even be good for your posture, if you are observant about how you move around them!

Given the chance, dogs orient toward balanced people like a compass needle to the North Pole. Are your role models and mentors this positive?

Several themes are interwoven throughout this book because they are the keys to getting the dog you have always wanted. They are:

- ❖ Calm, confident, matter-of-fact energy.
- ❖ Recognizing the state of mind behind a dog's behavior.
- ❖ Smiling.
- ❖ Moving, as a means to move on.
- ❖ Living in the moment.
- ❖ Leadership.

Putting these concepts into action can help you to accomplish so much more, and be happier doing it. None of these things can hurt!

BE WILLING TO LEARN FROM YOUR DOGS

Jelli was Toni's first real love. The pit bull/retriever mix was also her first housemate, major confidant and chief boyfriend- scrutinizer before she met her husband, Anton (who passed Jelli's scrutiny with flying colors). When their daughter, Latesha, was born, Jelli joined Toni on long walks behind her stroller. When the baby took her first steps, Jelli was there to help her balance. And when Latesha, as a toddler of three, was developing confidence, she did so while on walks with Jelli and her mother.

Very early on, Toni started a family tradition. When issues needed to be talked out; when she and Anton found themselves at odds, or when Latesha needed some childhood re-focusing, everyone would take Jelli for a walk. One at a time, they would take turns holding her leash. The rule was: the person leading Jelli was allowed five minutes to speak, uninterrupted, but he or she could only do so in a calm and thoughtful manner.

Walking, with Jelli central to the action, helped Toni, Anton and Latesha organize their thoughts, and it prepared them to listen to one another. It calmed tempers, and it got the family moving at times when it served everyone to move on.

Sometimes, they walked around the block. Other times, they headed to a local walking trail. When nothing major was brewing and the walks simply reflected family-time, Jelli was urged to *go out* and explore.

Latesha, now an adult and a mother, herself, recalls knowing, when her mother called Jelli and the family together, it was time to find and build bonds, and time to come to a common understanding. She recalls moments that she loved her mother for doing this, and times when (as a willful teenager) she thought she hated her for it. But the process worked its magic, and Jelli's sage presence kept the peace, centered his people, and allowed them to move on to better things.

"I wasn't allowed to wallow in my teenage angst, with my head down in my technology, searching the ether for someone to tell me I was right, when I wasn't. My mother's "Jelli walks" (which she sometimes called "Jedi walks") and "Jelli meetings" kept me both physically and mentally fit."

PUT YOURSELF OUT THERE

We cannot hope to bring out the best in our dogs passively. The more engaged we are as individuals and dog-owning families, the more we reap the benefits.

Some of our shelter's favorite volunteers come to us in pairs. They are a husband and wife, a man and his girlfriend, a pair of sisters, and a mother and son. In every case, they visit once a week on schedule, leaving their cell phones, work lives, homework assignments and other worldly connections behind to connect, instead, with the animals. When they leave the Center after feeding, grooming and walking the animals, they often stop for lunch or dinner, the better to continue this special time together. No matter what else the rest of their week holds in store, their time with the dogs (and in some cases our cats) allows them to reboot, laugh and give back.

If you and a spouse, friend or family member would enjoy doing the same, and if you can dependably commit to a few hours one day a week for many months or longer, I urge you to contact a local shelter or rescue. The experience will broaden your horizons, and it just might change your life.

NOW WHAT?

You are only one chapter away from the end of this book. Once that chapter is read, what is your next step? Review the basic rules (Chapter 3), and begin applying them moment by moment. Go back to the Table of Contents, and reread the chapters that resonate most with you. View videotapes of your interactions with your dogs, to see yourself through their eyes. Occasionally peruse the Appendixes.

Above all, view your dogs' behavior as you would a mirror, and be willing (and hopefully excited) to fine-tune your own behavior, in order to bring out everyone's best. Consider how your dogs' routines reflect your own, and how their energy and state of mind do the same. And smile more (which leads me to the last chapter...)

CHAPTER 32
KEEP SMILING!

Smiles nourish us. They stimulate breathing, and breathing is life. Smiles bring oxygen into our lungs, endorphins and happy neurotransmitters into our bloodstreams and joy into our lives. Our smiles nourish those around us, too. Our dogs (and our children, and our spouses, and our co-workers) watch for them, and they give us their best when we are generous with them.

Smiles are contagious, even between strangers. You need only to smile to yourself as you walk through any store to see this. Want to drop someone's blood pressure a few notches? Send a smile in his direction. Want to set someone up for a better day? Send a soft smile her way. It doesn't have to be personal. "To Whom It May Concern" works well. Smiles do stuff like this for free, with no untoward side effects.

Smiles shouldn't be saved for happy occasions! Just as using a straw to sip water throughout the day helps our bodies regulate our blood pressure and hold on to hydration better than if we gulp entire glasses at a time, it just makes sense to spread genuine smiles throughout our days. (Curmudgeons take note: grimaces don't count.)

GOOD MORNING!

Ever wake up holding your breath? Doing this is more common than you think in our species, as silly as it sounds. To reverse it, simply smile. Just one soft smile will reset your breathing. Do you commonly wake with your mind spinning over tasks to do, to the point that you are frazzled before your feet hit the floor? Give yourself a personal smile. It will help you reboot your thought process, the better to assess your options in a more relaxed manner.

POWER UP!

Simple smiles empower us to let the small stuff go, allowing us to be better prepared to deal with the big stuff. This is true even when we are in the wrong. When we can laugh at ourselves at times when things go awry because of something we have done (or should have done), we are in a better position to recognize another one of life's little lessons, acknowledge responsibility gracefully, fix the problems at hand and move on. For some, spontaneous smiling may take practice, but it is a practice that will pay dividends quickly.

Know that I am not talking about grinning and bearing it (that is, forcing ourselves to accept unpleasantries with good cheer, as if they don't bother us). I am actually referencing the opposite! Smiles relax our facial muscles, which helps our other muscles unwind in moments when the act of pure enduring would only promote further stress. Giving ourselves an ear-to-ear and to-our-eyes smile can be the first step toward harnessing our power, in a tough situation!

TAMING TENSION

Tension stems from *what might happen* and *what may have happened* as much as, if not a lot more from *what just happened*. But when *what might happen* doesn't actually happen, and when additional facts show that *what may have happened* actually didn't, tension often remains. The mechanisms to shed it, when it is past the point of helping us, isn't as finely developed in our ethos, as it is in our dogs'.

Dogs know how to shake off tension. When was the last time you saw a person enjoy a thorough, nose-to-toes, tension-tossing shake?

This is where smiles can help. Big ones; little ones; gentle ones; goofy ones with your tongue hanging out… it matters not. Smiles are that powerful! I've said it before, but it is well worth repeating one more time…*really, I promise, this is the last time (grin)*: try giving yourself an extra smile when you notice tension lingering! Whereas tension can be immobilizing and self-perpetuating, it is easier to seize the next moment (and a lot harder to be miserable) when you are smiling.

REWARDING OURSELVES

You now know that smiles are some of the best rewards that you can give your dogs for good behavior. They are also a wonderful way to reward yourself for the same!

Put doing this to the test. For example, if your goals are to: eat more green leafy vegetables and less sugar-laden foods, take your vitamins on a more regular basis, drink more water and not let certain exercises go, be sure to smile whenever you do these things. Smile when you start, and smile when you finish.* Enjoy the kick of oxygen your body receives in each case. Before long, and without much thought, you just may be doing each of these things more often and be <u>looking forward</u> to them! Too, since eating better foods, taking your vitamins and getting regular exercise all offer benefits of their own, your steps toward a healthier lifestyle will progress at a pleasant and very natural, stress-free pace.

Take it a step further! Smile when you decide to drive the speed limit, instead of forging ahead with an eye on the clock. You will more likely arrive at your destination. Smile when you let someone take a choice parking spot that you had your eye on. Losing a parking spot is never adequate cause to add stress to your day! Smile when you take the time to cook dinner for yourself, using carefully chosen ingredients, as opposed to heavily-processed foods. It is a double gift to yourself.

Remember that being kind to yourself doesn't equate to being indulgent. Being powerful doesn't always mean pushing ahead. And winning doesn't always mean taking first place. Winning can mean staying the course while helping others to do the same.

Your dogs will agree: rewarding yourself can be as simple as smiling, for no other reason than to be grateful for being alive.

* *A little spontaneous dancing works well, too!*

LAST WORDS

Smile when you see your dogs having a good time being dogs...when they fly off the ground in an all-out sprint, or when they plant their noses deep in the earth, searching for bugs. Smile when they howl at far-off sirens, and never forget to smile when they choose to curl up quietly across the room from you.

Smile to better connect with life, and aim to die with laugh lines, not frown lines!

www.givesmiles.us

If you have enjoyed this book, please tell your family, friends and co-workers about it! 100% of its proceeds benefit canine rescues and public libraries.

Woof!

APPENDIX 1

The Canine KISS Rules

1 - Create and nurture your dog's healthy associations with things, commands and experiences. Old associations can be changed and, if they are unbalanced, the dogs will support changing them <u>if you lead the way</u>.

2 - Be your dog's leader. Remember that dogs become leaders by default. They lead the way where there are leadership voids, but most would rather be happy four-legged followers!

3 - Dogs mirror the energy around them. If your dogs are out of balance, check your energy and state of mind before you correct theirs.

4 - Be aware of what your posture, positions and body language say to your dogs.

5 – When introducing dogs, minimize excitement for the sake of excitement, and don't force face-to-face interaction. Walk them side-by-side first, to promote calm curiosity and acceptance, and to trigger their noses (as opposed to their eyes).

6 - Remember not to reach for, talk to or initiate direct eye contact with new dogs until they have accepted you. Save the hugs, handshakes and how-do-you-do's for your fellow humans.

7 - Use yellow tape ribbons on collars and leashes to help dogs in need of personal space get what they need from the public. Explain what these ribbons indicate, in a positive way, to anyone who comes too close.

8 - Timing is everything! Cause and effect are not linked when the effect comes too long after the cause. Dogs naturally live in the moment.

9 - Utilize the forward movement of group walks to keep the peace amongst individuals. Dogs are not good multitaskers. If they are moving forward, at your direction, it is hard for them to rabble-rouse.

10 - Exercise first, and then teach good disciplines. Don't expect your dogs to learn new things when they are full of pent-up energy. Help them to release their extra energy in a productive way first, <u>then</u> work on your lesson plan.

11 – Promote level-one energy. Patiently wait out higher levels of energy, so you can reward the calm you want.

12 - Reward what you want, and reward it in a calm way that doesn't get your dog excited.

13 - Stop rewarding behaviors that you don't want (for instance, with conversation, petting or emotion).

14 - Use repetitions when introducing new skills. Make a game out of learning!

15 - Pick equal-energy responses. Corrections that are too low in energy will be ineffective, and you will lose a dog's respect. Those that are too high in energy will generate resentment, fear or revolt.

16 - Minimize your vocal energy. Dogs communicate best when they communicate non-verbally.

17 - Correct the instigator to calm his cohorts.

18 - Encourage leadership in others (confidence, consistency, calm assertiveness and quiet awareness). The right people really make all the difference. When in doubt about a person's level of competence, watch how the dogs respond.

19 - When in doubt about what a dog is doing, watch the responses of other dogs around him. How they respond can be a good indicator of how you should respond.

20 - Smile! It is the best reward that you can give to your dog and to yourself.

APPENDIX 2

Common Handler Errors

1 - Looking down while walking dogs.

2 - Maintaining tension on leashes that should be loose.

3 - Speaking in an excited voice, or being vocal when it isn't required.

4 – Walking on, before the dogs at your side exhibit level-one energy. (It only reinforces an excited state of mind.)

5 - Mistiming rewards or corrections.

6 - Holding a grudge from one moment into the next.

7 – Over-correcting or under-correcting.

8 - Allowing negative pictures to prevail in your mind. You are going to get more of what you expect to get!

9 - Confusing mitigation (very good) with micromanagement (not good).

10 - Not using thresholds and mealtimes to teach.

11 - Not correcting unwanted energy before it fuels unwanted behaviors.

12 - Setting treadmill speeds at too fast a pace. Dogs do better at a slower, 'thinking' pace that is varied.

13 - Leaving a dog in a state of tension (especially when less than a minute of patience will defuse it).

14 - Allowing dogs to claim your space and resources. Use calm assertion to take them back.

15 - Letting dogs mark territory when walking.

16 - Letting your dog lead the way when you haven't directed him to go out.

17 - Not smiling enough (the best way to reward and connect with your dogs!)

INDEX